NAPLES

Valerio Ceva Grimaldi and Maria Franchini

photographs: Fernando Pisacane

JONGLEZ PUBLISHING

travel guides

"The real voyage of discovery consists not in seeking new landscapes, but in having new eyes," said Marcel Proust. During this voyage of discovery to a Secret Naples, Valerio Ceva Grimaldi and Maria Franchini achieve this small miracle: they offer us a new way of looking, leaving us under the spell of the ancient city of the Siren. A revelation for tourists, for all those unfamiliar with Naples, but also for Neapolitans, who'll be able to rediscover themselves and their identity. I've always thought that we Italians are both lucky and a little lazy, the beauty of our artistic cities being rather too familiar. A beauty that we shouldn't take for granted, but rediscover every day. Because beauty lessens our daily concerns and will finally redeem the world.

The co-authors of this invaluable guide (in collaboration with the Geositi project of Napoli Servizi – Comune di Napoli) thus take us by the hand to lead us on a mysterious journey into the belly of Naples, its grottoes, passages, crevices, cisterns, a curious labyrinth in the style of Escher. I must admit that I too have discovered unlikely things. The levels of meaning, the layers that make up Naples, probably have no equivalent: a porous city, it has absorbed a thousand cultures, a thousand suggestions, a thousand styles – Baroque, Gothic, Oriental. Naples must be decrypted. This is an intelligible though esoteric process: like the symbols engraved on the diamond-point projections of the church of Gesù Nuovo or the alchemical mysteries of Raimondo di Sangro, Prince of Sansevero. An atmosphere not only magical but almost pagan, as borne out by the cult of the capuzzelle at the church of Santa Maria del Purgatorio ad Arco or at the Fontanelle, but also deeply spiritual and Christian. Naples succeeds in synthesising opposing and pluralistic traditions to compose a unique and fascinating mosaic wherein the pieces are all different. Welcome to the city of which I'm mayor!

Luigi de Magistris
Mayor of Naples

When in 2014 I discovered the first edition of *Secret Naples*, I immediately felt a great admiration for its two authors, Valerio Ceva Grimaldi and Maria Franchini, who, thanks to their deep culture and great sensitivity, succeeded in collecting in a guide so many secret and unknown aspects of the city. This book, a real guide that leads you from place to place, from secret to secret, seemed to me even more unusual than Naples is by its very nature — a mysterious, strange, unconventional and peculiar city, which seems to conspire ironically against logic and common sense.

What is even more extraordinary is that this book, a true treasure of daily erudition, is not only a guide, but also an enlightened synthesis of what is the essence of Naples and its most emblematic places; its «soul», I'd dare to say, or even its «nature», depending on whether one prefers scientific language or religious rhetoric. These two ways of interpreting the world divide the intelligentsia of the city from time immemorial: on the one hand San Gennaro and Orsola Benincasa, on the other Giambattista Vico and Domenico Cirillo, just to state the most famous names. On the one hand mysticism and its impenetrable powers, on the other, philosophy and science, the great medical tradition and the Enlightenment thinking. It is ultimately the myth that constitutes the truth of Naples; superior or inferior truth, it is nonetheless an "other" truth wherein the dead continue to deal with the business of the living. But it is also a city where one does not fear to affirm: "It is not true, but I believe it". That is the essence of its secret, the logic of its originality. Read this unusual book and Naples will have no secrets for you.

Sylvain Bellenger
General Director of the Museum and Royal Park of Capodimonte

Of Naples so much has been said that it seems pointless to list its wonders; visitors can enjoy it any time of the year. The first of our concerns today is to defend at all costs the historical, artistic and anthropological heritage of this city; a composite heritage, material and immaterial, caused by reciprocal contamination of a great variety of peoples that have occupied it in turn.
Since, for so many today, the Mediterranean is rather a barrier, sometimes even an abyss, the home of Parthenope, which overlooks this old sea, can become a bright beacon, a docking point for the lander. And if this «warm embrace» is possible, it is in the name of the welcome and sense of hospitality of its inhabitants and the degree of civilisation that the city has reached since the arrival of the Greeks.
The one who has already seen everything can afford to also offer a «secret» aspect. So much of the cultural wealth produced is abundant, and so much of it is overflowing with the generosity to share its treasures with strangers. But a work of this kind, written with passion and competence by Valerio Ceva Grimaldi and Maria Franchini, is above all a precious instrument for new generations of Neapolitans, for whom it will help to recapture knowledge and pride, a sense of participation and the spirit of protecting their motherland. And that's not all: the secret Naples guide also helps institutions and tourists to understand the immense responsibilities shared by everyone, so it may perpetuate and renew the miracle of beauty. Culture is the only instrument that allows this prodigy to be accomplished. These precious pages offer a serious contribution to this journey of intellectual enrichment by familiarising readers with the details and the chiaroscuro, while sparing them a banal and predictable visit, instead plunging them into a refined and cultivated world.

Paolo Giulierini
Director of the National Archaeological Museum

Valerio Ceva Grimaldi Pisanelli di Pietracatella
belongs to an old noble Neapolitan family. A journalist by
profession, he worked on the staff of the governor of the
Province of Naples, Professor Amato Lamberti, then for
the Assessorato all'Ambiente del Comune di Napoli. He
also spent two years with Rai TV's Gap programme. He
was editor-in-chief of the newspaper Notizie Verdi and
deputy editor of Terra, the first environmental daily with a
wide distribution. He has published numerous articles and
surveys on the City of Naples. For RAI he was the technical
advisor for the programme *Ulysses, the Joy of Discovery*,
under the direction of Alberto Angela, for the episode
entitled "The Thousand Secrets of Naples". Those who
would like to be accompanied by the author when visiting
some places in this guide may write to the following
address: cevagrimaldi@gmail.com.

Maria Franchini who has been a guide and lecturer on
the monuments of Campania for fifteen years, was born in
Naples. A journalist and the author of several books, she is
passionate about Neapolitan culture and is also a specialist
in Roman civilisation. She works for the Italian Cultural
Centre in Paris, where she runs courses in the Neapolitan
language, gives lectures and organizes seminars on her
favourite subjects.
www.sgdl-auteurs.org/maria-franchini/index.php/pages/
Biographie

We have taken great pleasure in drawing up
Secret Naples and hope that through its guidance
you will, like us, continue to discover unusual,
hidden or little-known aspects of the city.
Descriptions of certain places are accompanied
by thematic sections highlighting historical details
or anecdotes as an aid to understanding the city in
all its complexity.
Secret Naples also draws attention to the multitude
of details found in places that we may pass every
day without noticing. These are an invitation to look
more closely at the urban landscape and, more
generally, a means of seeing our own city with
the curiosity and attention that we often display
while travelling elsewhere …

Comments on this guidebook and its contents,
as well as information on places we may not have
mentioned, are more than welcome and will enrich
future editions.
Don't hesitate to contact us:
Jonglez Publishing, 25 rue du Maréchal Foch,
78000 Versailles, France
E-mail: info@jonglezpublishing.com

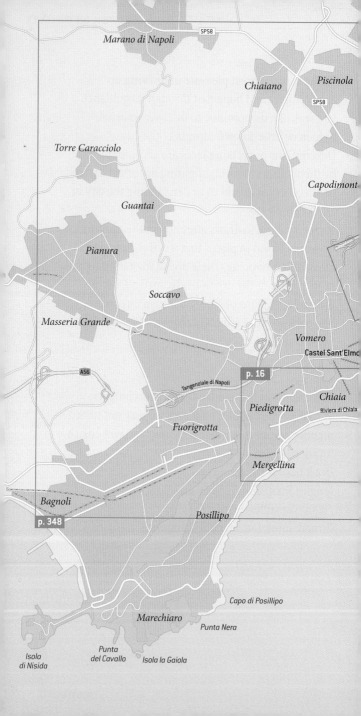

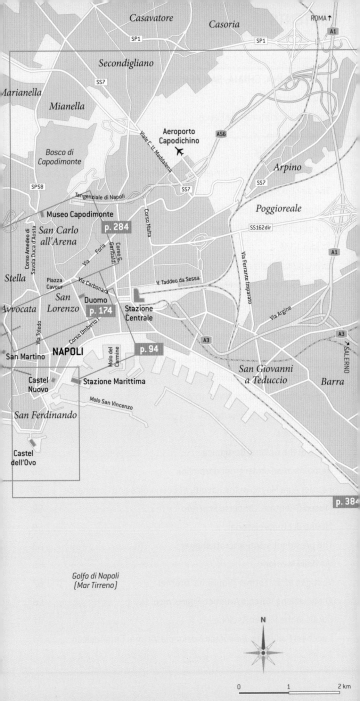

CONTENTS

MERGELLINA, CHIAIA, SAN FERDINANDO

TOLEDO, UNIVERSITÀ, BOVIO, GARIBALDI

CONTENTS

MONTESANTO, DANTE, CAVOUR, DECUMANI

CONTENTS

MATERDEI, SANITÀ, CAPODIMONTE

CONTENTS

OUTSIDE THE CENTRE WEST

OUTSIDE THE CENTRE NORTH AND EAST

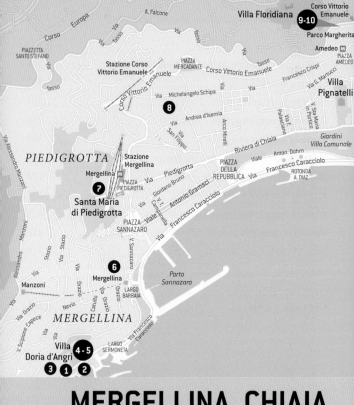

MERGELLINA, CHIAIA, SAN FERDINANDO

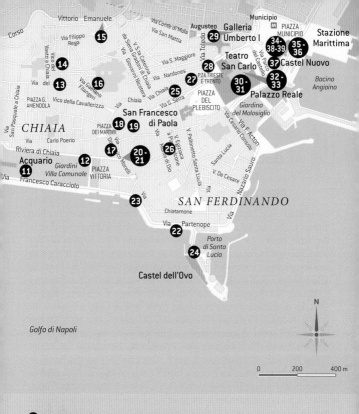

KAYAK TOURS ❶

- Bus: 140
- Booking essential: 331 9874271, 338 2109978
- info@kayaknapoli.com
- www.kayaknapoli.com (Non-swimmers welcome)

> **Discovering
> the city
> from the sea**

A kayak tour along the bay of Capo Posillipo (the city's most scenic district) can't be too highly recommended. Since Roman times these wooded hills overlooking the sea have been dotted with patrician villas concealed among the lush greenery. The tour takes in a stretch of rugged coastline where, nestling in the many creeks, are secluded beaches and grand villas, such as the one commissioned for the Spanish viceroy's wife Donn'Anna di Carafa in the 17th century but never completed. After a few kilometres you reach the beautiful Villa Rosebery, built in 1801, which has become one of three official summer residences of Italian presidents. A little further along is the fishing village of Marechiaro and the famous *"finestrella"* (little window), which inspired the song of that name by the great poet Salvatore Di Giacomo. Next you glide past Palazzo degli Spiriti (Palace of the Spirits), the remains of the nymphaeum of a fabulous Roman villa dating from the 1st century BC. The villa's owner, Publius Vedius Pollio, called it Pausilypon (from the Greek for "the place that brings an end to pain"): the 9-hectare grounds (which Emperor Augustus inherited on Pollio's death) included the two islets of Gaiola, on which stands a 19th-century villa (see p. 19), and extended to the small bay of Cala di Trentaremi where the tour ends. Sometimes these tours are available in the evening. By kayak you can also reach a traditional fishing boat, which serves lunch and dinner.

At certain times of the year you can visit the underwater park of Gaiola in a glass-bottomed boat. As well as offering a great view of the seabed, some of the submerged remains of Villa Pausilypon can also be seen.
Info: 081 2403235; info@areamarinaprotettagaiola.it.

Another company has recently started to organise boat trips along the coast, from a little further out.
Info: 081 4972249; www.alilauro.it.
Villa Pausilypon (36 Discesa Coroglio) can also be reached on foot.
Info: 081 2301030.
Guided tours: 081 2403235; info@areamarinaprotettagaiola.it

THE CURSED VILLA OF GAIOLA

The villa built in 1874 on the twin islets of Gaiola has never enjoyed a good reputation due to the series of misfortunes that have befallen all who lived there. A business established in the villa by its first owner, Luigi Negri, foundered. In 1911, Marquis Gaspare Albenga grounded his armoured cruiser, the *San Giorgio*, on a nearby sandbank while attempting to give one of his guests a closer view of the coast.

During a storm in 1926 the cable on the funicular linking the mainland with the villa gave way, causing the death of the passenger, a German lady named Elena Von Parish. She had been the guest of the villa's occupants Otto Grumbach and Hans Praun, who both committed suicide, one immediately and the other on returning to Germany. In the 1950s Maurice Sandoz, owner of the well-known pharmaceutical company, lived there for a few years before being admitted to a psychiatric clinic where he too committed suicide, convinced that he'd gone bankrupt. The next owner, Paul Karl Langheim, ended up ruined.

The villa was then bought by Giovanni Agnelli, who, during the few years he owned it, had a number of bereavements in his family. In 1968, Agnelli sold the property to the oil magnate Paul Getty, whose son was kidnapped and had an ear cut off by the kidnappers in 1973.

The last "lucky winner" was Gian Pasquale Grappone, who bought the estate in 1978 but was jailed after complaints from his many creditors. So the villa was auctioned and, on the same day, Signor Grappone's wife died in a car accident.

The villa of Gaiola is now owned by the Campania Region.

IS VIRGIL BEHIND THE CURSE?

Until the 19th century, before it was submerged, you could still see part of a building belonging to Villa Pausilypon that from the Middle Ages was known as "Virgil's school". Virgil, considered a benevolent god in antiquity (see p. 28), was "downgraded" and classed as a necromancer as Christianity asserted itself. To scare the people, who persisted in their belief in the great poet's beneficial powers, a rumour was put about that these ruins were part of the school where Virgil taught black magic, so the place was bewitched.

FONDAZIONE CULTURALE EZIO DE FELICE

Palazzo Donn'Anna
Largo Donn'Anna a Posillipo, 9
• Open Monday to Friday 9.30am–1.30pm
• Visits by appointment (contact architect Roberto Fedele)
• Tel: 081 5751121
• Check calendar of events on website
• www.fondazionedefelice.it
• segreteria@fondazionedefelice.it

Theatre
by the sea

No other Neapolitan building has been so violently affected by historical events as the Palazzo Donn'Anna. In the 17th century, these ranged from the splendour of the lavish court of Anna Carafa and her Spanish viceroy husband to the ravages of the insurrection against Spanish rule led by Masaniello. The extraordinary Baroque palazzo has changed hands a number of times and was once a factory making crystal. It is now the home of the Ezio De Felice Cultural Foundation, set up in the name of the architect, university professor and restoration expert (1916–2000), unanimously recognized as one of the founders of Italian museography/exhibition design. The venue hosts cultural meetings and exhibitions and offers guided tours of the 17th-century theatre, as well as the ingenious cave formations in the tuff cliffs. The foundation has a well-stocked library and interesting photographic archives.

The underground passages were designed so that boatloads of nobles invited by Anna Carafa could attend the theatre and participate in the sumptuous courtly feasts, known as "*spassi di Posillipo*" ("Posillipo musical parties").

The Chiaia district saw the wedding celebrations of Ramiro Núñez de Guzmán, Duke of Medina de las Torres, and Anna Carafa della Stadera, Duchess of Stigliano, in 1636. Afterwards the couple planned a private villa by the sea as an alternative to their official residence. They commissioned Italian architect and sculptor Cosimo Fanzago to renovate Palazzo Donn'Anna. In 1644, when the east wing was about to be completed, King Philip IV recalled Don Ramiro to Madrid. The magnificent villa is still unfinished, as you can see along the road out of the city centre, right on the seafront.

OSPIZIO MARINO ❸

Via Posillipo, 24
• Bus: R2 from Napoli Centrale station; 140 from Piazza Municipio (Donn'Anna stop)
• Visits on reservation: napolisegreta@gmail.com (authorization required)

**A hospice
with a view**

In the most beautiful district of Naples, on the peninsula of Posillipo, an enterprising monk founded the beautiful and little-known Marine Hospice in 1883. Antonio Curri, who was responsible for the construction work, chose an Arabist neo-Gothic style inspired by the famous Cloister of Paradise (Amalfi cathedral) for his beautiful portico of Moorish arches.

To reach the church, which stands just above the beach, you have to descend several long and unusual flights of "Holy Steps" (not a single flight as tradition dictates – see p. 199), with the Stations of the Cross depicted on the walls. The splendid ceramic decoration of the church, site of the founder's tomb, is the work of Brother Angelico Calabrese. On the floor above you can visit the cell where Brother Ludovico (see below) lived, with all his personal effects and a private chapel in polychrome wood.

The complex, which housed sick children and destitute old fishermen, was built on the ruins of a building that had been used as a lazaretto, bought by the founder in 1873. Today the hospice is run by Franciscan nuns who care for the elderly poor.

BROTHER LUDOVICO DA CASORIA, AN EXTRAORDINARY CHARACTER

Arcangelo Palmentieri (later Brother Ludovico) was born in Casoria, on the outskirts of Naples, on 11 March 1811. After a mystical experience in the church of San Giuseppe dei Ruffi in Naples, he devoted himself to saving African children from slavery. He spent the rest of his life fighting for the recognition of the rights and dignity of the poor, inventing such concepts as "professional training" before it was fashionable, placing disadvantaged children with practising artisans.

To finance his Marine Hospice, Palmentieri opened a resort for the clergy on the nearby beach that was even patronised by the Archbishop of Naples. "For my poor people," he would exclaim, "I've even gone into trade!" He was indeed an astute manager and founded over 200 similar institutions without having a penny to his name. He was a friend of King Ferdinand II, who financed a mission in Africa on his behalf, yet when the Bourbon dynasty fell he said: "On behalf of the poor, I kiss the forehead of the Grand Turk and of Victor Emmanuel." Palmentieri also founded the Order of the Grey Friars of Charity, who lived in absolute poverty but took no vows, not even that of celibacy. Brother Ludovico died in Naples on 30 March 1885 and was beatified in 1993 by Pope John Paul II.

VILLA DORIA D'ANGRI

4

Via Petrarca, 80
• Metro: Line 2 or 6 Mergellina, then Bus: C21 from Piazza Sannazzaro
• Tel: 081 5475418
• antonio.alviani@uniparthenope.it
• Visits by appointment

> *The villa where Wagner finished Parsifal*

Located in the old village on the heights of Posillipo, in a park of around 2 hectares with sweeping views of the bay, the splendid villa of the Doria d'Angri princes was built in 1833 in a neoclassical style inspired by Palladio and decorated with extravagant Pompeian and oriental frescoes. The villa was put up for sale in 1857 and purchased by the Santa Dorotea boarding school for girls. Since 2000, it has housed the "Parthenope" University of Naples.

The original decoration, preserved in only a few rooms, was carried out by renowned artisans such as Gennaro Maldarelli and Gennaro Aveta, who drew their themes from the classical repertoire, closely emulating the style chosen for Palazzo San Teodoro (see p. 41).

There is a plaque in a first-floor corridor in honour of Wagner, who composed the final notes of *Parsifal* during his stay at the villa. The summer house on the terrace overlooking the bay is shaped like a Chinese pagoda, a fashionable style at the time. Its decoration has been lost with the exception of the small bells on the roof.

The church of Santa Dorotea, opposite the main entrance to the villa, can be visited on request. Tel: 081 5475418.

NEARBY

5

NAVAL MUSEUM OF THE "PARTHENOPE" UNIVERSITY OF NAPLES
• Visits: contact museum director, Prof. Antonio Scamardella: antonio.scamardella@uniparthenope.it

Villa Doria d'Angri also has a very interesting naval museum with 160 model boats, parts of ships and nautical instruments. The museum was established at the time of the founding of the university, which inherited the collections of the arsenals and naval cadet school; it has since been enriched by various other pieces donated by Neapolitan workshops and the C and TT Pattison shipyard.

THE DEVIL OF MERGELLINA 6

Church of Santa Maria del Parto - 9/b Via Mergellina
• Metro: Line 2 or 6 Mergellina; Buses: R3, 140 (Mergellina stop)
• Open 8.30am–1pm and 4pm–7pm (ring bell at 9/b next to the elevator or to the left of the church)

The cardinal's demons

Santa Maria del Parto (Holy Mary of Childbirth), sited far from the beating heart of old Naples, is not much visited although it is of great interest. Its name probably comes from *De partu Virginis* (Childbirth of the Virgin), a poem by Jacopo Sannazaro who had the church built on his land (see opposite).

In the sacristy, the five life-size figurines of saints form part of a magnificent Christmas crib of 1520, when characters other than Mary and Joseph first appeared.

The sculptor was Giovanni da Nola, a leading artist of the Neapolitan Renaissance. Behind the altar stands Sannazaro's imposing tomb, clearly inspired by Michelangelo, with a bas-relief depicting a scene from the poet's major work, *Arcadia*. The monument is entirely covered with pagan motifs, leading one of the Spanish viceroys to order its destruction. The monks of the adjoining monastery saved it *in extremis* by engraving the names of David and Judith under the figures of Apollo and Minerva.

The most intriguing detail of this church is the painting of Saint Michael killing the dragon/devil, shown with a woman's head with lovely features. This is in fact the face of Victoria d'Avalos with whom Cardinal Diomede Carafa had fallen hopelessly in love. Initially tantalised and then rejected by the beautiful Victoria, the prelate lost his reason. So he decided to commission this painting from Leonardo da Pistoia in which his female tormentor is killed by the archangel. According to legend, the cardinal's anguish was eased as soon as he could act out his fantasy. He then had this legend inscribed below the canvas: "*et fecit victoriam alleluja*" (I finally won, Hallelujah) – words with a double meaning that may well relate to the victory of faith over the devil.

This is the legend from which the Neapolitan saying "beautiful as the Devil of Mergellina", referring to man-eaters, is derived.

After the suppression of religious orders in the Napoleonic era, part of the monastery was bought by an impresario for the use of Gioachino Rossini – here he could give free rein to his passion for beautiful women and the pleasures of life.

JACOPO SANNAZARO (1457–1530): THE POET OF *ARCADIA*

The poet Sannazaro, famous in his day, was widely imitated by Ronsard and Leopardi as well as other great poets. He was like a brother to King Frederick I of Aragon, who offered him a property at Mergellina, a magical place not far from Virgil's tomb. Sannazaro had a villa built there as well as founding the church of Santa Maria del Parto. Having gone into exile with the king, he returned to Naples in 1505 after the kingdom had been conquered by Charles V. In spite of his resounding success, he stayed loyal to the Aragonese and always kept his distance from the court of the viceroys. A great humanist, he discovered and transcribed the texts of Latin poets. He was extremely versatile and wrote poems as well as plays (known as *farces*) to entertain the Aragonese court. His poem *Arcadia*, where he sings of the beauty of Naples, is considered the archetype of the modern pastoral. In the last years of his life, he wrote only in Latin. *De partu Virginis* enjoyed great popularity with the papacy, as well as in France.

Sepolcro di Virgilio sul Monte Posilipo
poco lungi dalla Grotta di Napoli

EPITAPH ON VIRGIL'S TOMB

❼

Roman columbarium
Via Puteolana – behind Mergellina train station
• Metro: Line 2 Mergellina
• Open daily 9am to 1 hour after sunset
• Closed 1 January, Easter Monday, 1 May, 25 December

*Virgil's
magical laurel*

The Roman columbarium on Via Puteolana, close to the Crypta Neapolitana (see p. 31), is reputed to be the site of Virgil's tomb. The greatest poets of all time gathered there. The epic poet Statius, who was Neapolitan, recounts that the tomb was a sacred place and he made a pilgrimage there himself.

Close to the tomb there once stood a laurel that was said – in both the written and the oral traditions – to have grown spontaneously. According to a belief that endured until the 20th century, women picked the leaves and chewed them for their miraculous powers, as borne out by an epitaph of 1668. This belief was so strong that even Neapolitan emigrants to America were asking for branches from the tree. The demand was so great that the laurel had no chance to regenerate.

Laurel has always been part of the Virgil myth: according to his biographer Donatus, before the poet's birth his mother had dreamed of a laurel branch that grew to full size as soon as it was planted in the ground. However, laurel embodies a profusion of magico-religious symbols. For example, the tree is sacred to Apollo, whose priestesses, the Sibyls, chewed the leaves before prophesying.

As the tree bears no fruit, it incarnates virginity. It is also "eternal" because it doesn't shed its leaves in winter. Finally, it symbolises the underworld kingdom of Persephone, daughter of Demeter, the Great Earth Mother: to escape from her suitor Apollo, Daphne invoked the Great Mother, who turned her into a laurel. Through this tree Virgil brings together all these values: virginity, eternity, fertility and the underworld.

Doubts still linger about Virgil's actual burial site. According to some ancient chroniclers, the poet's remains were placed for safekeeping in the foundations of Castel dell'Ovo (Castle of the Egg), where Virgil had hidden a magic egg (laid by the bird-woman, the Siren, see p. 153). Be that as it may, as expressed in these lines engraved on a marble slab: "*If the tomb was opened, if the urn was broken, what does it matter? This place will always be celebrated for the name of the poet.*"

"POETRY TREES" IN VIRGIL'S HONOUR

In 2012 the municipality bestowed this title on an initiative designed to honour the great Latin poet on his 2,082nd anniversary. Along the path leading to the tomb and crypt were planted some of the trees and shrubs Virgil mentions in his works, among them the male dogwood (*Cornus mas*), which according to the *Aeneid* was used to build the Trojan horse.

VIRGIL, POET AND MAGICIAN

Born in Mantua, Virgil (70–19 BC) spent much of his life in Naples, where he set several episodes of the *Aeneid*. He also asked to be buried there.

Carved on his tomb (p. 27) are verses he is thought to have composed: "*Mantua gave me birth; Calabria took me away; and now Naples holds me; I sang of pastures, farms, leaders*." It was undoubtedly this detail that built up the immense popularity of the Virgil cult in this region, traces of which are still visible today.

His boundless knowledge, the perfection of his poetry and his interest in magico-religious language earned Virgil such admiration from his peers that, according to Pliny the Elder and Ausonius, the Ides* of October were dedicated to him shortly after his death (he was born on 15 October).

In Campania, people even began to associate him with the major cults of the time: the Great Mother (fertility), Apollo (the Sun), the Siren Parthenope (virginity) and the Sibyls (prophecy), so countless supernatural powers were eventually attributed to him.

The poet's saintly aura intensified over time, due largely to the Donatus biography derived from the work of Suetonius.

The early Christians themselves saw in his writings – especially in Eclogue IV of the pastoral poems, the *Bucolics* – the orphic and solar elements found in Christianity. Thus, while of the pagan world, Virgil was not rejected by the emerging religion, especially as the Emperor Constantine himself had formalised the acceptance of Christianity: Virgil (and the Sibyls) were henceforth represented among the prophets (notably in the Sistine Chapel in Rome).

Even Virgil's homosexuality, real or imagined, was considered a virtue. He was so chaste, insists Donatus, that he was called Parthenias, the "little virgin". And it is therefore no coincidence that the oral traditions of Campania often mention a "*verginella*" (little virgin) – always a man. The transvestite or hermaphrodite does indeed encapsulate the masculine and the feminine, and therefore the universe. Even today, Neapolitan transvestites play a fundamental role in some popular rites.

The Virgil cult remained in vigour until the year 1000. Then the myths linked to the poet were gradually replaced by legends of saints or madonnas, and the church demoted even Virgil to the role of necromancer. But belief in his benevolent powers was too deep-rooted in the Neapolitan spirit: his memory would often be evoked where churches were established, built in their turn on the ruins of pagan temples.

*Ides: from the Latin word *iduare* (divide), referring to the mid-month position of the Ides. In the Roman calendar, the Ides are reference days falling on the 13th (January, February, April, June, August, September, November, December) or the 15th (March, May, July, October) of each month.

SYMBOLISM OF THE CRYPTA NEAPOLITANA

Following Virgil's death in 19 BC, the construction of the tunnel known as the Neapolitan Crypt was attributed to him. The poet-magician is said to have pierced the hill with a sunbeam in a single night, to give the poor the chance to go through it to have their ailments treated at the Phlegraean Fields (Campi Flegrei, "burning fields"), the site of the defeat of the Titans, where many therapeutic hot springs still bubble.

Many other myths give meaning to this place. Caves, in the popular imagination, have always been associated with the origins of life. This tunnel carved out by Virgil, "the virgin" (see opposite), who is both man and woman at the same time, he who lies at rest close to the crypt, can only be a thousand times more sacred. With its east–west orientation, it is also an initiatory path, because he who takes that route from Naples is heading west and ritually dies with the Sun. But when he returns to the east, "resurrected" by the miraculous waters of Virgil, he is reborn like the sacred star. The crypt thus became one of the main places of worship of the ancient city, where initiatory rites were held for Mithras, Demeter and Dionysus, the deities associated with the Sun and fertility. Even less surprising is the later syncretism with the Madonna of Piedigrotta and the basilica dedicated to her "at the feet of the grotto" (see p. 32).

In the 8th century, when Christianity spread more widely, a chapel dedicated to the Madonna of Idria was erected in the crypt. Idria is derived from *Ogiditria,* meaning "indicates the way". The allusion to the path of the Sun couldn't be clearer. In addition, new mothers and brides gathered at the feet of the Virgin, just as they used to pray to the Sun and the Great Mother.

A fresco representing the Madonna of Idria can still be seen to the left of the tunnel entrance, while on the right a saint, probably Luke, is depicted. In the course of various excavations (15th and 17th centuries), a relief from the 3rd century AD was found showing the god Mithras sacrificing the bull (on view at the National Archaeological Museum).

In reality, the 705 m long tunnel, illuminated by two light wells, was built by the military architect Lucius Cocceius on the orders of Emperor Augustus (1st century BC) to connect Neapolis to Puteoliso, which at the time was the most important commercial port of the empire. The crypt has seen tremendous changes over the centuries and was closed in the early 20th century to be replaced by a modern tunnel, which connects Mergellina to the Phlegraean Fields.

WHEN OUR LADY LOST HER SHOE: WHY IS SANTA MARIA DI PIEDIGROTTA SO CALLED?

Maria Santissima
di Piedigrotta.

It was after an apparition of the Virgin to three nuns in 1353 that the basilica of Santa Maria di Piedigrotta was built. Although the word *piedi* (feet) originally referred only to a geographical position (the Madonna "at the feet of the grotto", the legendary cave created by Virgil – see p. 29), it soon took on another sense: the foot and the shoe (a woman's) are an allegory of the path in all its meanings, but also of fertility (as they trample the earth) and the cave (symbol of death and birth).

We also find this attribute in a local legend that the Virgin would appear to fishermen at night, leaving a shoe to mark her passage. Now Persephone, in Greek mythology, before she returned to the underworld at the end of summer, also left a shoe in token of her promise to fertilise the land the following year. And until recently a little shoe (called "*'o scarpunciello d''a Maronna*") was offered to pregnant women to ease the pains of childbirth, and to brides to ward off sterility. Prayers were also written inside a footprint.

From its earliest days, in order to be accepted more widely, Christianity tried to assimilate and transform pagan cults rather than eradicating them: besides Persephone, here the Virgin replaced a certain Virgil, who was also a "virgin" (see p. 30), and whose crypt (Crypta Neapolitana) is nearby.

So it is no surprise that the greatest festival of the year was dedicated to the Madonna of Piedigrotta: the date of 8 September was chosen because it corresponded to other pagan feasts in honour of solar and underworld deities, always in the name of fertility and all united under the sign of Virgil. Even the representation of the Madonna of Piedigrotta brings together key magico-religious elements: the babe in arms like the Great Mother, the Sun to the right and the Moon to the left, allegories of Heaven and the underworld, and with the bare foot showing.

This ritual chant recorded by Roberto De Simone (see p. 341) in 1970 makes clear allusions to the shoe as symbol of the path travelled by the Sun:

The sun has risen behind the mountains
There are shoemakers
Who know how to make shoes
With golden tips like the Sun ...

The great festivities in honour of the Madonna of Piedigrotta took place on the night of 7–8 September, and were not far removed from Dionysian rites: torchlight processions to the sound of loud instruments, erotic dances and songs. Cheering crowds wended their way to the church on decorated floats, men and women separately.

Everyone then gathered before Virgil's tomb, where chanting took place. Then came dancing in the cave where, for one night, all taboos were swept away.

Outside the tunnel/cave, the festivities adopted the same symbols but in a more refined manner. All Neapolitans participated, including the bourgeoisie.

Carts decorated in carnival style rolled through the streets, banter was allowed but must never exceed the bounds of propriety. The traditional torches were replaced by sumptuous lighting; music and songs took pride of place. From the 19th century onwards, the best-known Neapolitan songs had been composed for this occasion.

Today this Madonna is still celebrated, but the festive events have become much more low-key since the 1970s.

CINDERELLA WAS BORN IN NAPLES

The tale of Cinderella with her famous glass slipper comes from Naples (the storytellers called her "Cinderella Cat"). The first written version (in the Neapolitan dialect) is attributed to Giambattista Basile, author of the *Pentameron* (17th century), a collection of folk tales from the oral tradition.

PRIVATE COLLECTION OF PIAGGIO VESPAS ❽

• Booking essential: napolisegreta@gmail.com

*A rare
wartime Vespa*

A very secret private garage in the depths of a building occupied by the town hall of the Chiaia–San Ferdinando–Posillipo district houses one of Italy's most extraordinary – and virtually unknown – collections of motorcycles. It contains around seventy Piaggio Vespas dating from the 1940s to the 1990s. The collection specialises in models produced by Piaggio plants abroad, particularly in France, Spain, Germany and the UK. But there is also an extremely rare Ape, made in the USSR in the 1950s.

All the Vespas on show are in working order and have a certificate of origin. The oldest, the "Vespa 98" (number corresponding to engine size), dates back to 1946 and is one of 15,000 units produced by the Sestri Ponente factory (near Genoa) between 1946 and 1948, before a 125 cc engine was developed.

The most interesting example is undeniably the "Vespa TAP" (Airborne Troops), produced for the French troops who fought in Vietnam. These very light two-wheelers with reinforced parts were parachuted in behind enemy lines, and allowed soldiers to ride over terrain that was very steep and difficult to access. These incredible "war Vespas" were manufactured from 1956 by ACMA (Ateliers de Construction de Motocycles et Automobiles), already a Piaggio franchise.

The bikes were armed with a cannon similar to the "Super Bazooka" that could pierce armour-plating up to a centimetre thick. The gun was mounted under the seat at a slight angle, extending more than a metre beyond the windshield that supported it.

The TAP could carry two riders and the luggage rack held six large missiles. The removable support could be converted into a tripod for aiming the weapon. Six hundred of these Vespas were produced, all painted in the camouflage colours of green and beige.

STUDIO 137A

❾

(former City Hall Café)
137A Corso Vittorio Emanuele
• Metro: Line 2 Amedeo
• Funicular Chiaia: Parco Margherita
• Visits on reservation
• info@137a.it

> *Arts workshop in a historic meeting place*

Following the "coworking" principle, several artists, designers, architects, photographers and stylists share the large open-plan space at 137A, where a wide range of events is organised: arts workshops, cinema sets, exhibitions ...

137A occupies the premises that belonged a few years ago to the famous City Hall Café, a historic location where Andy Warhol met Joseph Beuys and where Chet Baker, Paolo Conte, Dizzy Gillespie, Stan Getz, Dave Holland, Sam Rivers and many other big names performed.

The current occupants have kept the original architecture, but added vintage artefacts, photographs and contemporary artworks. You can ask to have a coffee or an aperitif in the lovely small garden/terrace.

NEARBY

❿

EVERY PICTURE TELLS A STORY

A few steps away, at No. 141C, is a small workshop for restoring vintage objects. On request, the owner Giovanni Rinaldi will give you a slide show with a French stereoscopic device from the early 20th century. The extremely rare images show significant events in the city's history during the last century, such as the eruption of Vesuvius in 1944 and numerous views of Naples of yesteryear. For reservations, phone Signor Rinaldi: 347 3839827.

FRESCOES AT THE STAZIONE ZOOLOGICA ANTON DOHRN ⑪

Villa Comunale
• Metro: Line 2 Amedeo • Funicular Chiaia: Parco Margherita
• Open 9.30am–6pm; closed Mondays
• Visits to frescoes on reservation
• Tel: 081 5833111 / 081 5833218
• www.szn.it • stazione.zoologica@szn.it

> **A beautiful reading room in the aquarium**

The Stazione Zoologica Anton Dohrn, which houses Europe's only 19th-century aquarium still open to the public, also has spectacular frescoes on the walls of the library's reading room: the themes coincide perfectly with the ideology of its founder, German zoologist Anton Dohrn. As a supporter of Darwin's evolutionary theories, he aspired to combine science with art, so in 1873 he asked the painter Hans von Marées and the architect Adolf von Hildebrand to decorate the room accordingly.

In a decor featuring loggias surrounded by a frieze of marine plants and animals, a number of different scenes are painted: to the right of the entrance, muscular fishermen roll up their nets and push a boat out onto the water; they are next seen with a mysterious woman at the end of their working day.

Fishermen push the boat out

The other wall features *Pergola*: a group of friends seated in a tavern near Palazzo Donn'Anna in Posillipo (Anton Dohrn with his colleagues, Kleinenberg and Grant, as well as the two artists, von Marées and von Hildebrand, are recognisable).

Finally, on the wall opposite the entrance is an orange grove where two women chat while three male figures, an allegory of the three ages of man, are working.

This frescoed room is directly above the aquarium, which – almost uniquely – has kept its original 1874 structure. Here you can admire all the marine species from the Mediterranean, including some that are extremely rare.

The orange grove: the three ages of man

PALAZZO SAN TEODORO

281 Riviera di Chiaia
• Metro: Line 2 Amedeo • Funicular Chiaia: Parco Margherita
• Visits on reservation
• Tel: 081 3604134 / 081 3604135
• info@palazzosanteodoro.it

> *A palazzo in Pompeian style*

Built in 1826 in a style reminiscent of Roman patrician houses by the Florentine architect Guglielmo Bechi, a great admirer of antiquity, the beautiful residence which belonged to Duke Caracciolo of San Teodoro is unknown to most Neapolitans.

Much of the palazzo is now private apartments, with the exception of the first-floor rooms which can be hired for receptions and are therefore open to the public. At the top of an elegant marble staircase, you enter the large lavishly decorated dining room with terracotta tiles in imitation of Pompeian houses. In the middle of the ceiling hangs an imposing chandelier, a gift from King Ferdinand II. Walk through into the music room, which gives the impression of being in a Roman villa: columns, frescoed mythological themes dominated by Pompeian red, a ceiling decoration emulating Nero's Domus Aurea (Golden House) ...

FEMALE CENTAURS THAT CAUGHT THE ATTENTION OF THE METROPOLITAN MUSEUM OF ART

Guglielmo Bechi, known for his anti-conformism, had female centaurs painted on the ceiling of one of the rooms leading from the dining room to the music room. The fresco so impressed the directors of New York's Metropolitan Museum that they published a long article on the subject.

PALAZZO LEONETTI STAIRCASE AND ELEVATOR

❸

40 Via dei Mille
• Metro: Line 2 Amedeo
• Funicular Chiaia: Parco Margherita
• Visits during caretaker's working hours

A staircase and an elevator "suspended in space"

The self-supporting staircase of Palazzo Leonetti, built in 1910 by architect Giulio Ulisse Arata, is a work of great ingenuity. The steps of the Liberty-style staircase, whose elegant railing is decorated with floral motifs, seem to emerge from the wall, giving the impression of being suspended in space along with the elevator structure which is supported by the steps.

This system is used in both wings of the building, which is U-shaped, an unusual architectural form for Naples.

Palazzo Leonetti, one of the city's most elegant palazzi, is home to two consulates – British and Spanish. While initially designed as a luxury hotel, it was then used to accommodate the residents of the Pendino neighbourhood when it was demolished during the Risanamento. For financial reasons it was sold to the family of the Leonetti counts in 1916.

NEARBY

GAY-ODIN MUSEUM OF CHOCOLATE

❹

12 Via Vetriera
• Metro: Line 2 Amedeo • Funicular Chiaia: Parco Margherita
• Tel: 081 417843
• info@gayodin.it
• Visits during shop opening hours

Fabbrica Cioccolato Gay-Odin, one of the oldest chocolate manufacturers in the city, was founded in 1894 by a Piedmontese couple, Isidoro Odin and Onorina Gay. It has occupied the current premises since 1922. Besides the house specialities, visitors are offered the chance to visit a small museum with a collection of old wooden and bronze machines that show the different stages of manufacturing chocolate: a large bean grinder from 1837, a measuring device for liqueurs, etc. Visitors are shown how the machines work: the cocoa powder was separated from the fat (cocoa butter) in the beans, then, with the bronze wheel heated in the fire, the hot ingredients were mixed to make the chocolates.

Among the specialities is the "*foresta*" (forest), a small log composed of superfine layers of chocolate fashioned with a granite roller. Gay-Odin is also known for its 3 m tall Easter egg, displayed every year in the shop window and decorated with a different greeting every time.

Gay-Odin was sold in the 1950s to the Maglietta family, who still produce their chocolates in the traditional way. It was declared a national monument in 1993.

MUSEO DEL TESSILE E DELL'ABBIGLIAMENTO ⓯ *"ELENA ALDOBRANDINI"*

18 Piazzetta Mondragone
• Metro: Line 2 Amedeo • Funicolar Centrale, Corso Vittorio Emanuele
• Tel: 081 4976104 • www.fondazionemondragone.it
• Visits Monday to Friday 9.30am–1pm and 3pm–5pm;
Saturday 9am–1pm (but telephone in advance to check opening hours)
• Admission: €5

> *A trip through the history of Neapolitan haute couture*

Since 2003, the rooms on the first and second floors of the building occupied by the Fondazione Mondragone – set up in 1655 by Elena Aldobrandini, wife of the Duke of Mondragone and Prince of Stigliano – have housed the Museum of Textiles and Clothing. There are major collections by famous Neapolitan fashion designers, together with photographs and various documents that trace the evolution of local fashion from the end of the 19th century up to the mid-20th century. You can also admire beautiful upholstery fabrics, all manufactured in Neapolitan factories between the late 19th and mid-20th centuries, as well as robes and sacred objects from the church of Santa Maria delle Grazie a Mondragone, which is part of the foundation.

Be sure not to miss the fabulous garden whose beauty was praised by a number of chroniclers in antiquity – access is by a flight of steps in the courtyard. Outdoor concerts are organised here in summer.

TRADITIONAL NEAPOLITAN CHIC

The international fame of Neapolitan couture is due in part to the existence of London House, frequented by celebrities such as the princes of Savoy, Eduardo De Filippo, Vittorio De Sica and many others. The establishment was founded in the early 1930s by Gennaro Rubinacci, whose grandfather imported silk fabrics from the East in the first half of the 19th century.

PALAZZO MANNAJUOLO STAIRCASE

36 Via Filangieri
• Metro: Line 2 Amedeo • Funicular Chiaia: Parco Margherita
• Visits during caretaker's working hours

Palazzo Mannajuolo, built between 1909 and 1911, takes its name from one of the three engineers who designed it.

An Art Nouveau gem

This beautiful piece of architecture, located on the city's most exclusive street, is not on the tourist trail or even on the itineraries that cultural associations organise for locals. However, the corbelled, elliptical marble staircase, with its wrought-iron railings in Art Nouveau style, is a real gem.

The whole design is one of great boldness and elegance: seen from below, the curved flights blend with horizontal planes against a fake blue sky.

THE EARLY DAYS OF EDUARDO, "A GIANT OF EUROPEAN THEATRE"

In 1925, part of Palazzo Mannajuolo was converted into a cinema/theatre (the Kursaal), now the Filangieri cinema. It was here in 1931 that one of the giants of Italian theatre, Eduardo De Filippo (1900–1984), known to Neapolitans simply as "Eduardo", made his debut as a worthy successor to Pirandello. His plays, nearly all in the Neapolitan dialect, have always met with resounding success worldwide, as far away as India and Japan. In the UK it was Laurence Olivier who, through Eduardo, triumphed with *Saturday, Sunday, Monday*; in the US, critics heralded him as "a giant of European theatre". Such was the playwright's fame (and that of his company, which included his brother Peppino and sister Titina) that under the fascist regime, when the law banned "dialects" and Eduardo blithely ignored this censorship, Mussolini himself was obliged to declare: "We don't touch the De Filippo family!"

PIANO NOBILE OF PALAZZO NUNZIANTE

Fideuram Bank
7 / 15 Via Domenico Morelli
• Visits can sometimes be arranged on application to:
• ocardarelli5@fideuram.it
• gbalsamo@fideuram.it

Palazzo Nunziante is certainly one of the masterpieces of 19th-century Naples. Although the exterior of the monumental building is impressive, the real treasure is its *piano nobile* (main floor), with a ceiling height of 7.5 m and an area of 550 m², including a grand salon of 120 m² reached by a superb monumental staircase. The frescoes are by Vincenzo Paliotti.

Hidden wonders

The palazzo was built in 1855 on the initiative of Alessandro Nunziante, Duke of Milan, who commissioned the project from Milanese architect and urban planner Enrico Alvino. The vast size of the building is the result of the architect's desire to complete the triangular Piazza dei Martiri (Martyrs' Square). Together with its large walled "garden of earthly delights", it does indeed define the layout of the piazza.

A private chapel contains works by Paolo Vetri and Antonio Busciolano, as well as a beautiful painting of *Our Lady of the Assumption* by Domenico Morelli.

PALESTRA "FITNESS & BEAUTY" ⑱

26 Vico Santa Maria a Cappella Vecchia
• Metro: Line 2 Amedeo • Funicular Augusteo
• Visits on request during opening hours
• Tel: 081 7646580

A sports venue in a deconsecrated church

In what is now the chic neighbourhood of Piazza dei Martiri, the early Christians built a chapel near a cave which, according to some writers (such as Jacopo Sannazzaro, see p. 27), was dedicated to the Egyptian god Serapis. Later, Basilian monks enlarged the chapel, which became a church and then a monastery. The complex then passed to the Benedictines and the Olivetans. In the 19th century, the monastery was sold to the Marquis di Sessa (owner of the neighbouring palazzo). The church itself was handed over to a religious congregation. Now deconsecrated, it has become a gym and sports centre, although the 18th-century stucco and the Gothic portico can still be seen.

CARAFA CAVES

30/M Vico Santa Maria a Cappella Vecchia, c/o Gran Garage
• Metro: Line 2 Amedeo • Funicular Chiaia: Parco Margherita
• Monday to Saturday open 24/7; best to visit during daylight hours
• Admission free

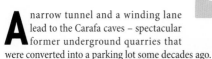

A magical site

A narrow tunnel and a winding lane lead to the Carafa caves – spectacular former underground quarries that were converted into a parking lot some decades ago.

To see their full extent, go up to the second level (artificially created to make better use of the space), from where you can appreciate the impressive height of the vaults supported by huge stone arches.

Since antiquity, the people of Naples have excavated the local yellow and grey tuff, a soft but durable volcanic stone that is ideal for all kinds of construction work. The Romans used it to build water tanks for their fleet.

According to some sources, during the Angevin domination in the 13th century this quarry supplied the materials to enlarge the port and build Castel Nuovo (New Castle, the royal palace of the time).

The Military Academy of Nunziatella, the Military Archives, the Madeleine bridge (which spanned the Sebeto river at the entrance to the city) and Palazzo Carafa (hence the name of the caves) were all built with tuff from these quarries.

THE OLD CITY AND ITS FERRUGINOUS WATER

The Carafa caves were cut into the hill of Pizzofalcone (formerly known as Monte Echia), part of the territory where, in the 7th century BC, the Greeks founded a place they named after the Siren Parthenope (see p. 153). In Roman times the hill became the setting for the sumptuous residence of General Lucullus, famous for his proverbial banquets. The remains of his villa are still visible from the most panoramic viewpoint of Pizzofalcone.

The natural caves at the foot of the hill, inhabited in the Neolithic period, were closed in the 17th century. Monte Echia was the source of the ferruginous water much enjoyed by Neapolitans, which was collected and stored in earthenware pot-bellied jugs – part of the memories of old Naples – to be sold from small kiosks dotted around the city. The source, which was suspected of being polluted, was sealed off in the 1970s.

TOURS OF THE GALLERIA BORBONICA

"Standard" tour organised by the Associazione Culturale Borbonica
Sotterranea
40 Via Domenico Morelli (entrance in Morelli parking garage)
• Metro: Line 1 Municipio; Line 2 Piazza Amedeo
• Funicular Parco Margherita
• Tel: 366 2484151, 081 7645808 • mail@galleriaborbonica.it
• www.galleriaborbonica.com
• Guided tours: Friday, Saturday, Sunday and public holidays 10am,
12 noon, 3.30pm, 5.30pm (duration 1 h 20 min)
• 60% of the route is wheelchair accessible

> *The king's secret passage*

The Bourbon Gallery is part of a strategic design by the Bourbon King Ferdinand II: in 1853 he commissioned architect Errico Alvino to excavate an underground passage beneath Monte Echia, between Palazzo Reale and Piazza Vittoria, which as well as opening onto the sea was also close to the barracks. The passage was designed to allow the troops stationed in the barracks on Via Pace (today Via Domenico Morelli) quick access to the royal residence; it was also a means of escape for the royal family if they were in danger from a foreign invasion. The work, carried out entirely by hand, was often delayed by technical problems, such as the huge cisterns over which bridges had to be built and which can still be seen today. The 431 m long tunnel ran down to Piazza Carolina, behind the columned portico of Piazza del Plebiscito, but it was never completed due to the excessive cost and the unstable political situation.

The tunnel had no exit until the Second World War, when it was used as an air-raid shelter and fitted with electricity and toilets, still there today. After the war and until 1970, the tunnel was used by the city council to store objects found in the rubble of buildings destroyed by the 200 bombardments the city had suffered. These abandoned objects are still there – cars and motorbikes by the dozen, many statues from different eras, and the funerary monument of Captain Aurelio Padovani, founder of the Neapolitan branch of the Fascist Party.

The association runs three different tours exploring this section of the "underground city": Standard (see above), Adventure (*Avventura*) (see p. 54) and Caving (*Speleo*) (see p. 63). The Adventure option includes a raft ride through part of the tunnel, whereas the Standard tour lets you walk the full length of it.

REMAINS OF AN UNDERGROUND TRAMLINE

"Adventure" tour organised by the Associazione Culturale Borbonica
Sotterranea
40 Via Domenico Morelli (entrance in Morelli parking garage)
• Metro: Line 2 Amedeo • Funicular Chiaia: Parco Margherita
• Tel: 366 2484151, 081 7645808
• mail@galleria borbonica.it • www.galleriaborbonica.com
• Guided tours: Saturday and Sunday 10am, 12pm, 3.30pm and 5.30pm
(duration 1 h 20 min)

On a raft 20 m below Piazza del Plebiscito

In the late 1980s, a metro line was planned below Piazza del Plebiscito, or rather an underground tram line that was supposed – on the occasion of the 1990 World Cup – to connect the western districts to the city centre and run on to the east side. The work was never completed. As the tunnel is partly flooded from the groundwater table, a raft ride is part of this tour in the "underbelly" of Naples.

A short walk through the tunnel leads to a jetty where you board a raft for the crossing (which only takes a few minutes), before continuing on foot as far as a gallery where you can still see traces of the construction site.

The "Adventure" tour helps you understand the extent of this underground city. Naples in fact sits on an unimaginable maze of tunnels, aqueducts and cisterns carved out of the tuff over the centuries since the founding of the Greek city, and even earlier, as the first traces of human presence date back to the third millennium BC.

At all periods the excavated volcanic stone was reused for building at street level. The cisterns, which were in use until the 19th century, were closed in 1885 during a severe cholera epidemic and replaced by a modern aqueduct.

During the Second World War, some of the tunnels were used as air-raid shelters.

The association runs four different tours exploring this section of the "underground city": Standard (see p. 51), Adventure (*Avventura*) (see above), Caving (*Speleo*) (see p. 63), and "Via delle Memorie" (see p. 65). The Adventure option includes a raft ride through part of the tunnel, whereas the Standard tour lets you walk the full length of it.

FORMER AULA MAGNA OF THE FACULTY OF ECONOMICS AND COMMERCE

㉒

Centro Congressi Federico II - 36 Via Partenope
- Bus: C25 or 140
- Metro: Line 1 Municipio • Funicular Chiaia: Parco Margherita
- Visits by appointment: 081 2535706
- Monday to Friday 9am to 7pm

A ceiling worthy of a royal palace

The Conference Centre of the University of Naples Federico II, built by Roberto Pane in 1937, boasts ambitious architecture typical of the Mussolini era: a vast columned hall with a grand staircase and a room with a stunning coffered wooden ceiling 22.5 m long. The current occupants are recent, as the building formerly housed the Faculty of Economics and Commerce – the first in Europe (see opposite).

NEARBY

MUSEO ORIENTALE "UMBERTO SCERRATO"
61/62 Via Chiatamone (entrance on Via Partenope)
• Funicular centrale: Augusteo
• www.museorientale.unior.it • museorientale@unior.it
• Admission free • Open Thursday and Friday 11am–2pm; other days by appointment

The Umberto Scerrato Museum, which belongs to the University of Naples "L'Orientale", opened in November 2012. It brings together over 300 pieces in addition to various collections previously acquired by the university but scattered around different sites and not open to the public.

Among the most interesting is a collection of Mesopotamian seals (2002 BC–5th century AD) that is unique in Italy. Some gemstone seals served as good-luck talismans, as borne out by the inscription on one of them: "Long life to the owner of this seal." In the 19th century it was very fashionable to set such objects in jewellery. The collection of Egyptian and Islamic stelae is also

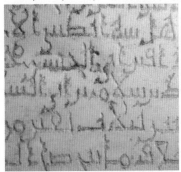

interesting: the smallest of the Islamic steles, displayed at the museum entrance and dating from AD 819, is among the oldest found to date. The University of Naples "L'Orientale", founded in 1732, is Europe's first seat of learning dedicated to the study of non-European cultures and remains one of the most important in Italy.

MUSEO DI ETNOPREISTORIA
• Tel: 081 7645343 • museo@cainapoli.it
• Open Saturday and Sunday 10am to 1pm; other days by appointment

Since 1972 the wonderful Castel dell'Ovo has housed the "Alfonso Piciocchi" Ethno-Prehistory Museum run by the Neapolitan Speleological Association (Naples branch of the Club Alpino Italiano, CAI).

The displays include artefacts from the Lower Palaeolithic to the Iron Age. Of particular note are the fossil animals and many Villanovan ceramics from the Catena site. The museum also offers visitors an innovative approach to archaeology that reveals how our ancestors lived.

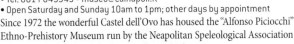

BYZANTINE REMAINS IN CASTEL DELL'OVO
Traces of the Byzantine church of San Salvatore (a stone arch, two pillars and three small Roman columns) can be found in the Castle of the Egg. Access to this part of the fortress is only authorised on certain occasions such as Maggio dei Monumenti (Monuments in May). Info: www.comune.napoli.it.

For the connection between Castel dell'Ovo and Virgil's egg, see following double-page spread.

FROM VIRGIL'S EGG TO THE CASTLE OF THE EGG

The name Castel dell'Ovo (Castle of the Egg) derives from a legend known only in outline. Virgil, the great benefactor of Naples, is supposed to have placed an egg in a glass carafe, then locked the carafe in a cage hung from the roof of a tunnel over which this castle was later built, right in the city centre near the waterfront.

The egg is a recurring symbol in many religious rites in Naples and elsewhere. It is the ultimate symbol of life and, with its perfect shape, a representation of the universe: part of it is yellow like the Sun and part is white like the Moon, the two celestial bodies that personify male and female respectively.

In Naples the egg is linked to various cults, notably that of the Siren Parthenope (see p. 153), the founder of Naples, a deity half-woman and

PORTO DI NAPOLI

Castello dell OVO

half-bird who, before dying, had laid a sacred egg at the spot where they later built her tomb. So it would be a very inauspicious omen if the egg was stolen or broken.

This belief persisted until the 14th century, a time when attempts were being made to eradicate the pagan cults.

It is said that when Queen Joan I of Anjou rebuilt the castle after it was destroyed by a tidal wave, she hung a cage containing an egg in the tunnels under the fortress in order to save the city. In any case, the islet was renamed "Il Salvatore" (The Saviour) after the church, which was incorporated into the fortress. A chapel dedicated to the Madonna dell'Uovo (Our Lady of the Egg) was also built to keep both clergy and people happy. Today, no trace of the chapel remains, though the legend continues to haunt the castle vaults.

The Castle of the Egg was built by the Normans (12th century) on the ruins of a Basilian monastery, built in turn on the remains of an estate that belonged to the Roman general Lucullus.

The huge estate stretched from the existing islet to the hill of Pizzofalcone and probably as far as Castel Nuovo (Piazza Municipio).

Lucullus bred moray eels in saltwater lakes dotted around his grounds. In his splendid gardens he had planted the very first peach trees to be imported from Persia, as well as the first cherry trees from Pontus, a region bordering the Black Sea. This love of gastronomy earned Lucullus such a reputation that the word "Lucullan" now means "lavish" or "gourmet".

THE PRESIDENT'S ANTI-AIRCRAFT SHELTER

"Caving" (Speleo) tour organised by the Associazione Culturale
Borbonica Sotterranea
4 Vico Grottone
• Funicular Centrale: Augusteo, metro Linea 1 Municipio
• Tel: 366 2484151, 081 7645808
• mail@galleria borbonica.it
• www.galleriaborbonica.com
• Guided tours: Saturday and Sunday at 11am and 4pm (duration
2½ hours)

> **Hoisted
> by cable 35 m
> underground**

The Caving tour organised by the Associazione Culturale Borbonica Sotterranea requires equipment that is provided by the association itself (helmet with lamp, overalls and harness). You start down a narrow 17th-century staircase that leads to the cisterns 35 m below. You then go through a maze of pipes and cisterns once used to supply the city with water, before reaching a bomb shelter used during the Second World War by the famous writer Curzio Malaparte and the current President of the Italian Republic, Giorgio Napolitano.

Next is a small gallery with thousands of shells piled high, thrown out from a 19th-century goldsmith's that specialised in buttons and cameos: the workshop was located just above the tunnel and was linked to it by means of a well. Then you have to crawl along increasingly narrow tunnels belonging to the ancient Bolla aqueduct, where in some places there are mysterious (religious?) signs on the walls, probably made by the *pozzari*, the men who looked after the underground aqueducts. Finally, you cross a huge cave via a wooden bridge suspended 6 m above the ground and return by cable lift.

The association runs four different tours exploring this section of the
"underground city": Standard (see p. 51), Adventure (*Avventura*) (see
p. 56), Caving (*Speleo*) (see above) and 'Via delle memorie' (see p. 65).
The Adventure option includes a raft ride through part of the tunnel,
whereas the Standard tour lets you walk the full length of it.

VIA DELLE MEMORIE

Itinerary of the Associazione Culturale Borbonica Sotterranea
14 Via Monte di Dio, Palazzo Serra di Cassano, Int. A14
• Central funicular: Augusteo; Chiaia funicular: Parco Margherita
• Metro: Line 1 Municipio; Line 2 Piazza Amedeo
• Guided tours on Fridays, Saturdays, Sundays and public holidays at
10am and 4pm (duration 1h 15mins)
• Tel: 366 2484151 / 081 7645808
• mail@galleriaborbonica.com
• www.galleriaborbonica.com

> *An underground flight of 115 steps that leads to an air-raid shelter and a huge cistern*

The historic Palazzo Serra di Cassano was built with tuff excavated from its foundations: the resulting caves were formerly used for aqueducts, cisterns and air-raid shelters. These vast galleries can be reached from the Bourbon Tunnel on the Via delle Memorie (Memory Lane) guided tour.

At the start of the descent, the first site you come across (former stables converted first into a carpentry workshop and more recently into an exhibition space) is filled with dozens of objects. These were found by volunteers cleaning up the tonnes of residue from the palazzos above that were blocking the passageways. Many everyday items such as footwear, glass flacons, little vases, etc. were also discovered.

Next stop is the deepest vault, straight down a flight of 115 steps, which leads to the former air-raid shelter installed during the Second World War to accommodate over 2,600 people.

Down there you'll see a huge and spectacular stairway that connects the underground aqueduct tank to the surface quarries. It was built by the army to help the thousands of people seeking shelter from the bombardments to climb up and down easily.

The tour continues through a network of quarries, tunnels and galleries before ending abruptly at the edge of a huge cistern, partly filled with waste material (it was 5–6 m deeper than it appears today) but once again full of water from the original aqueduct, now restored and working again.

VESTIGES OF THE FORMER "SUPREMA" BROTHEL

Chiaja Hotel de Charme - Antica Casa Lecaldano Sasso La Terza
216 Via Chiaia – 80121 Napoli
• Metro: Line 1 Municipio • Funicular Centrale: Augusteo • Bus: R2 from Napoli Centrale station
• Tel: 081 415555 / 081 422344 • info@hotelchiaia.it

De Crescenzo said: 'The evening before, Saint Januarius failed to work his miracle'

The up-market "Suprema" brothel in the Spanish quarter was one of the most elegant and luxurious in the city. Although at the time you entered by the door which now leads to the kitchen of the famous Pizzeria Brandi, access today is via the Chiaja Hotel de Charme (address above), whose staff are happy to show visitors around.

In 1958, the Suprema was closed, like all the brothels in Italy, to the chagrin of many fans, including Luciano De Crescenzo. This illustrious Neapolitan author wrote that on 19 September 1958, Saint Januarius (the city's patron saint) had failed to work his biannual miracle, presumably in protest at the unjust closures that would take place next day.

But fate had decided that the Suprema would live again. One day, a contractor who was converting a large apartment block into a hotel heard that the adjacent premises were being offered for sale at auction. He managed to buy the place only to discover that it was the former brothel.

Given its historical value, the hotel's interiors have been restored in spirit, with their garish colours and even a price list. You can see some original objects such as mirrors, a small piece of furniture and the bidet where prostitutes washed their clients (in the first half of the 20th century, venereal disease was widespread and greatly feared). Don't miss the original sign, which has been carefully restored.

The rooms with their flashy decor – around ten in all – have plaques with the "stage name" of each girl. They read: Mimì of Vesuvius (alias the anti-fascist, Gelsomina), Anastasia the Friulian, Dorina of Sorrento …

At the beginning of the corridor, to the left, a little bridge connects two small terraces that used to overlook the courtyard: from here the girls would display their charms while the clients, down below in the lobby, made their choice. Further along the corridor you can admire a beautiful Art Nouveau glass door, which has also been restored. A staircase, which now leads to the hotel's emergency exit, at the time led to a door reserved for personalities or celebrities who didn't want to be seen in such a place.

ASSOCIAZIONE "CIRCOLO ARTISTICO POLITECNICO" 28

48 Piazza Trieste e Trento
• Metro: Line 1 Municipio
• Funicular Centrale: Augusteo • Bus: R2 from Napoli Centrale station
• segreteria@fondazionecircoloartistico.it • Tel: 081 426543
• www.fondazionecircoloartistico.it

> *A meeting place under the sign of art and culture*

Established on 22 December 1888 under the name Società Napoletana degli Artisti by a group of famous artists including Antonio Mancini and Domenico Morelli, the Circolo Artistico Politecnico association, housed on the second floor of the palazzo of Cardinal Zapata (viceroy of Naples in the 17th century), has a museum, historical archives, a library and a photographic collection. It also awards scholarships and organises cultural events, art exhibitions, concerts and plays.

The elegant Liberty-style salon dates from 1912 and was designed by the architect Giovan Battista Comencini. The museum displays over 500 works by Neapolitan painters and sculptors of the early 19th to early 20th centuries. The photographic collection includes signed portraits of famous people such as Enrico De Nicola, Giorgio Napolitano, Enrico Caruso, Eduardo De Filippo and Giacomo Puccini. The library is dedicated to the poet, journalist and writer Ferdinando Russo, a founder member of the circle. It holds 3,000 volumes, including rare editions from 1687.

GIOSUÈ CARDUCCI'S REVENGE

The guest of honour at a poetry conference held in 1887 was the great Tuscan poet Giosuè Carducci, who was visiting Naples with his girlfriend Annie Vivanti. Ferdinando Russo was struck by her beauty and straightaway wrote a song especially for her, *Scetate* (Wake Up), set to music by Mario Costa. One night, Russo sang his composition below the balcony of the hotel where Carducci and his girlfriend were staying. When he attended the conference next day, the furious Carducci declared that poetry "was the prerogative of people living in cold and meditative regions".

MASCAGNI, A POOR LOSER

The Italian operatic composer Pietro Mascagni was a tireless card player, and could spend all night at "*Lo Scopone scientifico*" (see the 1972 film of that name directed by Luigi Comencini), which is played by two couples with Neapolitan cards. Mascagni always claimed he was unbeatable at this game, but whenever he happened to lose he attacked his partner, calling him "a nullity who deserves an end like Turiddu", alluding to his opera *Cavalleria rusticana*.

HORNS AGAINST THE EVIL EYE

The number of Neapolitans who have never owned a red horn can be counted on the fingers of one hand. Even fewer have never mimicked horns, pointing the index and little fingers towards the ground, an automatic gesture for them as soon as they feel threatened by a curse, real or imaginary.

And the phrase "I'm making the *corna*" (sign of the horns) is used instead of "Touch wood". The people of Naples certainly didn't invent this symbol, which was once almost universal, but have simply developed it in their own way and perpetuated its use over time, to make it the ultimate "talisman".

Animal horns were displayed over house entrances as far back as the Neolithic period. They were believed to be a powerful natural weapon in driving out enemies and the forces of evil. By warding off misfortune, they brought happiness and therefore fertility, which was indispensable for survival.

Warriors in most parts of the world wore horned helmets and the animals that supplied the horns themselves became objects of worship.

In ancient Egypt, horns also became an attribute of female fertility: Isis, the Great Mother, a very popular deity in Rome and Naples, wore horns on her head with the Moon set between them. In addition, many goddesses are represented with a crescent Moon, an allusion to the horn.

The little Neapolitan version, in order to be effective, must be red, hollow, twisted, pointed and received as a gift. It derives from the Roman phallus, attribute of the god Priapus, a ubiquitous amulet in Roman culture. At Pompeii, phalluses were carved on doors, walls and even the cobbled streets. In people's homes, many objects were decorated with huge priapic symbols in marble or bronze. Women wore the symbol around their necks as red coral pendants.

With the coming of Christianity, propriety required the phallus to be replaced by a horn. In the Middle Ages, Neapolitan jewellers were renowned for their necklaces made from miniature red horns, which were exported throughout Europe.

CUCKOLD'S HORNS

Whereas to ward off the *iettatura* (curse of the evil eye, from Neapolitan *jettare*, to throw, or hurl), the two-fingered gesture points to the ground, pointing the fingers up at someone is to treat them as a cuckold. Originally this gesture branded a man as an ox and therefore impotent.

In Italy, Saint Martin, Bishop of Tours, became the patron of deceived husbands. Each city has its own legend to justify this practice. In Naples it is said that the husbands of unfaithful women would lock themselves in the Certosa di San Martino (Saint Martin's Charterhouse, see p. 371).

CORALS IN THE MUSEO ASCIONE ㉙

Ascione 1855 SrL - 19 Piazzetta Matilde Serao (inside Galleria Umberto I)
• Metro: Line 1 Municipio • Funicular Centrale: Augusteo
• Visits on reservation • Tel: 081 421111
• napoli@ascione.com • www.ascione.com

> *A coral display in the city centre*

I n premises located on the second floor inside Galleria Umberto I, in the museum run by the house of Ascione, you can admire over 300 designs in coral, lava stone (very popular with Queen Victoria) and cameos – so many choice pieces from a production that spread over a century and a half from the early 19th century to the 1940s. The Ascione workshop is the oldest in the town of Torre del Greco (between Pompeii and Naples), world capital of coral and cameos.

Here you'll find a superb chain created in 1938 for Princess Maria José on the occasion of her visit to Naples; a precious coral necklace presented to Queen Farida of Egypt (two copies of this were made in case the original was lost); and a 1920 cameo considered to be one of the prettiest in the world, *Immortal Love*, by Antonio Mennella. Note also a splendid medusa in coral, emblem of the house, which alludes to the Medusa of Greek mythology whose blood turned into coral when she was killed by Perseus.

A browse through the information section will reveal corals of different types and provenances, ancient techniques for collecting the coral (which used to be found in abundance along the coast) and tools for working the precious material ... an entire room is devoted to cameos and the art of engraving them.

LUCCHESI PALLI WING, *BIBLIOTECA NAZIONALE* VITTORIO EMANUELE III

1 Piazza del Plebiscito
- Metro: Line 1 Municipio, Line 2 Montesanto • Funicular Centrale: Augusteo
- Bus: R2 from Napoli Centrale station
- Tel: 081 7819266 (administration), 081 7819240 / 7819267
- bn-na.lucchesipalli@beniculturali.it
- Open Monday to Friday 8.30am–6.45pm (last distribution 5.30pm)

> **A splendid but virtually unknown collection**

This wing of the Victor Emmanuel III National Library holds the valuable and little-known Lucchesi Palli collection, established in 1888 when Count Febo Edoardo Lucchesi Palli of the Campofranco (Sicily) noble family donated his extensive library to the state. The count gave not only his books and manuscripts, but also furniture and shelving from his library, having them transported and adapted at his own expense. The rooms were then embellished by the city's most sought-after artisans.

The original collection consisted of over 30,000 volumes (librettos, theatrical works and Japanese literature in the original language). It has since developed considerably as a result of acquisitions and other donations,

to become a reference for music, theatre and cinema.

The collection includes many letters in Giuseppe Verdi's own hand; all the manuscripts and publications of the celebrated poet Salvatore Di Giacomo (see p. 78), who was also the librarian of this section; some 2,500 scripts of plays from the early 19th century; the Raffaele Viviani archive (see p. 333), tracing the entire career of the great Neapolitan actor and writer; as well as a collection of over 25,000 *Piedigrotte* – Neapolitan songs mainly written for the Piedigrotta festival (see p. 30).

AOSTA COLLECTION AT THE *BIBLIOTECA NAZIONALE* VITTORIO EMANUELE III

1 Piazza del Plebiscito
• Metro: Line 1 Municipio, Line 2 Montesanto • Funicular Centrale: Augusteo
• Bus: R2 from Napoli Centrale station
• Tel: 081 781 19 31
• The visit is not for the faint-hearted!

> **The enchanted Africa of Hélène, Duchess of Aosta**

A tiger skin and head, the heads of an elephant and a rare three-horned rhinoceros, antelopes, giraffes and other stuffed animals of the savannah together with weapons (daggers, machetes, spears, guns, a sword with a horn hilt and an emerald set in the blade), African musical instruments, Inca artefacts, a rock inscription in the Berber language from the 11th century BC (one of the oldest in the world, found in the Algerian Sahara) ... All these objects were donated to the National Library by the Duchess of Aosta, Princess Hélène of Orléans, a world traveller (known as "the Bedouin princess"), photographer, hunter and benefactor (she was an inspector for the Red Cross). She died at Naples in 1951, aged nearly 80, and is buried in the church of Santa Maria Incoronata at Capodimonte.

The extraordinary Aosta collection was originally assembled in the Reggia (royal palace) at Capodimonte, where the duchess lived with her husband, Prince Emanuele Filiberto of Savoy-Aosta. In 1947, everything was entrusted

to one of her friends, Guerriera Guerrieri, the museum's director. It is now displayed in the five frescoed rooms that formerly comprised the private cabinet of King Ferdinand I of Bourbon.

The collection also includes 11,000 books and 10,000 photographs: private documents that reveal a unique image of the cadet branch of the Savoy dynasty. Hélène of Orléans was a precursor of the Danish Baroness Karen Blixen, who was also a writer and inspired the film *Out of Africa*. In Hélène's memoirs, she describes her journeys and continues to dream of Africa, where "my wandering soul could stop, live, enjoy the passing of time".

TEATRO SAN CARLO CLOCK

32

98/F Via San Carlo
• Metro: Line 1 Municipio • Funicular Centrale: Augusteo • Bus: R2 from Napoli Centrale station
• biglietteria@teatrosancarlo.it
• promozionepubblico@teatrosancarlo.it
• Booking office opening hours: Monday to Saturday 10am–7pm; Sunday 10am–3.30pm • Tel: 081 7972331

The clock face turns, not the hands

In the San Carlo theatre, the clock under the proscenium arch has a feature that few Neapolitans know about: instead of the clock hands moving, as tradition dictates, here the dial rotates around a fixed pointer in the form of the right arm of a winged female figure.

The most plausible explanation for this is that the Siren (lower left) is inviting Time to stop and enjoy the pleasure of the arts, while pointing out to him the Muses of poetry, music and dance. Time, in the centre and surrounded by six female figures, indicates the passing of the hours, which are represented as signs of the zodiac.

Originally, the predominant colours of the San Carlo theatre were blue and silver: these colours are still displayed on the royal coat of arms above the proscenium arch. The current red and gold decoration dates from 1849.

ROYAL ACCESS
The San Carlo theatre is linked to Palazzo Reale by an underground passage excavated on the orders of the Bourbon King Charles III. The passage, intended to connect the royal family's apartments to the box reserved for the king and his entourage, was commissioned from the architect Antonio Medrano by the king himself, who paid 32,000 ducats from his own pocket for the privilege.

THE NEW "GIARDINI ROOM" IN THE DISUSED CARPENTRY WORKSHOP
In 2011, the premises formerly occupied by the San Carlo theatre's carpentry workshop were converted into rehearsal and recording rooms. Below the "romantic garden" of Palazzo Reale, they can be glimpsed through a window near the sculpture *Prova d'orchestra* by Mimmo Paladino.

For more on music in Naples, see following double-page spread.

NAPLES, WORLD CAPITAL OF MUSIC

Of course, not all Neapolitans are musicians or singers, but music and singing are deeply rooted in their culture. In this region people pray, protest and even sell their wares in song.

In the 19th and 20th centuries, song production was in full swing and some melodies travelled from one end of the planet to the other in the baggage of the world's most famous tenors. The lyricists of this period were often poets of great stature such as Salvatore Di Giacomo to whom we owe, among other works, the delightful *Marechiaro*. It is said that E. A. Mario wrote about two thousand songs, among which is the hugely popular *Santa Lucia luntana*.

Many of the lyrics revolve around love, but there are others that celebrate Naples as its people are attached to their city in a way that borders on the absurd. Songs such as *Santa Lucia luntana*, dedicated to emigrants torn apart by homesickness, are a poignant testimony to this.

The echo of Neapolitan music spread around Europe from the early 16th century, when the first *villanelles* – pastoral songs – were transcribed and recovered by professional composers.

From the late 16th century onwards, Naples never ceased to produce great composers. Carlo Gesualdo, Prince of Venosa, was an innovative and unparalleled madrigalist, despite having been involved in a horrific crime: in his palazzo at 9 Piazza San Domenico, the prince surprised his wife Maria d'Avalos with her lover, Duke Fabrizio Carafa, and brutally murdered them both.

In the following centuries, the four Neapolitan conservatories (the first of which, Santa Maria di Loreto, was founded in 1537) echoed to the music of Pergolesi, Vinci, Scarlatti, Jommelli, Porpora, Cimarosa, Paisiello, Bellini, Leoncavallo, Cilea ... almost 300 of them in all.

Jean-Jacques Rousseau exclaimed in his 1768 *Dictionnaire de musique*: "Run, fly to Naples and listen to the masterpieces of Leo, Durante, Jommelli, Pergolesi ..." The 18th-century French writer Charles de Brosses called

Naples the "world capital of music". For Stendhal, writing in the first half of the 19th century, the San Carlo was simply incomparable. This theatre, built in 1737, was also the world's first opera house (Milan's La Scala dates from 1778 and Venice's La Fenice from 1792).

By the 15th century, music had already charmed the Aragonese (Spanish) court, and in the 13th and 14th centuries musical plays, predecessors of the lyric opera, were heard in the royal castle of the Angevin (French) dynasty. From the time of the founding of the city by the Greeks, the people had never stopped singing. Only a few pieces of this very early musical heritage have been recovered by the maestro Roberto De Simone (see p. 341) because it belonged to a strictly oral tradition.

Even today, during religious festivals, the words of ritual songs are improvised by the performers who, although following a traditional model, can't repeat what they have just sung. During these celebrations, the tarantella or "*tammurriata*" dance is performed in a frenzy, in bygone days with the aim of inducing a trance and communicating with the gods. These dances, considered "diabolical" by the Church, were even banned at one time, before ending up in the traditional music repertoire. Nowadays, in certain small towns of Campania, devotional dances are still performed as in Graeco-Roman times. The instruments are the same too – large and small tambourines, castanets, the double flute and vertical flute, and others with untranslatable Neapolitan names (*putipù, scetavajasse, triccabballacche*). When street vendors still walked the city, you could hear rhythmic poetry chanted to advertise their wares, with lines such as: "*Maiateche 'e cerase! Che belli voce! Sientele, segno c'abbrile trase*" (I'm selling these cherries in pairs! Listen to their beautiful voices! They say that April has arrived). The religious songs and the street vendors' voices are very similar to ancient Greek monody, even directly emulating it.

In their day, both Livy and Virgil recorded that they were moved by the wonderful songs they heard at Naples. Seneca complained of Neapolitans deserting places of high culture to squeeze into theatres where singers were performing. Nero came to Naples in a public relations exercise and recruited hordes of Alexandrians to his cause, because they applauded by making a terrific din with their instruments (hence the derivation of those untranslatable names above) – so it was Nero who invented "rent-a-crowd" applause on his visit to Naples.

This passion for music is rooted in the founding myth associated with the Siren Parthenope (see p. 153), one of the first deities of the ancient city. Just as the Sirens sang to sweeten the passing of the dying, the priestesses who worshipped at their shrine chanted prophecies. No wonder that singing is considered sacred in Naples.

Modern technology has not dried up the musical vein of ancient Parthenope. Excellent musicians and singers carry on the tradition. Riccardo Muti is a product of the Neapolitan music schools, as is maestro Roberto De Simone, one of the most eclectic geniuses of our time.

CIRCOLO NAZIONALE DELL'UNIONE

99 Via San Carlo
• Funicular Centrale: Augusteo
• Access only on request during Maggio dei Monumenti: phone or email to get authorization
• Tel: 081 415693 / 081 413329 • circolonazionaleunione@yahoo.it

A historic club faithful to ancient traditions

The Circolo Nazionale dell'Unione, considered the most beautiful private club in the city, has hosted numerous heads of state in its extremely lavish rooms.

An ancient wooden elevator with velvet-covered seats leads to the first floor with its reading room, meeting room, library, and the large salon of breathtaking riches – crystal chandeliers, vast mirrors in golden frames and stucco decoration. From the terrace of this salon you can enjoy an incomparable view of Palazzo Reale, Castel Nuovo and Piazza del Plebiscito.

This place was built to host the court on the orders of King Ferdinand IV (who became Ferdinand I after the Congress of Vienna) by the architect Antonio Niccolini, who was also responsible for the reconstruction of the San Carlo theatre after it burned down in 1816. Later, King Francis I of Bourbon gave the building to the Accademia delle Dame e dei Cavalieri (Academy of Dames and Knights), an aristocratic association that organised receptions, especially in honour of foreign dignitaries visiting Naples.

After the unification of Italy, Victor Emmanuel II hired out the building to a new association, the Casino dell'Unione, founded by union supporter Carlo Poerio. In 1947, the Casino and the Circolo Nazionale merged to create the Circolo Nazionale dell'Unione, whose vocation is still hospitality in the form of receptions in honour of high-ranking visitors. The club is members only but visits can be arranged on request or during the Maggio dei Monumenti open day in May. Certain rules are mandatory, such as the dress code (black tie for gentlemen, formal dress for ladies).

BAS-RELIEF OF A WOMAN

Triumphal arch at the entrance of Castel Nuovo – Piazza Municipio
• Metro: Line 1 Municipio, Line 2 Montesanto
• Funicular Centrale (Augusteo) or Funicular Montesanto (Montesanto)

> *Lucrezia d'Alagno, lover of King Alfonso I?*

The monumental gateway of the Arco di Trionfo (Triumphal Arch) at Castel Nuovo (the royal palace in the Angevin and Aragonese periods), a masterpiece of the Neapolitan Renaissance, commemorates Alfonso of Aragon's victorious entry to the city in 1443.

He is followed by pages, eminent citizens, soldiers, horsemen ... and one woman – the only one. She is shown in the foreground just in front of the horses pulling the triumphal chariot. Given the height of the arch, you won't be able to see her with the naked eye.

Historians are in agreement that the suggestion of her being an allegory of the Siren Parthenope is highly unlikely as she has never been shown fully clothed like this mysterious female figure: most experts think she represents Lucrezia d'Alagno, King Alfonso I's great love.

She was 18 and he was 53 when they met for the first time on 23 June 1448. On this Saint John's Eve, it is said, the beautiful and noble Lucrezia was begging in the street with the other girls, as tradition required. The king, who was passing by, accepted the small plant that the lovely beggar handed him and in exchange offered her a purseful of Alfonsos, the gold coins of his reign. Lucrezia opened the purse, pulled out a single coin and gave the rest back to the king, saying that one Alfonso was enough for her. Even if the story of this meeting is shrouded in legend, the king was indeed deeply in love with Lucrezia. Their love story lasted for ten years, until the death of the monarch. All those who knew her, even Pope Paul II, were ready to swear to Lucrezia's virtue as she never allowed Alfonso to share her bed. Be that as it may, the beautiful lady not only became immensely rich and powerful, but she was introduced to the king's court and he had her sit at his right hand during official ceremonies. But he could never marry his beloved, because, although he was separated from his wife of thirty years, the pope obstinately refused to grant him an annulment. Lucrezia, emboldened by her many influential connections, even tried her luck by going to Rome herself. Alfonso provided her with an escort of the noblest ladies of the kingdom, an army of servants and 500 horsemen, such were the depths of his passion. But Calixtus III was unimpressed and unyielding. On the king's death, Lucrezia's power diminished and she ended her days in a convent.

CASTEL NUOVO: A POPE IMPRISONED, CAMPANELLA TORTURED, GIOTTO'S FRESCOES, THE ESCAPADES OF JOAN OF ANJOU ...

It is said that the future Boniface VIII ordered his spies to intimidate the rather gullible Pope Celestine V while he was being held at the court of King Charles II of Anjou in Castel Nuovo. So under cover of night these minions introduced a long speaking tube into the room of the pope, who believed he was hearing the voice of God commanding him to renounce the papacy.

Celestine made his decision to abdicate in December 1294 and died two years later while interned on the orders of Boniface VIII.

Giotto, who in 1328 was the official court painter, completed no less than three cycles of paintings in Castel Nuovo: a series of portraits of famous people in the Great Hall, scenes from the Old and New Testaments in the Palatine Chapel and a number of frescoes in the king's apartments. Everything was lost in a fire before the castle was rebuilt in the 15th century.

Joan I (1327?–1382) of Anjou (Queen of Naples and titular Queen of Jerusalem, Countess of Provence), the granddaughter of Robert the Wise, had four husbands and, it is said, several lovers. Her reputation as a lustful woman was such that people attributed her death to a horse she had tried to mate with in the castle stables (when in fact she was dethroned, imprisoned and assassinated). For centuries, playwrights, writers and historians, Spanish, English, French and German, perpetuated these defamatory rumours. Joan, however, was simply the victim of her youth (propelled onto the throne at only 16), the libertinism at court and a very disadvantageous historical context.

Joan II of Anjou-Duras (1371–1435) acceded to the throne at the age of 41 on the death of her brother Ladislas. She, too, had a renowned libido and it was she who, according to legend, got rid of her discarded lovers by having them fall into a trap that led to the "crocodile pit" (see opposite). Dethroned in her turn, she was buried in the church of the Annunziata at Naples, unlike Joan I whose body simply disappeared.

It was also in a Castel Nuovo cell that the philosopher Tommaso Campanella was imprisoned and brutally tortured, accused of inciting his countrymen to revolt against Spanish rule. He survived by feigning madness, which demanded incredible courage given the constant supervision to which he was subjected. In 1602, having recovered from the injuries inflicted by his torturers, he was incarcerated for twenty-seven years in a cell where he wrote the utopian treatise *La Città del sole* (The City of the Sun).

THE CROCODILE THAT DEVOURED PRISONERS

Prints of Castel Nuovo up to the mid-19th century show a stuffed crocodile hanging above the main doorway. No historian has ever been able to provide a rational explanation of what this exotic animal was doing or when it was put there.

A symbolic act, some say. But to symbolise what? It is true that in the castle's underground passages a trapdoor leads to a well of some kind which is connected with the sea, and this place, from an unspecified period, was known as the "crocodile pit".

Chroniclers of different eras (including Alexandre Dumas *père* in his history of the Bourbons of Naples) reported that Queen Joan II of Anjou cast the lovers she tired of into the pit. The unfortunate suitors were then devoured by a huge crocodile which, after being imported by traders in exotic animals, had escaped and hidden in a cave on the shore next to the castle.

This very reptile would probably have dealt with any number of prisoners who needed to be "disappeared" with no fuss. Later – exactly when is not known – it was decided to kill the animal using a horse's thigh as bait. Might the mummified remains of the beast then have been placed at this strategic spot to feed the legend and discourage enemies of the kingdom?

The mystery remains, and still haunts Neapolitans to such an extent that, on 21 March 2004, they immediately jumped to the conclusion that evidence had been found of the famous crocodile's existence when the skeleton of a large animal was discovered during excavations for the construction of a metro station in Piazza Municipio. The daily *Il Corriere della Sera*, which heralded the sensational discovery, published a retraction the next day, as soon as it was clear that this was simply a mammal whose bones happened to be there.

STATUE OF ANTONIO TOSCANO

Museo Civico di Castel Nuovo
Piazza Municipio
• Tel: 081 7957722, 7957713
• Funicular Augusteo • Metro: Line 1 Municipio
• Visits Monday to Saturday 9am–7pm

Portrait of an intransigent republican

Among its numerous works of art, the Museo Civico di Castel Nuovo's second-floor display of portrait busts includes a little-known statue by Francesco Jerace (1857–1937), depicting a man with his left arm raised to protect his head.

Antonio Toscano was a Calabrian priest and committed republican who sacrificed his own life and that of his companions to avoid falling into the hands of the enemy. In 1799, with the proclamation of the Parthenopean Republic, Toscano was entrenched with his garrison at Fort Vigliena, south of the city. On 13 June of the same year, Cardinal Fabrizio Ruffo, at the head of his troops supporting the king (known as Sanfedisti, i.e. members of the "Holy Faith"), gave the order to attack the fort and broke down the walls. Seeing that all was lost, Toscano managed to reach the powder magazine and blew it up.

In the same room, the glass floor allows you to see the Roman remains (1st century BC and 5th century AD) found beneath the castle.

NEARBY

SOCIETÀ NAPOLETANA DI STORIA PATRIA

Castel Nuovo
Piazza Municipio
• Funicular Centrale Augusteo • Metro: Line 1 Municipio
• Tel: 081 5510353
• info@storiapatrianapoli.it
• Open Tuesday and Wednesday 10am–6pm

Housed in the "San Giorgio" and "di Mezzo" towers of Castel Nuovo (also known as Maschio Angioino), the Neapolitan Society of National History, founded in 1875, holds the first book to be printed in Italy: Saint Augustine's *De Civitate Dei* (The City of God), published in 1467 by C. Sweynheym and A. Pannartz at Subiaco (near Rome).

This private library, which also organises conferences and cultural events, has the richest literary heritage in southern Italy, consisting of about 350,000 works ranging from monographs to manuscripts, scrolls, prints and drawings. One of the most important collections is that of the library of French seismologist Alexis Perrey (1807–1882), which includes a letter written to him by Charles Darwin.

CASTEL NUOVO TOURS

Piazza Municipio
• Central funicular: Augusteo • Metro: Line 1 Municipio
• Visits only on reservation (email or phone)
• www.timelinenapoli.it (faussebraye, arsenal and panoramic terrace)
• info@timelinenapoli.it; Tel: 331 7451461
• info@projectivi.it (Holy Grail at Maschio Angioino / Castel Nuovo);
Tel: 348 3976244
• hkavventura@gmail.com (rope descent into pit): Tel: 331 7451461

> **Between the Holy Grail and a pit carved out of the rock**

Castel Nuovo, whose construction began in 1279 on the orders of Charles I of Anjou, now offers totally unexpected tours that are little known, even to Neapolitans. Thanks to the new itineraries organised by various associations, you can discover places that were hitherto inaccessible (although not to cats: one was found dead in the crack of a wall inside the castle, where it remains "mummified").

For example, during Timeline Napoli's tour, just underneath the arsenal you can see some archaeological remains and a fascinating geological display of pyroclastic deposits from the Vesuvius and Phlegraean Fields volcanic eruptions. Next you come to the retaining wall of the Beverello Tower, grafted onto the corner of the great hall by the Aragonese to repel the enemy's heavy artillery. The tower had ramparts with arrow slits so that crossbowmen and archers could double their defensive fire, from the garrison on the upper tower and the light artillery stationed below.

Next stop is the North Terrace with its breathtaking panorama of Piazza Municipio.

For an extra adrenaline rush, choose the HK Avventura tour and swing down a rope (with professional help) into a vast pit carved out of the rock.

ALL TOURS

La fortezza del tempo (The fortress of time), Timeline Napoli. Reservations at 331 7451461. *Graal tra storia e mistero* (Holy Grail between history and mystery), offered by IVI (Itinerari Video Interattivi), where participants discover an esoteric route through the castle, from the Triumphal Arch to the Barons' Hall. *Il segreto celato* (The hidden secret), IVI's video presentation – viewed through OLED glasses – relives the story of Lucrezia d'Alagno, favourite of Alfonso of Aragon, "in the flesh".

La fuga di Re Carlo (The flight of King Charles), an adventure trail run by HK Avventura, which retraces the French King Charles VIII's infamous retreat from Naples in 1495, safely descending into the emblematic pit, accompanied by a professional caving guide.

PLAQUE IN VICO PENSIERO

Società Napoletana di Storia Patria - Castel Nuovo, Piazza Municipio
• Metro: Municipio or Montesanto; Funicular Piazza Augusteo or Montesanto
• Funicular Centrale (Augusteo) or Funicular Montesanto

A lover's despair engraved in stone

In the ancient heart of Naples, where almost 3,000 years of stratified history is frozen in time, part of Via dei Tribunali (the main east–west axis crossing the Graeco-Roman city) is closely associated with stories of witchcraft (see below). Here (before it was swept away by the wave of modernisation that engulfed the city in 1890) was Vico Pensiero (Thought Lane), a dark alley so called because of a plaque bearing the enigmatic Neapolitan lines "*Povero pensiero me fu arrubato pe no le fare le spese me l'à tornato*" (Poor thought stolen from me and then returned to avoid paying the price). No one yet knows either the origin or the author, or even the date of this plaque, now kept in the premises of the Società Napoletana di Storia Patria (SNSP, Neapolitan Society of National History).

The active Neapolitan imagination couldn't ignore such a mystery, so people took it upon themselves to find an explanation: one evening in the year 1500, a young poet strolling through the neighbourhood came upon the alley in question. Suddenly he heard a meow and saw a kitten crouched in a corner. He picked it up and sheltered it under his coat. Before he had even turned away, a door opened and a girl came out. She had jet-black hair down to her hips and jade-green sparkling eyes. In the voice of an angel, she thanked the young man for taking care of her cat. Literally thunderstruck, he stayed for a long while chatting with the beautiful stranger, who arranged to meet him the next day at the same time.

For months on end the poet lived for these nocturnal meetings, obsessed with one idea: to marry the sublime creature who had captivated him. One day, however, she vanished without warning. Enquiries around the neighbourhood came to nothing: no one had ever seen this girl. He had surely been the victim, he was told, of a witch who wanted to capture the spirit of a handsome young man for her own amusement. But the poet would have none of it and almost went insane: emaciated, in scruffy clothes, he spent all his time sitting at the place where he'd met the girl. One night, in the depths of despair, he took up a stone and engraved the words that can still be read today, then disappeared without a trace.

NEARBY

THE THINKER OF VICO PENSIERO

Above the plaque in Vico Pensiero, a bas-relief called *Thought* depicts a seated man with a pensive air. Could the mysterious plaque-inscriber have written these words after the theft and subsequent return of the sculpture? This is the hypothesis put forward by Ludovico de la Ville-sur-Yllon (one of the founders, with Benedetto Croce, of the prestigious journal *Napoli Nobilissima*), when he wrote an article about it in 1893. The "*poor thought*" would actually have been the statuette that was thought to have been "stolen and then returned to avoid paying the price", i.e. to avoid punishment by the law.

DIANA AND THE WITCHES

The ruins of the temple of Diana below the church of Santa Maria Maggiore (see p. 93), a short distance from the site of Vico Pensiero, are not unrelated to the web of legends woven by the popular imagination over the centuries. The cult of Diana, followed by women who celebrated nocturnal rites, was demonised by the early Christians, who associated these moonlit ceremonies with the witches' sabbath. In the Neapolitan dialect, in fact, the word *janara* (wicked witch) derives from *dianaria* (follower of Diana).

NAPLES, A CITY STEEPED IN SPELLS

The celebrated writer Matilde Serao (1856–1927), who understood the Neapolitan soul so well, wrote in her book *Il Ventre di Napoli* (The Belly of Naples, 1884): "The Neapolitans, women in particular, believe in witchcraft. The *fattura* [spell] has its fervent adherents: *fattucchiere* [witches] abound.

"A woman wants her husband to remain faithful while away from home? The *fattucchiera* gives her a piece of cord knotted in several places to stitch into the lining of her husband's jacket. Another wants a man to fall in love with her? The *fattucchiera* burns a strand of her hair, pulverises it and mixes it with other ingredients to dissolve in a glass of wine and give it to the uninterested man to drink. You want to win a lawsuit? You have to psychologically tongue-tie the adversary's counsel: make fifteen knots in a length of string and invoke the devil, a terrible incantation.

"Do you wish for the death of a faithless lover? You must fill a small pot with poisonous herbs and boil them up in front of his door at midnight precisely. Do you wish for the death of a woman who's your rival? Pierce a fresh lemon with a few pins to form the silhouette of your enemy, then attach a scrap of her clothing to the fruit, and finally throw the whole lot into her well. The *fattura* … is found in all districts of the city, she has a solution for every need, emotional or violent, and can satisfy all desires, well-meaning or cruel.

"That's all. Or rather, that's not all. If all that has just been said was multiplied twentyfold, you still might not be near the mark."

THE *JANARA*: THE LEGENDARY WITCH OF NOCTURNAL EVILDOING

In the towns and villages of Campania, where people worshipped the goddess Diana – known also as Hecate by the Romans – the legend arose of the *janare* (probably a corruption of *dianare*), diabolical and supernatural creatures, so different from the very real *fattucchiere* (see opposite).

Hecate, a lunar deity like Diana, embodied both fertility and the Black Moon, which was associated with darkness, ghosts and nightmares.

The *janare* originated in Benevento, 80 km east of Naples. There, under a walnut tree in a deep gorge of the Sebeto river (probably the source of the word sabbath as associated with witches), these fearsome she-devils assembled on Saint John's Eve.

In Naples, on the very spot where the church of Santa Maria Maggiore stands today, was a temple dedicated to Diana/Hecate. With the advent of Christianity, the women who performed nocturnal rites in honour of the deity began to be demonised and called *janare*.

In both town and country they were greatly feared: it was said that after 11pm every Tuesday and Friday (unlucky days for the superstitious), when their husbands and children were sleeping, they stripped off completely, smeared their bodies with magical olive oil and rode out on their broomsticks to spread evil.

As they could liquefy their bodies, they'd find their way into homes through the keyhole of the door, leaving behind sickly babies with stunted growth. If someone felt oppressed during the night, it was the *janara* leaning with all her weight on the unfortunate victim's chest. When a horse looked half-dead and its mane was tousled, that was because a *janara* had exhausted it by galloping all night. These terrifying creatures could also metamorphose into women of great beauty to drive men wild with desire (see Vico Pensiero, p. 90).

At dawn their powers would disappear and they again became ordinary women. But there were tricks to confuse them. If you managed to catch one in the act, you just needed to say: "Come and fetch some salt tomorrow." The next day the witch, in her normal guise, had to come and ask for a handful of salt. If you dared grab her by the hair, you had to be shrewder than her and not reply "Your hair" to her question "What are you holding me by?" Otherwise she'd vanish.

To ward off evil spells, metal objects and a pious image were hung around children's necks. A broom made from rice straw was also placed in front of the door: the *janare* were compelled by their infernal rules to count the stalks one by one. As this task took them until dawn, you could easily stop them without fearing their powers, which would be neutralised by daylight.

It seems that the Russian composer Modest Mussorgsky, after staying at Montecalvo Irpino (near Benevento), in the palazzo of the Duchess Isabella Pignatelli, daughter of Tsar Nicolas II's adviser, was so impressed by these legends that he was inspired to compose the symphonic poem *Night on Bald Mountain* (Montecalvo means "Bald Mountain").

TOLEDO, UNIVERSITÀ, BOVIO, GARIBALDI

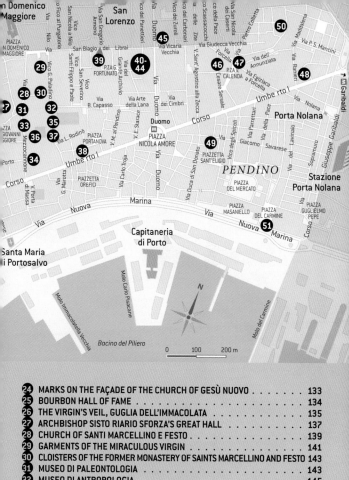

MUSEO DEL GIOCATTOLO DI NAPOLI

Università degli Studi Suor Orsola Benincasa
10 Via Suor Orsola
• Funicular: Centrale or Montesanto (Corso Vittorio Emanuele)
• Visits on reservation: 081 2522225

The Suor Orsola Benincasa Institute has four museums (see following double-page spread), of which the most unusual and unexpected is the Museo del Giocattolo (Toy Museum). The collection brings together 1,238 historic items from Italy and abroad: dolls and dolls' houses with a vast range of accessories, wooden and tin toys, board games and lead soldiers.

Yesterday's toys in an unexpected place

The museum also has a doll manufactured by the house of Kämmer & Reinhardt in the 1930s, bought in Germany by the great Neapolitan philosopher Benedetto Croce for his daughter Silvia. She later donated her doll to the museum where it can be seen today, perfectly restored.

GIARDINO DEI CINQUE CONTINENTI ❷

Istituto Suor Orsola Benincasa
10 Via Suor Orsola
• Funicular: Centrale or Montesanto (Corso Vittorio Emanuele)
• Open Monday, Wednesday and Friday by appointment: 081 2522288

A hanging botanical garden

In 2001, a "Garden of the Five Continents" was planted on the top-floor terrace of the former convent of Suor Orsola Benincasa, featuring rare species of trees and flowers from around the world. It is accessed through a rose garden with thirty different varieties, in a place that was once devoted to the meditation of nuns. The convent, which was founded in 1582, was converted in the early 20th century to an academic institute specialising in education and the natural and human sciences.

NEARBY

SISTER ORSOLA BENINCASA'S CELL
• Visits on reservation: 081 2522203

A small staircase in the Immacolata Concezione leads from Saint Michael's chapel, which Sister Orsola (1547–1618) had built, to the cell where she lived. In a room near the sacristy is a clothed wooden statue of Sister Orsola sitting in a wheelchair. The sculpture was made soon after the death of the renowned founder of the Order of the Oblates of Santissima Concezione. As the nuns of the order were bound by the most rigorous rule of seclusion, Sister Orsola's motto was: "To live in bliss, you must live in silence and solitude."

ANTICO LABORATORIO SCIENTIFICO DI SCIENZE NATURALI, FISICA E CHIMICA
Istituto Suor Orsola Benincasa
• Visits on reservation: 081 2522288 / 335 5855499

The Laboratory of Natural Sciences, Physics and Chemistry holds a collection of scientific instruments that were still in use at the end of the 19th century

MUSEO DELLA FONDAZIONE PAGLIARA
• Visits on reservation: 081 2522463
• servizi.musealli@unisob.na.it

The Rocco Pagliara collection of prestigious art includes Old Masters such as El Greco, Claude Lorrain, Camille Corot, Giacinto Gigante and Antonio Mancini.

MUSEO STORICO
• Visits on reservation: 081 2522308

In the Historical Museum of Suor Orsola Benincasa, many objects trace the history of the former convent and the school that succeeded it. One of the most remarkable pieces is probably *Descent from the Cross*, a wooden sculpture by Giacomo Colombo dating from 1698. There is also a notable painting of Orsola Benincasa interceding with the Virgin on behalf of the Neapolitans, who vowed to worship this woman to such a point that they placed her among the patron saints of their city. The museum is housed in the former parlour where you can see a perfectly preserved rotating pass-through hatch, the nuns' sole point of contact with the outside world.

REPRODUCTION OF LOURDES GROTTO

Monastic complex of San Nicola da Tolentino
9 Via Suor Orsola
• Funicular: Centrale (Corso Vittorio Emanuele)

Built in 1618 by Neapolitan architect Gian Giacomo da Conforto, the monastic complex of San Nicola da Tolentino has a small shrine dedicated to the Virgin of Lourdes, as well as a reproduction of the cave in which she appeared to Bernadette Soubirous in 1858.

A stone from the original grotto

In 1873, the monks displayed an image of the Virgin for the first time in their church.

A group of the faithful, returning from a pilgrimage to Lourdes, brought back a statue of Mary which was installed on its present site and a stone from the grotto into which a marble plaque was set.

The monastery is also home to about 3,000 marble ex-votos. For lack of space, the monks are now obliged to refuse all new ex-votos that the worshippers continue to offer.

From the monastery belvedere you can enjoy a stunning view of the Bay of Naples.

NEARBY

A KITCHEN GARDEN DECLARED NATIONAL HERITAGE

The impeccably maintained kitchen garden of San Nicola da Tolentino monastery, laid out on two terraces, is always shown in old maps and sketches of Naples such as the famous "Tavola Strozzi" (on view at the San Martino Museum). The garden was declared national heritage in 2010.

CHAIR IN THE CHAPEL AT SANTA LUCIA AL MONTE

❾

Hotel San Francesco al Monte
328 Corso Vittorio Emanuele
• Funicular Centrale and Montesanto (Corso Vittorio Emanuele)
• Tel: 081 4239111
• info@hotelsanfrancesco.it • www.sanfrancescoalmonte.it/

A miraculous chair for pregnant women

The charming Hotel San Francesco al Monte, set on the hillside just below the San Martino vineyard (see next page), was built over the remains of Santa Lucia al Monte monastery, built in the 16th century by the Friars Minor Conventual. Among the well-preserved structures that have been incorporated into the modern building, you can visit the chapel of San Giovanni Giuseppe della Croce, built in the 18th century in the cell where the saint lived. Here, miraculously unmarked by the passage of time, is the chair where he prayed and which is linked to the legend of the "apricot prodigy" – one winter's day, in the presence of the holy man, a pregnant woman was seized by an irrepressible desire for apricots, which were out of season. Saint Giovanni Giuseppe then gave her a little tree on which apricots immediately began to grow.

When this monk was beatified in 1789, the chair became a cult object which, it was believed, had the power to protect pregnant women who came to sit there from time to time.

The convent developed from a small cell dug into the tuff hillside by Friar Agostino Maglianico that became the church of Santa Lucia al Monte, which can still be visited. Later, with the help of Father Francesco of Perugia, a monastery was built around the church. In this still tranquil place, Saint Giovanni Giuseppe della Croce lived for twelve years until his death in 1734, when he became the patron saint of the island of Ischia.

In a corridor dug into the tuff is another chapel, the site of the original cell that gave rise to the church and monastery.

In the former refectory there is still a huge fresco depicting Jesus offering food to Saint Peter of Alcantara and Saint Pascal, with Saint Teresa of Ávila. Behind this room was the entrance, now sealed up, to a secret passage leading to the Certosa di San Martino (Saint Martin's Charterhouse, see p. 366).

From the hotel terrace the view takes in the entire city, to such an extent that during the popular insurrection of 1647 led by Masaniello, Spanish soldiers used this monastery as a base from which to bombard the dissenters entrenched in the city centre.

SAN MARTINO VINEYARD

Communità Rurale Urbana Vigna di San Martino
340 Corso Vittorio Emanuele
• Funicular Centrale and Montesanto (Corso Vittorio Emanuele)
• Tel: 338 5621757
• www.piediperlaterra.org • piediperlaterra@gmail.com
• Open all year round (but obtain authorization first)

> *A verdant oasis of peace*

Although the San Martino vineyard was once part of the Charterhouse of the same name (see p. 366), these 7 hectares (privately owned) lie on the slopes of Vomero, a densely populated residential neighbourhood. It's hard to imagine that behind a gate on a busy avenue is an agricultural business with terraces bounded by ancient supporting arches of tuff.

Orchards, vegetable gardens, olive groves, vineyards, herb gardens and even donkeys and farmyard animals make this place a verdant oasis of peace that has miraculously escaped real-estate speculation thanks to its owner. It has been declared a national monument by the Ministry of Culture.

Within the farm, the association Piedi per la Terra (Feet on the Earth) has for several years organised walks and courses on environmental culture for children, as well as other events. The association and the farm have partnered to create the Urban Rural Community of San Martino, a centre for disseminating an ecological culture and alternative economy, building a relationship between the land and the city. The Community offers a range of initiatives organised around environmental protection, not to mention artistic events.

The vineyard also boasts an exceptional and unusual view of the city: between the high walls that flank Suor Orsola Benincasa University is a sweeping vista of the bay in which the island of Capri seems to be suspended.

THE MUNICIPALITY OF NAPLES HAS THE SECOND-LARGEST AREA OF CULTIVATED VINEYARDS IN EUROPE (AFTER VIENNA)

Few people know that the municipality of Naples is the second largest terroir in Europe, after Vienna, by the number of hectares given over to vineyards. Most of these are in the Agnano, Camaldoli, Posillipo and Vomero neighbourhoods. The network of urban vines isn't the only local curiosity in terms of wine – thanks to the composition of its soil, Naples is one of the few regions in the world that uses directly planted rootstock (*franc de pied*), i.e. without recourse to grafting onto an American vine. A rare situation, appreciated by oenologists and wine lovers alike, because it preserves the purity of grape varieties, and traditional cultivation methods, and is a rather romantic miracle of nature. This wine is genetically the same as the original vintage that came from Greece to Naples and Cumae, witness to a long history of some 3,000 years. Some of the producers who strive to develop this generally unknown terroir are mentioned below. You can visit their vineyards and discover their precious heritage.

Raffaele Moccia (Azienda Agricola Agnanum, Via Vicinale abbandonata agli Astroni 3, Tel: 081 2303507, www.agnanum.it). Above the ancient village of Agnano near Pozzuoli, this family vineyard encapsulates the history of "heroic viticulture" – in other words, winemaking in areas at risk of degradation or where the landscape is of particular value, so is stubbornly kept alive. This grape variety was planted well before Italian unification and Raffaele is one of the last local references for work in the vineyards and the tools of the trade.

Gerardo Vernazzaro manages Cantine Astroni (48 Via Sartania, Tel: 081 5884182, www.cantineastroni.com). Ask him to talk about his wine

or his vines and the answers may surprise you: digressions on the legends linked to the name Astroni, anecdotes about Greek and Roman denominations, quotes from the wine literature, chemical formulae, geological and geographical concepts, etc.

The vineyard of **Salvatore Varriale** (Azienda Agricola Varriale, 10 Via Santo Strato a Posillipo, Tel: 081 7691288, www.aziendavarriale.it) has its roots in the history of the Parthenopean Republic and is in an area subject to archaeological constraints. The sea is so close that the ozone mixes with the aroma of the *falanghina* and *piedirosso* grapes, two legendary Italian varieties.

Luca Palumbo (Cantine Federiciane Monteleone, 34 Via Antica Consolare Campana, Marano di Napoli, Tel: 081 5765294, www.federiciane.it) is the winery's oenologist. In a few minutes he can describe, step by step, the many months of preparation needed to make a bottle of sparkling wine and his vision of an organic future where the culture of earth and vine will spread.

The Neapolitan vineyard of **Aniello Quaranta** (Azienda Agricola Quaranta, 4 Via Pietra Spaccata, Marano di Napoli, Tel: 081 5873495, www. levigneflegree.com) is located on the slopes of Monte Prospetto, south-east of the hill of Camaldoli at a place called Pietraspaccata. This is a relatively unknown and little-explored suburb, with a view over a huge part of the city and, beyond, the Isole Ponziane (Pontine islands, an archipelago in the Tyrrhenian Sea). A land where silence reigns in the face of landscapes that, over centuries, have favoured the building of hermitages. Vertigo alert in this high-altitude hillside vineyard ...
It is possible to "discover" the city also by www.wineandthecity.it/

LARGO BARACCHE GALLERY

Largo Baracche
largobaracche@gmail.com
• Metro: Line 1 Toledo • Funicular Centrale (Augusteo)
• For opening hours and visits, enquire at 393 3641664

The Largo Baracche workshop and gallery is located in a small square at the heart of the Spanish Quarter. Originally a bomb shelter, it was occasionally used after the Second World War to store goods. It was restored in 2001.

A bomb shelter converted into an art gallery

Since 2006, young artists have joined together to rehabilitate the square and the underground space of 200 m², staging exhibitions, shows and even film festivals there. A staircase incorporated into a modern multi-coloured structure leads to the first gallery from which you can access other whitewashed areas, giving an impression of great clarity thanks to the very well-planned play of light.

INSCRIPTION ON PALAZZO MAJORANA ⓬

15 Via Carlo Cesare
• Metro: Line 1 Municipio

Caffarelli's monstrous ego

Caffarelli, whose real name was Gaetano Majorana (1710–1783), had one of the purest voices in the history of Italian opera. Apulian by birth (from the old Puglia), he studied in Naples where he was castrated, the price for keeping his magnificent voice. He is remembered in the city by the palace he built in 1754.

The extremely narcissistic singer had these words to his own glory inscribed on the gateway: *Amphyon Thebas Ego Domum* – literally "Amphion Thebes Myself this House" – by which he meant: "If Amphion built the walls of Thebes with the mere sound of his lyre, I have built this palace with the sound of my voice."

A number of contemporary writers, including Lalande in his *Voyage en Italie*, mention that a mischievous spirit had written this comment on the double doors: *ille cum, tu sine* ("him with, you without"), alluding to Amphion's intact male attributes, unlike those of Caffarelli. But no trace remains of this witticism.

Caffarelli, a cad and an insolent brawler, was the subject of much gossip that delighted all the scandalmongers of the time. A story doing the rounds in Europe claimed that he refused the gift of a valuable snuffbox from Louis XV on the pretext that it had no portrait of the king. When it was pointed out to him that His Majesty only granted such an honour to ambassadors, Caffarelli retorted: "Well, let His Majesty make the ambassadors sing!"

In 1739, during a concert at the prestigious church of Donna Regina, Caffarelli came to blows with his rival, Reginelli. In 1741, he had to be handcuffed and locked up because during an opera performance at the San Carlo theatre, he shouted at the audience, jeered the other singers and exhibited openly lecherous behaviour towards one of the women. Two years later, again on stage in front of the spectators, he changed the music to confuse his partner, just for the hell of it.

CASTRATOS: THOUSANDS OF CHILDREN SACRIFICED IN THE NAME OF *BEL CANTO*

The practice of castration, introduced to Italy by the Arabs, was adopted by the Church as it was anxious to cover the full range demanded by polyphonic music without using female voices, which had traditionally been banned since the Middle Ages.

The rise of melodrama, which demanded a vocal range inaccessible to women (the castrato voice was capable of an octave higher), was the origin of the exponential spread of this practice in the 17th and 18th centuries. If the career of these "angelic monsters" was decided in Naples, the Papal States held the record for castration (42%).

As the church prohibited the operation in monasteries (at the time, the four Neapolitan conservatories were religious institutions – see p. 178), children between 8 and 10 years of age were operated on in rural clinics or sometimes in large city hospitals. The operation took place in unspeakable sanitary conditions without anaesthetic.

At best, opium was given to the young patients but in the main they just had the carotid artery compressed until they lost consciousness. Most of these children came from poor families who were willing to sacrifice them for money or in the belief that it was the only possible future for their sons.

Of the thousands of children operated on, only a few kept an exceptional tone and some even lost their voice. Many of them were psychologically devastated and committed suicide, went crazy, shut themselves up in a monastery or ended up in the streets to swell the ranks of prostitutes.

Those who did become famous at the cost of exhausting work (four to six hours per day) would reap veritable fortunes. They were adored by powerful men and even by women, who had no hesitation in marrying them. Some are true legends in the style of Caffarelli, Porporino or Farinelli who, as President de Brosses wrote, "had seven notes more than a normal voice". And as for Gaspare Pacchiarotti, on some evenings

he made members of the orchestra weep with his angelic voice.

In 1798, castration was abolished although the last of the great castrati, Giovanni Battista Velluti, sang at the San Carlo from time to time until 1808. The reason for the demise of the castrati was not really a moral issue, but rather the advent of romanticism, which no longer required artifice, illusions or vocal ambiguity.

PALAZZO ZEVALLOS STIGLIANO GALLERY

"Gallerie d'Italia"
185 Via Toledo
• Metro: Line 1 Toledo, Line 2 Montesanto • Funicular Centrale (Augusteo)
• Tel: 800 454229 / 081 7917233 • info@palazzozevallos.com
• Open Tuesday to Sunday 10am–6pm, Saturday until 8pm
• Admission €4, concessions €3

**Ups
and downs
of Palazzo Zevallos**

The only remaining original feature of Palazzo Zevallos Stigliano (1637) is Cosimo Fanzago's gargoyled doorway. The palazzo is located in Via Toledo – of which Stendhal said in *Rome, Naples, and Florence*: "I shall not forget Via Toledo, nor any other of the parts of Naples; to my eyes this city has no equal and is the most beautiful city in the universe." The numerous changes in ownership have significantly altered the interior design, including the loss of frescoes by Luca Giordano (17th century). In the early 19th century, the palazzo was even divided into apartments. Finally, in 1898, it was bought by the Banca Commerciale, which undertook major work to convert the hall (formerly open to the sky), the monumental staircase and the first floor into what we see today. Only the *Apotheosis of Sappho*, the large fresco by Giuseppe Cammarano that decorates the ceiling, is from an earlier date (1832). Having been completely renovated in neoclassical style by the Cariplo e Intesa Bank, the building now houses a prestigious museum/gallery where you can see the last work of Michelangelo Merisi, better known as Caravaggio (see opposite), several landscapes by Gaspar van Wittel and Anton Smink Pitloo, two great masters who had a decisive influence on the Neapolitan school of the 19th century, and a fresco by Ezechiele Guardascione (1875–1948), which shows the palazzo as it was before being bought by the Banca Commerciale.

OBSCURE SAGA OF THE LAST CARAVAGGIO

Now displayed in the gallery of the Intesa Bank on the first floor of Palazzo Zevallos, *The Martyrdom of Saint Ursula*, the last work by Caravaggio painted just before his tragic death at Porto Ercole (Tuscany), has a troubled history. The picture, commissioned in 1610 by the son of the Doge of Genoa, Marcantonio Doria, who left it to his son Nicolò, Prince of Angri and Duke of Eboli, seemed to disappear during the 18th century. It abruptly reappeared in 1814, wrongly attributed to Mattia Preti, in the legacy of Giovanni Maria Doria. In 1854, it turned up at Naples in the Palazzo Doria d'Angri before being moved to this family's country estate at Eboli (90 km south of Naples). After the Second World War, the villa and the painting were sold to Baron Romano Avezzano. The badly damaged painting, its provenance still uncertain, was sold to the Banca Commerciale in 1972 for the modest sum of 8 million lire (equivalent to about 4,000 Euros).

Meanwhile, irrefutable evidence (letters, wills, etc.) were used to validate the thesis of Professor Bologna, who since 1954 had been fighting for the recognition of Caravaggio as the author of *The Martyrdom of Saint Ursula*. Caravaggio had, moreover, included his self-portrait, without any scars, in the guise of a soldier standing just behind the saint.

In 2004, the painting was painstakingly restored and finally recaptured its original radiance. It had suffered a number of accidents in its lifetime: Caravaggio, in a hurry to leave the city – because he'd been badly beaten up by thugs from the family of the man he killed in a duel at Rome – delivered the canvas without waiting for the varnish to dry completely. In order to expedite its transfer to Genoa, Prince Doria's agents in Naples left it out in the sun to dry, thinking they were doing the right thing. But the varnish softened further and the painter was asked to repair the damage. As the condition of the remaining paint was still unsatisfactory, however, it was subjected to much "tinkering" that partly led to those false attributions.

The Martyrdom of Saint Ursula is one of three Caravaggio paintings to be found in Naples (the others are *The Flagellation of Christ* in Capodimonte Museum and *The Seven Acts of Mercy* in the church of Pio Monte della Misericordia), although the artist completed dozens of works during the two periods he spent in the city (1606–1607 and 1609–1610). Two of them have fallen into oblivion (an altarpiece said to be commissioned by

Croatian merchant Nicholas Radulovic and *Judith Beheading Holofernes*); another three in a chapel of the church of Sant'Anna dei Lombardi were destroyed during the earthquake of 1805; *The Denial of Saint Peter* was smuggled out and sold to New York's Metropolitan Museum of Art; and others are scattered throughout Europe.

BUST OF THE GODDESS KNOWN AS THE "HEAD OF NAPLES" ⑭

Palazzo San Giacomo – Piazza Municipio
• Metro: Line 1 Municipio • Funicular Centrale (Augusteo)

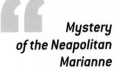

Mystery of the Neapolitan Marianne

The Palazzo San Giacomo (Naples town hall) was chosen in 1961 as a safe home for the marble bust of a woman's head previously found in the church of San Giovanni a Mare (where a copy can be seen today). Although the writers of antiquity attributed this head to a colossal statue of the Siren Parthenope, the mythical founder of Naples (see p. 153), it is actually Aphrodite/Venus whose temple was on the acropolis in Roman times. It is not known how the head came to be in a neighbourhood that was originally outside the city walls.

Although this first sculpture was initially known as *Marianna a capa 'e Napule* (Marianne, the Head of Naples), it took the name "Marianne" at an unknown later date.

Intriguingly, the area where the bust is now found is called "Caponapoli", literally "Head of Naples", in the sense that Naples begins here for those arriving from the south. Symbolically, this is also where the head would be of the Siren lying along the city that she personifies.

We also know that when the head was probably near the church of Santa Maria dell'Avvocata, this Madonna was celebrated on the feast day of Saint Anne, 26 July. The women performed a propitiatory rite, dancing around the sculpture, which they decked out with flowers and ribbons. The confusion between Mary and Anne (mother of the Virgin Mary) may have resulted in the name "Marianne".

This bust was meant to embody a very important symbol for the people, who sometimes honoured it and sometimes directed their anger against it, as in the popular revolution of 1799. In that year, a group of

intellectuals wanted to follow the French example by proclaiming a republic against the will of the people, who remained faithful to the king. The counter-revolutionaries then conflated the Neapolitan Marianne and the French Jacobin one. In each revolution, Marianne lost bits of her nose, which was fairly well repaired until she was quite disfigured and became associated with ugliness. The Neapolitans, who are always ready to mock, say that an unattractive woman with a large head looks like "Marianne, the Head of Naples".

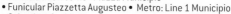

NEARBY

SECRETS OF NAPLES TOWN HALL

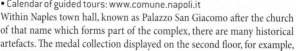

Palazzo San Giacomo - Piazza Municipio
• Funicular Piazzetta Augusteo • Metro: Line 1 Municipio
• Calendar of guided tours: www.comune.napoli.it

Within Naples town hall, known as Palazzo San Giacomo after the church of that name which forms part of the complex, there are many historical artefacts. The medal collection displayed on the second floor, for example, includes forty-five medals associated with notable events in the former capital as well as the symbolic keys to the city, which used to be handed over to successive conquerors as a sign of surrender.

The bow (handgrip) of each key is decorated with a wreath of laurel and oak leaves, together with a crown. An "unbridled" horse, the ancient symbol of Naples, is set inside the bow. The join with the shank is formed by a shield engraved with the monogram CDN for *Città di Napoli* (City of Naples).

A remarkable plaque in a room between the first and second floors shows the location of each of the numerous original offices. It was Ferdinand II's decision to have this building constructed to bring together all the state's ministries and secretariats, previously scattered around the city.

Palazzo San Giacomo, formerly known as the "Royal Building of Ministers of State", had seven entrances, six interior courtyards with two fountains, forty corridors and 846 rooms. It was built between 1819 and 1825 by the architects Stefano and Luigi Gasse, Vincenzo Buonocore and Antonio De Simone.

> The guided tour also includes access to the mayor's office, who welcomes visitors himself when available (otherwise his deputy fills in).

EMEROTECA-BIBLIOTECA TUCCI

Palazzo delle Poste – Piazza Matteotti – 2nd floor
• Metro: Line 1 Toledo • Funicular Centrale (Augusteo)
• Tel: 081 5513845 / 081 5511226 • info@emerotecatucci.it
• www.emerotecatucci.it
• Open Monday to Friday 8.30am–6.30pm
• Saturday 8.30am–2.30pm (except July and August)
• Admission free
• Some photographic reproduction is allowed

Newspaper library

The Tucci newspaper library, largely unknown to the general public, keeps 9,500 collections of newspapers, magazines and almanacs, mainly Italian but also French, English, German, Austrian, Russian, etc., published over the last five centuries.

Some 200 of these titles are thought to be the only copies in the world. A real treasure trove is held by this extraordinary library founded in 1909, for professional reasons, by a group of journalists (among them Vincenzo Tucci, correspondent of the *Giornale di Sicilia*, to whom the building was dedicated in 1953). The library moved to its present location in 1936 (previously it was in Palazzo Gravina, which used to be the central Post Office). It has been continually enriched with valuable donations from all over the world, becoming an international study centre of the first order. Periodically it organises literary meetings and round tables.

Furthermore, it publishes documents not for sale (the institution is non-profit), but for sending to researchers, universities and libraries around the world. The archives also contain secret military maps and documents, and signed letters from generals, politicians, writers and poets. Finally, you can visit a small postal museum displaying posters, prints and manuscripts of the 18th century. The very welcoming director, Salvatore Maffei, will be pleased to show visitors the otherwise unobtainable collection of the Neapolitan daily *Il Lampo* (1848–1849), a volume of rare news from various places (1692) and the first Italian edition of Vitruvius' *De Architectura* (1521). The spacious premises, whose showcases are packed with history, also has an art gallery where you can admire, among other works, a canvas by landscape artist Giuseppe Casciaro, *Grapevines*.

In 1999 the archives were declared to be "of remarkable historical interest" by the Ministry of Culture.

PASTRENGO BARRACKS

4 Via Mario Morgantini
• Metro: Line 1 Toledo, Line 2 Montesanto • Funicular Centrale (Augusteo) or Montesanto (Montesanto)
• provnacdo@carabinieri.it
• Visits by appointment (authorization required: military zone)

Four ancient cloisters in the carabinieri barracks

The four beautiful cloisters that used to be part of a monumental religious complex that included the adjacent church of Sant'Anna dei Lombardi (1411) are little known: since 1860, they have been incorporated into the carabinieri headquarters. As this is a military zone, only accompanied visits are allowed.

As soon as you cross the threshold you'd think you were in 16th-century Naples – the so-called Cloister of the Well, in perfect condition thanks to restoration work, is spectacular. Built in the late Renaissance, it is surrounded by arcades of grey volcanic stone (*piperno*) and completed with a beautiful garden in the centre of which stands a white marble well dating from the late 16th century. Even the original wooden bucket is attached to the well chain.

The great 17th-century cloister – known as the Cloister of the Post as one side belongs to the central Post Office – is equally beautiful. Designed by the architect Giacomo Conforto, it stands on a different level to the other three cloisters. The Cloister of the Carabinieri or of the Columns, and the Cloister of the Supreme Court (so called as it was formerly occupied by the judiciary) are also worth a visit.

The vast monastery belonged to the Oliveto monks until 1799, the

year in which this Benedictine Order was suppressed by the king for adhering to revolutionary ideas. It was subsequently occupied by several institutions: the Special Court for passing judgment on the revolutionaries (1799–1800), the Parliament in 1848 and the Education Board (Provveditorato agli studi). The size of the monastery, which originally consisted of seven cloisters, was significantly reduced during the redevelopment of the city in the late 19th century.

Italian epic poet Torquato Tasso wrote part of his *Gerusalemme liberata* (Jerusalem Delivered) a few years before his sojourn there.

UNDERGROUND ALTAR
OF THE CHURCH OF SANT'ASPRENO

(18)

Via Sant'Aspreno
• Metro: Line 1 Università
• Visits Monday to Friday 9am–1pm

*The "hole"
that cures
headaches*

Built in the 8th century on the site of a legendary cave inhabited by Saint Aspren, the church of Sant'Aspreno al Porto was incorporated into the current *Borsa* (Stock Exchange) in 1895.

In the crypt, which was probably part of some thermal baths in the Roman period, the altar against the wall is said to have therapeutic properties: people suffering from a headache should kneel down and stick their head into the square "hole" of the altar while invoking the saint's name and the pain will disappear.

You do notice right away the wear and tear caused by many heads rubbing on the stone. The phenomenon is unexplained, but many people believe in the effectiveness of this "therapy".

WHY DOES SAINT ASPREN RELIEVE HEADACHES?

Aspren, the first Bishop of Naples, was also the protector of the city before he was deposed by Saint Januarius in 1673. He is thought to have lived during the reigns of Trajan and Hadrian (1st–2nd centuries AD).

According to legend, Saint Peter, having founded the church of Antioch and before going to Rome with a group of disciples, stopped at Naples. He healed an old lady with an incurable disease who immediately converted to the Christian faith. Later, as Saint Candida the Elder, she begged Saint Peter to heal her friend Aspren, who was also sick. As soon as he was cured of his illness, Aspren embraced the new religion. Before leaving Naples, the apostle named the neophyte as first bishop of this city where the Christianised community was flourishing.

Some say that the gift of curing headaches comes from the fact that Aspren was beheaded because of his conversion to Christianity. Others say he placed a heavy stone on his head as a penance.

His body lies in the vast catacombs of Capodimonte hill, while his solid silver bust is in the Duomo (Naples cathedral) among fifty other busts of saints, also silver (including Saint Januarius).

The Duomo also possesses the staff with which Saint Peter healed Saint Aspren, and there is another site where this saint relieves headaches.

SAINT ASPREN: THE ORIGINAL ASPIRIN?

Apparently inspired by Saint Aspren, Bayer laboratories gave the name "aspirin" to the analgesic and anti-inflammatory drug they had just launched on the market in 1899.

GREAT HALL OF THE CHAMBER OF COMMERCE ⓓ

2 Via Sant'Aspreno
• Metro: Line 1 Università
• Visits on request
• Tel: 081 7607111, Fax 081 5526940

"Hall of cries"

The Chamber of Commerce, Industry, Crafts and Agriculture, built in 1895 over the ruins of the church of the early Christian Saint Aspren (see previous page) by the architect A. Guerra and engineer L. Ferrara, was opened in 1899. The building also housed the Stock Exchange until 1992, when all trading activities were centralised in Milan.

Few Neapolitans know that it's possible to visit the great "hall of transactions", which were known as "cries". The immense neo-Renaissance hall is surrounded by columns interspersed with caryatids bearing lanterns or anchors, symbolising maritime trade. The boards that listed the stock quotations for major Italian companies are also kept there.

The upper section has windows painted by Neapolitan artists representing allegories of trades and commerce. An imposing staircase leads to the first floor where there are offices, an entirely wood-panelled library with thousands of volumes concerning the activities of the Naples Chamber of Commerce and a beautiful meeting room now used for conferences. The Chamber of Commerce, founded in 1808 by Joseph Bonaparte, had its headquarters in Via Toledo in the Monte dei Poveri Vergognosi ("Shamefaced Poor") building, which was acquired in the 20th century by the Rinascente department store.

The Naples Stock Exchange was launched in 1778, at a time when transactions took place in the religious complex of Saint Thomas Aquinas (between Via Toledo and Via Medina), demolished in 1932. In 1826, the exchange was transferred to its present home in Palazzo San Giacomo. Because the city had a major port and enjoyed stable international relations, its trading activities were very intense, although they declined after Naples was annexed to the Kingdom of Italy.

GRIMALDI GROUP SIMULATOR

13 Via Marchese Campodisola
• Metro: Line 1 Università
• Visits only on special occasions
• Contact Commander Michele Siniscalchi, Tel: 081 496508
• www.grimaldi.napoli.it

View from the bridge

This cutting-edge bridge and communication simulator is an essential tool for the upgrading of the highly trained Grimaldi Lines maritime personnel who command their fleet of container ships. The powerful computer that controls this machine runs complex mathematical models of all the company's vessels (the most modern of which are over 300 m long and 38 m wide).

An extremely detailed reconstitution of what happens during all phases of navigation is projected onto huge screens covering three walls of a room in the Naples headquarters.

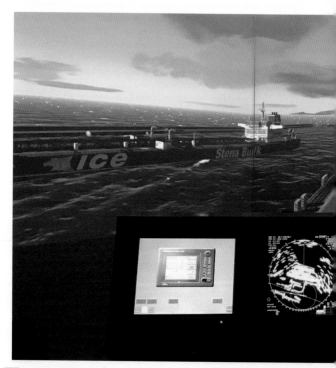

In front of the screens is an authentic control console fitted with indicator lights, radar, GPS, electronic charts, navigation systems and, of course, a rudder: reconstituting a ship's bridge down to the smallest detail.

The simulator provides an extremely high degree of realism, to the point that watching the navigation of a rough sea almost brings on seasickness. The 360-degree view, which accurately reproduces on-board visibility, gives a complete overview of the ship from bow to stern.

The simulator can be set with a number of different parameters to make the reconstruction even more "real": the type of vessel (each has its own navigational quirks), the port of arrival or departure (dozens of which have been perfectly reconstituted), weather, wind and sea conditions.

This complex simulator is also used by naval investigation officers: if problems are encountered during actual navigation – a ship running aground, for example – the ship and security officers meet and transmit information to the simulator to reconstruct the incident.

Analysis of this reconstruction will serve to determine the extent of the problem and prevent it happening again.

PALAZZO PENNE

㉑

24 Piazzetta Teodoro Monticelli
• Metro: Line 1 Università
• Admission free (courtyard)

Beelzebub's palace?

Palazzo Penne, built in 1406 for Antonio Penne, the private secretary of King Ladislas of Anjou, is a rare example of the architecture of this period with its blend of Catalan (doorway) and Tuscan (façade bosses) elements. The renowned Antonio Baboccio was probably the designer. Penne's influence at court was such that he was allowed to be buried along with his family in the church of Santa Chiara, a site reserved for the royal dynasty. To get an idea of the size of this building, just think of its stables (in the courtyard) that could accommodate forty horses and six cars. The lily (symbol of the royal dynasty) and the feather (the family emblem – *penne* means "feathers") are engraved all over the façade and entrance. Other carved symbols, revealing both the religiosity and the superstition of this eminent dignitary, probably excited the imagination of ordinary people, who spread a scurrilous tale about him. Above the doorway, right in the centre, clouds are pierced by rays of light (divine). On either side of this relief, a hand holds

a ribbon on which is engraved a phrase from the Latin poet Martial which warded off the evil eye by these words: "*Avi Ducis Vultu Sinec Auspicis Isca Libenter Omnibus Invideas Nemo Tibi*" (You who do not look favourably on this place, O envious one, then envy everyone, [because] no one will envy you).

The palace is traditionally said to have been built by the devil himself, to whom Antonio Penne appealed by signing a written agreement in his own blood. The noble fell deeply in love with a girl who, not knowing which of her many suitors to choose, imposed unrealistic conditions on all of them. She promised to marry Antonio Penne if he could build a grand palace in a single night. No sooner said than done: Penne charged Beelzebub with the task, although he took the precaution of asking for a small clause to be added. The poor devil, overjoyed to possess such a soul and sure that he was the smartest, accepted and carried out the job. When the next day he asked for his due, the noble Penne first demanded that his clause should be respected. This stipulated that before the debt was paid, the service provider must count grain by grain all the corn spilled in the courtyard of the palace, the number of grains having already been noted in a sealed letter. Beelzebub burst out laughing and in two ticks picked it all up.

But once the letter was opened, he realised that he was five grains short: Penne had very cunningly coated them with pitch so they'd stick under the devil's nails. Satan tried to protest but his overlord made the sign of the Cross and he was forced to disappear.

ISTITUTO MAGISTRALE ELEONORA PIMENTEL-FONSECA

㉒

Former Casa Professa
2 Via Benedetto Croce
- Tel: 081 2520054
- Metro: Line 1 Dante or Università; Line 2 Montesanto
- Funicular Montesanto
- Visits Monday to Saturday 9am–1pm

A rare edition

The former Casa Professa was a Jesuit monastery, another witness to their power in Naples. This beautiful building, now converted into a high school, adjacent to the celebrated church of Gesù Nuovo, still retains the original library with its collection of 50,000 rare volumes, mainly journals and essays concerning the Jesuit Order.

The library, which is on the second floor, is accessed by a monumental staircase leading to a splendid carved wooden door surrounded by a marble portico. This majestic salon impressed all visitors at the time, who considered this library to be the most beautiful in the city (and there were many of them).

The ceiling has frescoes by Antonio Sarnelli (1712–1800), who was also responsible for the very fine patterns on the tiled flooring. The books are arranged over two storeys on shelves set into the walls and decorated with wooden mouldings (1730). The upper storey is surrounded by a balustrade of pierced wood, decorated with medallions and carved birds.

The ensemble was not completed until 1750: between 1685 (when the building was constructed) and the time that serious work began on the fixtures and fittings, chickens were even kept there.

ANTONIO GENOVESI HIGH SCHOOL

House of Congregations
Piazza del Gesù Nuovo (left of Gesù Nuovo church)
• Metro: Line 1 Dante, Line 2 Montesanto • Funicular Montesanto
(Montesanto) • Tel: 081 5514756 • Visits (contact caretaker) Monday to
Saturday 9am–1pm (except public holidays)

Forgotten
vestiges
of the former House
of Congregations

The House of Congregations, occupied since 1888 by the Antonio Genovesi high school, was part of a complex composed of several buildings including the church of Gesù Nuovo. This grand ensemble dating from the 16th century fitted perfectly into the Counter-Reform movement, which promoted the exaltation of the greatness of God by decorative richness beyond measure. Although the church is still in one piece, adjacent buildings have retained only vestiges of their former splendour. Only the Oratory of the Ladies, the sacristy and the Oratory of the Nobles (or Knights) remain of the former House of Congregations.

These lay congregations for charitable work, initially five in number, were placed under the exclusive spiritual direction of the Jesuits, the most powerful order in Naples at the time. They had succeeded in ousting the Dominicans by being more tolerant as confessors to noble families, and taking the side of the Neapolitans (of all classes) who were fiercely opposed to the Inquisition. It was moreover thanks to these astute tactics of the Jesuits that the Inquisition never crossed the borders of the kingdom. The sacristy of the Congregation of Nobles is now the entrance lobby to the Genovesi high school. Its decoration was commissioned from Gian Domenico Vinaccia, a versatile artist among whose designs was the incredible solid silver carved altar of the Cappella di San Gennaro (Chapel of Saint Januarius, also known as the Chapel of the Treasury, in the Duomo). To the left is a bust of the philosopher Antonio Genovesi (see opposite). Next is the Oratory of the Nobles (now the assembly hall). The ceiling frescoes (1630) are remarkable, with a nativity scene by Battistello Caracciolo (1578–1635) in the centre. This artist, originally a faithful follower of Caravaggio, was seduced by the decidedly Baroque taste of the Carracci brothers while devising his own very personal style. Here Caracciolo created one of his masterpieces, despite the divergent opinion of some critics who accused him of having "stuck an easel painting on the ceiling". In 1640, the Jesuits had the decoration completed by Giovanni Lanfranco (1582–1647), a painter from Parma renowned for his light and delicate touch and to whom we owe the extraordinary fresco of the dome of the Chapel of the Treasury.

Finally you can visit the school library, located in the former Ladies Oratory, where the frescoes were executed by Belisario Corenzio, a painter omnipresent in Naples between the 16th and 17th centuries. Contemporary chroniclers accused him of using unorthodox methods to discourage rivals and win commissions.

ANTONIO GENOVESI (1712–1769): A PHILOSOPHER WHO BECAME THE WORLD'S FIRST ECONOMICS PROFESSOR

Genovesi, born near Salerno to a very modest family, was obliged to enter a religious order to be able to study. A figurehead of the Italian and European Enlightenment and passionate about philosophy, he shone particularly in economics. After teaching metaphysics and ethics at the University of Naples, in 1754 he became the world's first professor of political economics, when King Charles of Bourbon founded this faculty as part of his progressive reforms. Here, for the first time, education was no longer reserved for the clergy and Italian was made obligatory rather than Latin. His major work, *Lezioni di commercio*, was translated into German, Spanish and Portuguese. Catherine II of Russia even sent students to Leipzig, where the innovative theories of this great thinker were taught — he is still studied today.

According to Genovesi, education should be extended to all social classes so that a country could prosper. He was utterly opposed to the privileges of aristocrats, advocating the productivity of the individual for his own good and for that of society. He also took the side of those who sought separation between Church and State: for him the Church was only competent in matters of religion. These ideas earned him accusations of atheism and heresy, although he was never prosecuted. However, at his death he was buried in the church of Sant'Eframo Nuovo (Saint Ephraem) with no epitaph on his tomb.

MARKS ON THE FAÇADE
OF THE CHURCH OF GESÙ NUOVO

Piazza del Gesù Nuovo
• Metro: Line 1 Dante, Università; Line 2 Montesanto
• Funicular Montesanto
• Tel: 081 557 8111

24

*An
Armenian
musical score?*

The façade of the church of Gesù Nuovo (all that remains of Palazzo Sanseverino, built in the 15th century) holds the key to a mystery that was a complete enigma until 2010: some of the diamond-point projections that decorate this façade are marked by incisions about 10 cm long which have been variously interpreted. According to one theory, these marks were thought to have the power to attract positive energy and were part of a secret language known only to the medieval master builders and their descendants. But in justification of the number of natural disasters suffered by this building over the centuries, it is said that the diamond points were installed facing in the wrong direction, which would have distorted the benevolent influence of the incisions.

In 2010, after five years of research, the art historian Vincenzo de Pasquale, supported by two Hungarian researchers, Jesuit Csar Dors and musicologist Loránt Renz, suggested that these marks are actually letters of the Aramaic alphabet, the language spoken by Jesus of Nazareth, which correspond to musical notes. If read from right to left and bottom to top, they would form the extraordinary exploded score of a 45-minute concerto that its discoverers named *Enigma*.

However, this theory is not accepted by many art historians.

Diamond-point rustication, hitherto little known in the Kingdom of Naples, was depicted on the 10,000 lira notes issued from 1976 to 1984.

BOURBON HALL OF FAME ㉕

Church of Santa Chiara
49/c Via Santa Chiara
• Metro: Line 1 Dante, Università; Line 2 Montesanto
• Open 7.30am–1pm and 4.30pm–8pm

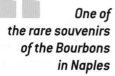

> ## One of the rare souvenirs of the Bourbons in Naples

It has not been established how the bodies of the last of the Bourbons of Naples – the exiled Francis II and his wife Maria Sophia of Bavaria – were repatriated in 1984 and interred alongside their family in the Chapel of Saint Thomas in Santa Chiara, the church that had been chosen by the Angevin kings as their final resting place. This is one of the few reminders of the Bourbons in Naples.

For some time now, the reputation of the Bourbon dynasty (which ruled Naples from 1734 to 1860) is starting to be reassessed: it is known, for example, that the King of the Two Sicilies, Ferdinand II (died 1859), was so renowned for his liberal ideas that when the early unificationists offered him the throne of Italy he refused, faithful to his non-expansionist policy.

Religious ceremonies in honour of the kings of Naples are regularly held at Santa Chiara.

THE VIRGIN'S VEIL, GUGLIA DELL'IMMACOLATA

Piazza del Gesù Nuovo
• Metro: Line 1 Dante, Università; Line 2 Montesanto
• Funicular Montesanto

A menacing shadow over the square

The 30 m monument to the Immaculate Virgin, right in the middle of Piazza del Gesù Nuovo, is regarded as one of the most outstanding examples of Neapolitan Baroque.

Legend has it that if you look at the back of the Virgin's statue on top of the spire, you get a menacing feeling of being watched that can only be shaken off some distance away. The veil that covers her head does indeed seem to bear the outline of a face, staring at

passers-by, which could be a carbon copy of death.

According to the most superstitious local residents, this sinister joke was orchestrated by the family of the Princes of Sanseverino, who had been forced to give up their palace to make way for the church of Gesù Nuovo on that site.

The Jesuits kept only the façade as a reminder of the greatness of the Sanseverinos, who were disgraced for joining a conspiracy against Don Ferrante of Aragon (King Ferdinand I of Naples) in the late 15th century.

WHEN THE VIRGIN BELONGS TO THE CITY AND NOT TO THE CHURCH

Every 8 December the city of Naples, represented by the mayor, pays tribute to the Virgin Mary by offering her a bouquet of roses placed in the arms of the copper statue by firemen on an extending ladder. The monument is owned by the city and not by the Jesuits who commissioned it, as indicated on the shield carved on the surrounding railings. This decision sprang from an agreement signed by Pope Pius VII and the Bourbon King Ferdinand I in 1818.

ARCHBISHOP SISTO RIARIO SFORZA'S GREAT ㉗ HALL

Decumani Boutique Hotel
15 Via San Giovanni Maggiore Pignatelli
• Metro: Line 1 Dante or Università • Funicular Montesanto (Montesanto)
• Tel: 081 5518188 • info@decumani.com

> *One of the most sumptuous salons in Italy*

In the palace that was once the residence of Sisto Riario Sforza (1810–1877), the last Archbishop of Naples before the unification of Italy, you can see one of the vastest salons in Italy, with its 9 m high ceiling. The prelate's magnificent reception room was first used for the official presentation of certificates to graduates of the University of Naples "L'Orientale" before it became part of a high school, during which time the palace deteriorated somewhat. Today, the superb salon – decorated with frescoes and enriched with stucco and fine gold-framed mirrors – has a new lease of life, thanks to the restoration work (undertaken in collaboration with the authorities) by a private company that has converted part of the palace into a hotel.

In the vaulted ceiling of the hall, note the fresco with the arms of the Riario family and those of the powerful Sforza family (sky-blue viper).

THE ARCHBISHOP WHO INVENTED MICROCREDIT BEFORE ITS TIME

Sisto Riario Sforza was very popular: during his long sojourn as archbishop (1846–1879), he greatly helped the poor, whose number continued to grow after three eruptions of Vesuvius and four cholera epidemics. After giving away all his personal property, the archbishop borrowed 12,000 ducats from Baron Rothschild, who lived in Naples. With these funds he created a "bank for the poor", which lent small sums to people without means who wanted to start a small business. On learning what his money was being used for, Baron Rothschild refused any repayments.

The current Cardinal of Naples has also set up a privately funded "bank for the poor" and named it after the archbishop.

CHURCH OF SANTI MARCELLINO E FESTO

University of Naples Federico II
10 Largo San Marcellino
• Metro: Line 1 Università • Bus: R2 from Napoli Centrale station
• Visits on reservation (authorization required, by phone or email):
081 2537395 / 081 2535706 (Ufficio eventi Rettorato); eventi@unina.it

Sacred art in the heart of the university

The church of Saints Marcellino and Festo, now incorporated in the Faculty of Sciences at the University of Naples Federico II (founded in 1224), was part of a large religious complex for women which was given its current name in 1565, when two adjacent monasteries, both built in the 8th century, were joined together: that of Saints Festo and Desiderio, which belonged to the Benedictines, and Saints Marcellino and Pietro, occupied by the Basilians (monks who follow the rule of Saint Basil of Caesarea or any Byzantine rite). The church, which is open only on special occasions or on reservation, is richly decorated with gilded stucco, carved woodwork and grandiose frescoes. The vault and dome feature paintings by Belisario Corenzio representing different saints and episodes from the life of Saint Benedict. The walls were painted by Massimo Stanzione. The wooden ceiling is breathtaking, as is the main altar bursting with precious marble and bronze. The remarkable tabernacle, with its statues of Saint Marcellino and Saint Festo, was carved in 1666 by Dionisio Lazzaro. The church was completed by Pietro D'Apuzzo, probably following a design by Giacomo di Conforto, and restored by renowned architect Luigi Vanvitelli in 1767.

Here it is based "Nuova Orchestra Scarlatti": for scheduled concerts and guided tours, check website www.nuovaorchestrascarlatti.it.

GARMENTS OF THE MIRACULOUS VIRGIN

Church of Gesù Vecchio
38 Via Giovanni Paladino
• Metro: Line 1 Università
• Closed on Sunday afternoons except the 11th of each month

> *Placido Baccher, "apostle of the Immaculate Virgin"*

On the altar of the church of Gesù Vecchio, the miraculous statue of the Virgin was commissioned by Don Placido Baccher, who disseminated the cult of Mary around Naples.

Placido Baccher (1781–1851) was a very pious man, his devotion to the Virgin so great that he was known as the "apostle of the Immaculate Virgin". During the 1799 revolution, when he was 18, he was unjustly arrested, sentenced to death and imprisoned in Capuano castle. The night before his execution, he dreamed of the Virgin, who promised to save him. The next day his judges, recognising their error, did indeed free him. But the presiding judge, seeing that there were only sixteen condemned men instead of seventeen, ordered Placido's re-arrest. He tried to escape the guards by climbing down a rope from a balcony but fell, seriously injuring his head. Again, the Virgin appeared in his dreams and healed him.

Placido was ordained as a priest in 1806 and came to the church of Gesù Vecchio five years later. At that time he instituted the cult of the Immaculate Conception and commissioned a statue of the Virgin wearing ornate gilded garments, just like those he had seen in his dream, from sculptor Nicola Ingaldi.

Today, that Madonna still watches over the tomb of Placido Baccher, who devoted his entire life to the cause of the poor and the sick, notably during cholera epidemics. Thanks to him, the cult of this Madonna is still very much alive in the church – the Saturday following 30 December is commemorated as the day when the Virgin, during the solemn crowning of her statue authorised by Pope Leo XII, spoke these words in the presence of the officials, the court and the devout: "Blessed be the priests who officiate at my altar and the faithful who take communion on the Saturday after my coronation." On that day, known as "Special Saturday", you can witness a veritable pilgrimage in which all the worshippers receive communion. Another very popular ceremony is that of 8 December, the Feast of the Immaculate Conception.

CLOISTERS OF THE FORMER MONASTERY OF SAINTS MARCELLINO AND FESTO

University of Naples Federico II
10 Largo San Marcellino
• Metro: Line 1 Università • Bus: R2 from Napoli Centrale station
• Tel: 081 2537231
• Open Monday to Friday 9am–5pm

A sublime yet forgotten cloister

Within the Faculty of Sciences of the University of Naples Federico II are two cloisters that belonged to the former monastery of Saints Marcellino and Festo. The largest of the two, built in 1567 by the architect Vincenzo della Monica, is square and surrounded by arches of grey volcanic stone (*piperno*); it is now part of the Faculty of Political Science.

The second cloister has an elegant double staircase. The Museum of Palaeontology (see below) is in the former chapter house.

NEARBY

MUSEO DI PALEONTOLOGIA
8 Via Mezzocannone
• Metro: Line 1 Università • Bus: R2 from Napoli Centrale station
• Tel: 081 2537587
• Open Monday to Friday 9am–1.30pm
• Monday and Thursday 2.30pm–4.50pm also
• Guided tours on request

Few people know that within the remarkable Centro Musei delle Scienze Naturali – the University of Naples Science Museums – the Palaeontology Museum holds the only dinosaur skeleton in central and southern Italy. It has been suspended from the ceiling of the chapter house of the former monastery of Saints Marcellino and Festo to preserve the magnificent 18th-century majolica floor covered with floral motifs and landscapes, a work of the Massa brothers. The giant skeleton (8.5 m long and 3.4 m tall) is that of an *Allosaurus fragilis* found in 1993 in the United States, on the border between Wyoming and Utah, and which lived about 140 million years ago.

In an adjoining room you can see the cast of Wolly, a small mammoth found in Siberia in 1977. Note also the Middle Triassic fossils of fish dating back over 210 million years from the Salerno region (at Giffoni Valle Piana).

NEARBY

MUSEO DI ANTROPOLOGIA

8 Via Mezzocannone
- Metro: Line 1 Università • Bus: R2 from Napoli Centrale station
- Tel: 081 2535205 • Open Monday to Friday 9am–1.30pm
- Monday and Thursday 2.30pm–4.50pm also

The Anthropology Museum opened in 1994 in one wing of the Jesuit college. Among the most interesting pieces are two human skeletons dating back 11,000 to 12,000 years, found in the Romanelli caves (Puglia/Apulia), an 8th-century mummy found at Tiwanaku in the Bolivian Andes, and stone artefacts of the 3rd millennium BC from an Anatolian-Aegean site: these were bequeathed to the museum by Heinrich Schliemann, the German archaeologist who discovered Troy and Mycenae, and died at Naples in 1890.

MUSEO DI ZOOLOGIA

8 Via Mezzocannone
- Tel: 081 2535164 • Open Monday to Friday 9am–1.30pm
- Monday and Thursday 2.30pm–4.50pm also

The Zoology Museum, founded in 1813, has an extraordinary, huge "mammals room" (47 m long and 10 m wide), surrounded by two levels of elegant walnut cabinets in neoclassical style. Notable in the large collection of vertebrates (consisting of rare animals) is the skeleton of a rorqual grounded on the beach of Maratea (Calabria) in 1846, and another whale, *Eubalaena glacialis*, the only museum specimen in the world and the sole member of its species to be killed in the Mediterranean. Hundreds of rifle and pistol rounds were needed to finish off the immense cetacean that had the misfortune to swim into the Gulf of Taranto in 1877.

The carcass yielded 3,521 kg of oil before its bones and internal organs were sold to the University of Naples. Other curiosities not to be missed: two mummified heads of Nile crocodiles (dating from 1758), and the skeleton of an Indian elephant offered in 1742 to Charles of Bourbon by Sultan Muhammad V in exchange for a few pieces of precious marble. The elephant, which was kept in the gardens of the Royal Palace of Portici (near Naples), died prematurely in 1756. Its presence and its death greatly affected the Neapolitans who, when a hand-out ends abruptly, exclaim *"Capurà, è muorto ll'alifante"* (Corporal, the elephant is dead), in memory of the poor soldier who guarded the beast and who, on its sudden death, no longer collected tips from the many onlookers jostling at the gates of the gardens to admire it.

CURIA NOBILIUM DE PORTU
HEIC UBI OLIM NAVIUM STATIO FUERAT
FUNDATA
INVENTOQUE IN EFFOSSIONIBUS ORIONIS SIGNO
DISTINCTA
NUNC SEDE IN ELEGANTIOREM URBIS REGIONEM
TRANSLATA
NE CONVERSO IN PRIVATOS USUS LOCO
LONGAEVA VETUSTATE FACTI FAMA ABOLERETUR
ÆTERNUM APUD SEROS NEPOTES TESTEM
HUNC LAPIDEM ESSE
UOLUIT
ANNO ÆRÆ CHRIST. CIƆIƆCCXLII.

BAS-RELIEF OF A HAIRY MAN   **34**

9 Via Mezzocannone
• Metro: Line 1 Dante, Museo, Line 2 Montesanto

> *Legend
> of the merman
> Cola Pesce*

An inscription at 9 Via Mezzocannone records that the bas-relief above, depicting a hairy man with a long knife in his hand, was found in the vicinity and became the emblem of the "Sedile di Porto", one of the city's administrative districts (see p. 254). The carving, the original of which is kept in the San Martino Museum (see p. 366), may represent the giant hunter Orion who, to escape the wrath of Apollo, took refuge in the sea. Here he was killed by an arrow from Diana who, repentant, transformed him into a constellation. Be that as it may, this character was commonly known as Cola (or Niccolò) Pesce, featuring in a popular legend.

Based on extensive research by Benedetto Croce, the great Neapolitan philosopher and historian, the first traces of this myth (with some variations) are to be found in 12th-century Spain (Cadiz). The legend then spread to France (Côte d'Azur), Sicily and Naples. In this city where it was still very much alive until the 17th century, it was said that a boy, as a consequence of spending all day in the sea, angered his mother who told him not to set foot on land again.

Cola (or Niccolò) Pesce travelled over long distances by being swallowed by a big fish – when it reached its destination he disembowelled it with his long knife. From time to time he left the water to talk to the fishermen, telling them that the caves under the island of Castel dell'Ovo (see p. 60) were bursting with treasure. One day the king, to whom Cola Pesce often presented gems he'd found underwater, wanted to test the boy's skills and asked him to fetch a cannonball fired from the top of the hill. The boy agreed, but just as he was about to reach his target, the water closed over him like a tombstone and he remained a prisoner of the sea forever.

The author of *Esoterica Napoli* (Esoteric Naples), Mario Buonoconto, gives his own version of this legend. He thinks that Cola Pesce belongs to a mysterious brotherhood formed in the early Middle Ages, whose members were followers of the cult of the Siren Parthenope and known as *e figli 'e Nettuno* (Neptune's children). According to Buonoconto, these men were the only ones to know the properties of a kind of seaweed with which they could stop their vital functions while remaining conscious. This allowed them to stay underwater for a long time, enrich themselves with the treasures lying at the bottom of the sea and practise their secret rites. Mating with the sirenians (sea-cows) who once inhabited the Bay of Naples was one of these ceremonies.

REAL MUSEO DI MINERALOGIA ㉟

8 Via Mezzocannone
- Metro: Line 1 Università • Bus: R2 from Napoli Centrale station
- Tel: 081 2535245 • Open Monday to Friday 9am–1.30pm
- Monday and Thursday 2.30pm–4.50pm also
- Guided tours by appointment: 081 2537587

*Rare
minerals
in the Jesuit
College*

The Royal Museum of Mineralogy, founded by the Bourbon King Ferdinand I, is a spectacular place. A library has been installed in the magnificent 17th-century hall where the Jesuit College met and the first meetings of the Chamber of Deputies were held when Ferdinand II granted the constitution of 1848.

Among the museum's 25,000 exhibits, note two hyaline (glassy) quartz

crystals from Madagascar, each weighing 482 kg (a gift to Charles III of Bourbon in 1740); several lava "bombs" from eruptions of Vesuvius; the fragment of a 7.5 kg meteorite found at Toluca, Mexico, in 1784; and cameos, a Neapolitan artisan speciality. Some of the cameos are carved out of lava stone, such as those depicting the faces of the Bourbon King Ferdinand IV and his wife Maria Carolina (sister of Marie Antoinette), and a satyr's head in white Carrara marble and quartz, the work of Antonio Canova.

NEARBY

MUSEO DI FISICA

36

8 Via Mezzocannone
• Tel: 081 2536256
• Open Monday and Thursday 9am–1pm and 2pm–5pm • Tuesday, Wednesday and Friday 9am–1pm

The Physics Museum has around 700 instruments dating from the 17th to 19th centuries: microscopes, electromagnetic, acoustic and mechanical devices, current testers ... Note the two astronomical telescopes, one of which was developed by the physicist and mathematician Evangelista Torricelli, inventor of the barometer (1608–1647).

ACCADEMIA PONTANIANA LIBRARY ③⑦

8 Via Mezzocannone
- Metro: Line 1 Università • Bus: R2 from Napoli Centrale station
- Tel: 081 5525015 • info@accademiapontaniana.it
- accademia@pontaniana.unina.it • sbordone@unina.it
- www.pontaniana.unina.it
- Visits on reservation by e-mail or phone

The oldest academy in Italy

The aim of the Accademia Pontaniana, housed at the University of Naples Federico II in architecturally austere rooms, is to promote cultural development in the Mezzogiorno (southern Italy).

Since it was founded in the 15th century, the academy has produced many major works of literature. Among its early members were the eminent man of letters Giovanni Pontano (after whom the institution is named), Pietro Summonte, Jacopo Sannazaro (see p. 27), Scipione Capece, Vincenzo Cuoco, Benedetto Croce, Renato Caccioppoli and Maria Bakunin.

The academy, originally known as the "Alfonsine", was set up around 1443 when King Alfonso of Aragon brought the leading researchers of the time to participate in round tables at Castel Nuovo. The first president was the poet, historian and writer Antonio Beccadelli, known as Il Panormita (a poetic form, meaning "The Palermitan").

FONTANA DI SPINACORONA

38

Via Guacci Nobile
Fountain on the wall of the church of Santa Caterina della Spinacorona
• Metro: Line 1 Università

> **The lactating fountain: Parthenope extinguishing the fires of Vesuvius**

The Spinacorona fountain, installed on the orders of Viceroy Don Pedro de Toledo in 1498, is the least known of the three Naples fountains representing the Siren Parthenope (see opposite). It is also the only one that has remained in its "original version", i.e. with wings and bird legs. Some historians of antiquity claim that there was already a fountain on this site dating back to a more distant time, but this hypothesis is disputed.

Jets of water spring from the breasts of the Siren Parthenope and flow down over Vesuvius carved in high relief. At the foot of the statue, a viola symbolises music, an inseparable element of the myth. A Latin inscription that used to

be there, *dum vesevi syrena incendia mulcet*, encouraged the divinity to extinguish the destructive fires of the volcano. It may seem that Don Pedro de Toledo was expressing his desire to calm the ardour of the very volcanic Neapolitans by gentleness. But they apparently didn't take the hint, because it has always been popularly known as the "fountain of the tits".

Don Pedro perhaps didn't know which way to turn at a time when Saint Januarius hadn't yet proved himself (see p. 354), the Virgil cult had waned and the Madonna had never before pulled off a miracle where eruptions of Vesuvius were concerned.

The statue here is a copy; the original is on display at the remarkable San Martino Museum, the museum of the history of Naples.

NAPLES AND THE MYTH OF THE SIREN PARTHENOPE

Homer tells how, after failing to shipwreck Ulysses, the three Sirens drowned and the lifeless body of one of them, Parthenope, was washed ashore near the island of Megaris (site of Castel dell'Ovo, now Megaride peninsula). The Greek colonists then erected a tomb to house the remains of the virgin Siren (*parthenos* = virgin in Greek) and gave her name to the city they founded near the monument.

Parthenope worship ran so high in Naples that festivities and gymnastic games were introduced in her honour – an unusual and unexplained phenomenon in Hellenic civilisation, as even in Greece there wasn't the slightest trace of such a cult. This reverence for the Siren partly explains the salient points of Neapolitan culture, which developed under the sign of a virgin who, in spite of her virginity, left the legacy of the egg/Palladium (Palladium being a symbol representing the city: see p. 60), thus becoming the mother of a city and a people.

Centuries later, the Virgin Mary gave birth to a child who was expected to save the world, a parallel that may throw light on the Neapolitan predilection for the Madonna.

The Siren dies, but the city is founded on her tomb. In Naples, death is therefore not a taboo but is respected as part of life. Worship of the dead is common and not a terrifying thing: people pray to the dead as they do to the saints.

The Siren accompanies souls to the underworld after bewitching the dying with her singing. She is a bird-woman (before transmutation into a mermaid in the Middle Ages) and, like all birds, encodes omens in her singing. As ships pass by, she sings with her companions: "... no one has yet passed by here with their black boat without hearing our song that flows from our lips like honey ... and we know all that is happening in every corner of this Earth ...".

Why then be surprised at the Neapolitans' great love of music and their predilection for premonitions? And doesn't the saying "See Naples and die" allude to Parthenope who, with her divine voice, enchanted those who had to make the final journey?

Even today, we find traces of the city being identified with the Siren. In the popular imagination, the parts of the prone body of Parthenope/Naples were in three districts of the city. Their symbolic names are still in use: the feet rest in the western outskirts, at "Piedigrotta" (see p. 32), while the head is at "Caponapoli" (Head of Naples) and the rest of the body lies in the centre of the old city, in the Nile district, known as the "Corpo di Napoli" (Body of Naples).

Moreover, Neapolitans are known as "Parthenopeans" and when at the beginning of the 20th century the city was extended down to the sea, the name "Partenope" was given to the new street running alongside Castel dell'Ovo. Three fountains are dedicated to the Siren: the first, which is very old, was restored in the 15th century (see opposite); the second, which dates from the 19th century, majestically dominates the centre of Piazza Sannazzaro near Mergellina marina (its original site was near the central station at the south entrance to Naples); and the third, which is ultramodern, graces the shopping mall at Napoli Centrale station that was refurbished a few years ago.

THE GIAMBATTISTA VICO FOUNDATION ㊟

35 Via San Gregorio Armeno
• Metro: Line 1 Dante, Line 2 Montesanto • Funicular Montesanto
(Montesanto)
• Tel: 081 19804664 • fondazionegbviconapoli@gmail.com
• Visits by appointment: Monday to Saturday 9am–1pm and 3pm–7pm

> *Foundation*
> *aid to reopen*
> *a church*

The 7th-century church of San Gennaro dell'Olmo, originally known as San Gennaro ad Diaconiam, was the first early Christian basilica dedicated to Saint Januarius in the city centre. In the 8th century, Basilian nuns persecuted by Eastern iconoclasts settled within its walls. Until the 14th century, Mass was celebrated there in Latin and Greek. Around that time the church was given its present name, Saint Januarius of the Elm, apparently because just in front of the building there stood an elm where tournament winners used to hang their prizes. In the 17th century, the church was completely rebuilt in the style of the time, although the neoclassical façade dates from the early 20th century. The church was closed and neglected for forty years, but reopened and restored thanks to the Giambattista Vico Foundation. Under the building are the remains of the temple of Augustus, not yet cleared of rubble.

The chapel that is now dedicated to San Biagio (Saint Blaise) originally belonged to San Gennaro dell'Olmo. The Basilian nuns had kept the skull of Saint Blaise there, brought back from the East with the remains of Saint Gregory. In 1543, the pope ceded the chapel to the confraternity of booksellers, of whom there were many in the area, hence the name of the street at a right angle to the church, San Biagio dei Librai (Saint Blaise of the Booksellers). The confreres were collecting funds for the upkeep of the chapel and for the dowries of poor young girls. As Saint Blaise was growing

in popularity, the present church was built (1631–1632). His success was due to a belief that attributed him with the power to heal sore throats. According to his hagiography, he is thought to have saved a child who was about to choke on a fishbone. Worshippers were falling over themselves to get into the chapel (and later the church) so that the priest would protect them from throat infections, in the name of the saint, by placing two crossed candles under their chin. Giambattista Vico was baptised in this church.

NEARBY

Giambattista Vico spent the early years of his life in this neighbourhood. Along with his eight brothers and sisters, he lived in a room above his father's small bookshop, as indicated by the plaque at 31 Via San Biagio dei Librai.

GIAMBATTISTA VICO FOUNDATION

Thanks to the perseverance of a group of enthusiasts, the two adjacent churches of San Gennaro dell'Olmo and San Biagio were saved from oblivion (see opposite). Now deconsecrated and restored, they host cultural events organised by the Giambattista Vico Foundation, which also has its headquarters there. This non-profit association, in addition to running exhibitions and conferences, aims to restore monuments and set up museums.

GIAMBATTISTA VICO (1668–1744): A GREAT BUT NEGLECTED PHILOSOPHER

Nothing seemed to predestine the young Giambattista to be the great philosopher he became. At the age of 7, after a severe fall that fractured his skull, he was bedridden for three years. This accident was probably the reason for his chronic melancholy. After studying with the Jesuits, he worked all his life to support his large family but never had a job that fulfilled his potential – he was appointed to the Chair of Rhetoric, the least well-paid post at the University of Naples. He died, consumed by throat cancer, before seeing the revised edition of his 1725 masterpiece, *Scienza nuova* (New Science), on the common cultural history of nations.

Montesquieu, unaware that Vico was dead, came to Naples to meet him. He bought a copy of *New Science*, which greatly inspired his *L'Esprit des lois* (The Spirit of Laws, 1750).

Vico is regarded as a prophet of modern thought. As an innovator, he completely ignored the philosophical currents of his time and denounced in particular the limits of Cartesian theories. He anticipated Marxist ideas in announcing the end of caste and the rise of social struggles which, according to his reasoning, would lead to social equality.

Vico rejected inequality between peoples, stating that all men have a common way of thinking and acting. In his far-sighted and progressive way, he wrote that a civilisation, even the most advanced, should never be considered as the best or even as unsurpassable. Although his work was neglected for over a century, he was extensively studied in the 19th and 20th centuries, notably by Hegel.

LAND REGISTRY OF THE STATE ARCHIVES ⑩

5 Piazzetta Grande Archivio
• Metro: Line 1 Universitá
• Tel: 081 5638256 or 081 5638301 • as-na@beniculturali.it
• Guided tours Monday and Thursday at 9am and 11.30am
• During Heritage Days and on 1 May, you can visit rooms normally closed to the public

*Temple
of art
and history*

The State Archives, opened in 1845, are housed in the premises of the Benedictine monastery of Saints Severino and Sossio, built in 902 and rebuilt in the 16th century.

The splendid old chapter house, which dates back to the 16th and 17th centuries (now the land registry), is decorated with frescoes depicting the precepts of Benedictine rule. The paintings were executed in 1608 by Belisario Corenzio who, the legend goes, fell to his death from the scaffolding while painting the transept of the church adjoining the monastery.

Some 9,000 volumes belonging to the *onciario* register are of great historical interest. This collection of documents, written between 1740 and 1752 as part of a reform initiated by King Charles III of Bourbon, identify all property, movable and immovable, belonging to the inhabitants of the kingdom, in order to impose fair taxation. This name *onciario* is derived from *oncia*, one of the currencies of the time used for the valuation of goods.

The monastery church, which has recently been restored, is occasionally open to the public.

FILANGIERI ROOM

41

5 Piazzetta Grande Archivio
• Metro: Line 1 Universitá
• Tel: 081 5638256 / 081 5638301 • as-na@beniculturali.it
• Guided tours Monday and Thursday at 9am and 11.30am
• During Heritage Days and on 1 May, you can visit rooms normally closed to the public

Former refectory of the monastery of Saints Severino and Sossio

In the stately Filangieri room, once the refectory of the Benedictine monastery of Saints Severino and Sossio (see previous page), the impressive fresco decorating the vault was painted in the 17th century by Belisario Corenzio: it depicts the multiplication of loaves and fishes, and Saint Benedict distributing bread to the religious

orders, the nobles and the people. One hundred and seventeen figures can be distinguished in all. Around the walls, filed on carved wooden shelves, are the *atti governativi* (royal decrees and dispatches) dating from the beginning of the 16th century until the unification of Italy (1861).

Other official documents, precious scrolls, watercolours and a very interesting collection of noble families' coats of arms are also kept in this room.

NEARBY

SOUVENIR OF THE TERRIBLE EXPLOSION OF 1943
In a corner of the first cloister of the archives (in the direction of the tour), known as the "Marble Cloister", you can still see the remains of huge chains belonging to a warship, the *Caterina Costa*. The ship was bombed while anchored in the harbour on 28 March 1943. Following the terrible explosion that ensued, the port was totally devastated and debris was hurled around the city, killing 600 civilians. On the outer left wall of Castel Nuovo (see p. 82), the scars left by the explosion can still be seen.

LO ZINGARO, THE BLACKSMITH WHO BECAME AN ARTIST FOR LOVE?

The remarkable frescoes that decorate the Chiostro del Platano (Cloister of the Plane Tree, built in 1460) in the former monastery of Saints Severino and Sossio – now the State Archives (see p. 157) – are attributed to Antonio Solario, nicknamed *Lo Zingaro* (The Gypsy). But this attribution cannot be verified as the artist is shrouded in a mystery that no expert has ever penetrated due to lack of documentation. Even his first name (Andrea or Antonio?) and his place and date of birth are uncertain: Abruzzo for some, Venice for others, whereas in Lombardy several artists can be found named Solari, Solaro or Solario. He is thought to have stayed in Naples, where several major works have been attributed to him without any supporting evidence. The art historian Bernardo De Dominici (18th century), a notorious raconteur whose biographies are filled with anachronisms and fanciful details, reported a romantic story about this artist: at the time of Ladislas of Anjou, King of Naples from 1386 to 1414, Antonio Solario was a blacksmith at the court (a trade usually followed by the gypsies, hence his nickname) and rather admired by the king's sister, Joan, who on the death of her brother became queen as Joan II.

Colantonio del Fiore, a renowned painter (another great artist whose biography is unclear) who was regularly seen at court, was enthused by the work of the young blacksmith and invited him home. Solario then fell deeply in love with his host's daughter, but Del Fiore stated that he would only give the hand of his daughter to a well-established and respected artist. Solario, determined to marry the young woman, accepted the challenge and obtained Colantonio's firm promise that he wouldn't marry off his daughter before the artist came back for her.

For ten long years *Lo Zingaro* paced Italy from north to south in search of the best teachers to learn the art of painting. Finally he made it back to the Naples court, where he showed a little picture he had painted to his patron, now queen, Joan II, won over by the beauty of the painting and familiar with

Solario's story, summoned Colantonio and showed him the picture without revealing the name of the artist. Del Fiore, who greatly admired the work, was commanded by the sovereign to consent to the marriage of the two lovers. Thus the blacksmith became a celebrated artist from whom works on a grand scale were commissioned. This story is scarcely credible because, on the one hand, the historical dates do not match the reality, and on the other, the obvious similarity to the story of Flemish painter Quentin Massys suggests that De Dominici took advantage of the lack of information on Solario and conflated the two artists.

SAINT BENEDICT'S PLANE TREE

The Oriental plane tree that dominates the courtyard of the main cloister replaced the thousand-year-old tree said to have been planted by Saint Benedict himself. The original, ravaged by pests and cut down in 1959, although it was indeed ancient, couldn't really have been planted there by Saint Benedict as he never came to Naples. The cloister is known as "del Platano" because a grove of plane trees was probably growing on the site and the monks kept one of them.

Around the cloister are beautiful frescoes depicting episodes from the life of Saint Benedict, executed at the end of the 15th or early 17th century by Antonio (or Andrea) Solario, nicknamed *Lo Zingaro* (see opposite).

TASSO ROOM

Near the Chiostro di Marmo (Marble Cloister) of the State Archives, you can visit a pretty room in which the poet Torquato Tasso (author of *Jerusalem Delivered*) lived from June to October 1594. On display is the Code of Saint Martha, a set of seventy-two illuminated sheets on which are reproduced the coats of arms of kings, queens and aristocratic members of the confraternity of that name between the 15th and 17th centuries. On the third floor, another unique object stands at the entrance to the director's office: the *Carta lapidaria* is an 8th-century marble table engraved on both sides with a contract for the sale of a building at Cumae (20 km from Naples).

SAINT GEORGE AND THE DRAGON FRESCO ㊺

Church of San Giorgio Maggiore
• Entrance to Piazza Crocelle ai Mannesi
• Metro: Line 1 Museo, Line 2 Cavour
• Tel: 081 287932
• Open 9am–12 am and 5pm–7pm
• To see the hidden fresco, contact the caretaker

One stunning image hides another

The choir of the church of San Giorgio Maggiore conceals an extraordinary secret: behind the main altar, the huge *Saint George Slaying the Dragon*, a 40 m² canvas, can be opened like the page of a book, thanks to a hinged mechanism (activated by the sacristan on request), to reveal a fresco by Aniello Falcone (see below) on the same subject. This was painted during the reconstruction of the church to a design by Cosimo Fanzago after the fire of 1640. The unfinished building work resumed a century later, when Alessio D'Elia executed his *Saint Severus* and *Saint George* under which, during further restoration work in 1993, Falcone's fresco was discovered.

San Giorgio Maggiore, founded by Emperor Constantine and enlarged by Bishop Severus in the 5th century, was one of the city's four main churches of the early Christian period. In the 1640 restoration the church's orientation was reversed: this explains the position of the entrance, which now leads directly to the apse, the only original section and of great architectural interest.

The paintings of Aniello Falcone, an artist famous for his depictions of battles and scenes of everyday life, are rare in Neapolitan religious buildings and they are clearly distinguishable from those of his contemporaries. The story goes (as revealed by the highly controversial De Dominici) that Falcone and his contemporaries belonged to a revolutionary group, the "Death Company", whose aim was to kill the Spanish occupiers of Naples.

LEGENDS OF PORTA NOLANA: FROM THE Y OF THE PYTHAGOREAN SCHOOL TO VIRGIL'S SERPENT

Porta Nolana is now opposite Circumvesuviana station (the first railway line in Italy, 1826). You can still see reliefs from the 15th century, when it was moved to this site. Previously it was in the Forcella ("small fork") district, whose emblem was a forked stick (still visible on the exterior of the church of San Lorenzo Maggiore, Via dei Tribunali, see p. 255). The letter Y echoed the topography of the site, i.e. a very long street (known as Spaccanapoli, cutting through the old city from east to west) that forked just at the site of the gate in question.

Today Forcella is a working-class district, teeming with life. According to some historians, it was once home to the Pythagorean school represented by Y. This letter embodies a plethora of symbols: in addition to the tree of life, it was associated with the Christian Cross as well as the golden bough that Aeneas had to seek before returning to the underworld (Virgil's *Aeneid*). Until the late 18th century, local residents carved a Y on their doors or their shields to exorcise evil. Y also has the same shape as a sorcerer's wand – which locates water and therefore life, as well as the type of stick used to catch snakes.

Several medieval chroniclers, from the 11th century onwards, recounted a legend whereby Virgil had chained a snake under Porta Nolana to rid the city of all creeping vermin.

In the 14th century this enduring belief was replaced by the story of a miracle performed by the Madonna, an extraordinary event that served as a pretext to build a church near the gateway. According to this legend, a worshipper, after praying to the Virgin, returned home safely although he had passed through a swamp where a monstrous serpent killer of men was lurking. The church was dedicated to Santa Maria dell'Agnone (Our Lady of the Swamp, a word derived from the Latin *anguis*). Today, the building is no longer there, but the alley that ran alongside it is still called Vico della Serpe (Snake Alley), and locals tell the story of a magician who killed a snake just as it was about to bite the king.

But Virgil had not only charmed the snakes, he had also placed two marble heads in niches flanking the gateway, on the right a grinning male and, on the left, a grimacing female. These two sculptures were useful in divination: if you go through the gate on the left, there'll be nothing but trouble, whereas if you go through the one on the right, everything you undertake will turn out well. The man's head clearly represented the Sun and therefore the light, while the woman embodied the Moon, and thus the night and darkness. The position of the two stars is the same in the painting of Christ and the Madonna (see Santa Maria di Piedigrotta, p. 32).

Note that in Roman times people were strongly discouraged from entering a city on the left foot (incidentally, even if the meaning is slightly corrupted, the English idiom is still "get out of bed on the wrong side"). Both sculptures were moved to the royal residence of Poggioreale, but all trace of them has been lost over the centuries.

AUGUSTISSIMA COMPAGNIA
DELLA DISCIPLINA DELLA SANTA CROCE

🔢46

9 Via Cesare Sersale
• Metro: Line 1 Garibaldi or Università
• Visits on reservation with Signora Stefania Como
• Tel: 339 8690373 • stefania.como@yahoo.it

**The
city's oldest
congregation**

F ounded in 1290, the August Company of the Discipline of the Holy Cross is the oldest congregation in the city. But it remains virtually unnoticed, access being through an anonymous building.

To reach the church, you pass through a lovely garden surrounded by walls decorated with 17th-century frescoes, in the centre of which stands a beautiful 16th-century well. The main entrance was blocked up after the 1980 earthquake.

The church, built in 1420 over part of an older oratory, was subjected to a number of alterations carried out by Dionisio Lazzari and Arcangelo Guglielmelli in the 17th and 18th centuries. Set into the majolica floor is a tombstone dating from 1367.

Through a door (now walled up) and spiral staircase leading to the dome, the church communicated with that of Sant'Agostino alla Zecca, one of the oldest and largest in the city (closed for repairs).

The real treasure of the congregation, which is awaiting restoration, is a canvas in the San Martino Museum: *The Deposition of Christ*. Painted in 1465 by Pietro Bifulco, it was a gift of Don Ferrante of Aragon (Ferdinand

I), who is depicted along with his court dignitaries.

Although the Compagnia della Disciplina, which preaches penance and charity, has secular origins, its members include many illustrious Neapolitans and three popes: Clement XIV, Pius IX and Leo XIII. According to some historians, one of the meetings of participants in the so-called "Barons' Conspiracy" against the Aragonese king took place within this institution in 1485.

Following this foiled plot, the congregation's activities were prohibited until the fall of the Aragonese dynasty at the beginning of the 16th century.

GREEK TOWER AT THE TRIANON THEATRE 47

9 Piazza Vincenzo Calenda
- Metro: Line 1 Garibaldi or Università
- Tel: 081 2258285 • trianon@teatrotrianon.org
- Open daily, except public holidays, 10am–1.30pm and 4pm–7.30pm
- Call or e-mail for current opening hours

> ### *The only Greek watchtower in the region*

The Trianon theatre, in the centre of a large building complex, is surrounded by houses whose balconies and windows can be seen from the auditorium and which overlook the dome surmounting the property. Apart from this curious feature, the theatre also possesses the remains of a watchtower, known as the "Siren's Tower", which was part of the Greek walls (5th–4th centuries BC). These ruins were incorporated into the theatre during its construction in 1911. The tower, enclosed by a glass screen and visible from the auditorium, is the only one in the Neapolitan area that survives from the Greek era.

The remains of the ancient Greek fortifications (which flanked Porta Herculanensis or Furcellensis) that can be seen in Piazza Vincenzo Calenda are known as "'*o cippo a Furcella*" (Forcella district cippus, or boundary stone) by the people, who see them as the ultimate symbols of antiquity – when Neapolitans want to accuse something of being obsolete (whether an object or an event), they say "*s'arricorda 'o cippo 'e Furcella*" (this dates back to the Forcella cippus). The term "cippus" probably derives from the pillars on either side of the door.

Other remains of a corner tower from antiquity can be seen at 14 Via Costantinopoli, in the courtyard of the Second University of Naples' Faculty of Medicine.

PAY FOR YOUR PIZZA EIGHT DAYS LATER

Pizzeria d"e Figliole
39 Via Giudecca Vecchia
Closed Sunday
Fried pizza + one drink, €6
Tel: 081 286721

Pizzeria d"e Figliole, founded in 1860, serves only fried stuffed pizzas for which, by tacit agreement, you can pay eight days later.

This old custom dates from the time when this kind of pizzeria was only open one day a week and the most loyal customers were allowed to pay their bill "'*a agge a otto*" (in a week starting from today), i.e. on the next opening day.

FALSE WINDOWS OF CORSO UMBERTO

272 Corso Umberto
• Metro: Line 1 Garibaldi

Aesthetic astuteness

Looking through the top-floor windows of the building at 272 Corso Umberto, it becomes obvious that you can't see the ceiling of an apartment but simply the sky. These are actually the windows of a fake storey that was added in 1884 to harmonise with its neighbours. At that time, the authorities of the newly unified Italy launched a city regeneration programme (the Risanamento) and built this new thoroughfare from scratch.

SARTORIA C.T.N. 75 – CANZANELLA COSTUMI ㊾

39 Via Solitaria; moving to 7 Piazza Sant'Eligio
• Metro: Lines 1 and 2 Garibaldi
• Visits by appointment • Tel: 081 7645173 • info@ctn75.com

Dream dresses for divas

Vincenzo Canzanella's haute couture workshop – Naples' oldest workshop specialising in costumes for cinema, theatre, opera and TV – opens its doors (booking essential) onto a magical world of silks, velvets, brocades, hats from another age and pearl-studded fans … all displayed among 19th-century console tables and gilded mirrors. Fifteen thousand costumes worn by A-list stars of cinema and theatre take the visitor on a journey through time.

Signor Canzanella is always proud to show people round, and loves to point out the famous dazzling white dress worn by Claudia Cardinale for the ball scene of Visconti's film *The Leopard*. Years later, Kim Basinger asked if she could borrow the dress (suitably altered to fit her) when she went to accept an award at Taormina (Sicily) – needless to say, the request was granted.

The list is long: you'll be bowled over by the countless other costumes, such as those of Sophia Loren in Vittorio De Sica's film *Il Viaggio* (The Journey, 1974), Ingrid Bergman in Roberto Rossellini's *Giovanna d'Arco al rogo* (Joan of Arc at the Stake, 1954) and Audrey Hepburn in William Wyler's *Roman Holiday* (1953).

The highlight is undoubtedly the ballgown ordered for a concert by Maria Callas, who in 1963 weighed 106 kg and wanted at all costs to appear slim. The obliging Signor Canzanella worked for over a month to satisfy the diva, who was thrilled with her dress embroidered with metallic thread, glass beads and sequins, despite its weighing 6 kg.

Besides these unique pieces there are costumes for numerous lyric operas and the plays of the great Eduardo De Filippo, in addition to those made for the Shah of Iran in 1968 and many others …

FONDAZIONE MADE IN CLOISTER

48 Piazza Enrico de Nicola
• Metro: Line 1 Museo or Garibaldi
• Metro: Line 2 Cavour or Garibaldi
• Tel: 081 447252
• Open Tuesday to Saturday 10am–7pm
• Check website for updated events calendar
• www.madeincloister.it/
• info@madeincloister.it

A rare example of Bourbon industrial archaeology

The monumental complex of the church of Santa Caterina in Formiello is an outstanding example of Neapolitan Renaissance architecture. After a lengthy restoration, this little-known gem can now be visited during exhibitions and cultural events.

In the 19th century, the complex was requisitioned by the Bourbon King Ferdinand II, who converted it into a factory for the manufacture of wool and military uniforms. The cloister and the site, known as the Lanificio (woollen mill), was a spectacular example of the "industrialisation programme" of the time, with over 400 employees.

In the central section of the 16th-century cloister (the smaller of the two existing ones), a wooden structure was built, a rare example of Bourbon industrial archaeology.

With the Italian unification of 1861 and the accession of the House of Savoy, orders for military uniforms at the Lanificio ceased. The Sava family, who were managing the business, failed to diversify and went bankrupt, and at the same time began protracted legal proceedings against the new Kingdom of Italy.

Before long the site was abandoned. The cloister was eventually divided into separate properties used for a range of activities (garage, carpenter's workshop, storage depot ...). All the arches of the portico were blocked up and the frescoes decorating the walls were covered over. A two-storey office building was even built in the main porch.

Recently, the 16th-century cloister was the starting point of the "Made in Cloister" conversion project: the masonry around the arches was removed, the little office building demolished and the frescoes recovered.

The Bourbon wooden lantern has also been restored, and can be seen in the centre of the ETFE (ethylene tetrafluoroethylene, a transparent and very resistant plastic) roofing.

The restoration work was carried out in collaboration with the Accademia di Belle Arti di Napoli (Naples Academy of Fine Arts).

THE MIRACULOUS CARMELITE CRUCIFIX

Basilica Santuario del Carmine Maggiore
2 Piazza del Carmine
• Metro: Line 1 Garibaldi
• Tel: 081 201196 / 081 201942 • info@santuariocarminemaggiore.it
• Visible from 26 December to 2 January, and Ash Wednesday

In the basilica of Our Lady of Mount Carmel, a 14th-century wooden crucifix displayed for only a few days a year bears an unusual figure of Christ with his head bent over to the right. The legend goes that on 17 October 1439, Christ leaned over to dodge a cannonball fired from a Spanish warship

> **When the crucified Christ ducked to avoid a cannonball**

when the Aragonese were trying to dislodge René of Anjou and his men, holed up in the church. The legend also says that the missile (still kept in the crypt) headed straight for the crucifix after smashing through the apse. At that moment Christ must have ducked, leaving his head as we see it today.

The order to fire on the church was given by Pedro of Castile, brother of Alfonso of Aragon, pretender to the crown of Naples. It seems that the next day, before again ordering the bombardment of the church, Peter's head was blown off by an enemy cannonball. Three years later, Alfonso triumphantly entered the city. Learning of his brother's blasphemous act, he decided to protect the crucifix by building a tabernacle. This was not completed until 26 December 1459, after the king's death. Since then, the crucifix has been on show to the public every year from 26 December to 2 January. It is also displayed on the first day of Lent to celebrate the day in 1679 when this very crucifix is thought to have saved the city as it was about to be destroyed by a violent storm.

BUNGLED LOOTING OF THE REMAINS OF CONRAD OF HOHENSTAUFEN

In the Carmelite church lies the tomb of Conradin (King Conrad the Younger), the last Swabian heir to the throne of the Kingdom of Naples and Sicily. Dethroned by the Angevins, he was executed in 1268 by order of Charles of Anjou. In September 1943, a group of German soldiers burst into the church to claim the remains of the king they considered one of their own. The sole guardian of the church, Father Elia Alleva, was forced to lead them to the tomb surmounted by Conrad's statue. On reading the epitaph, the soldiers thought they understood that the king was buried *dietro* (behind) the monument, so they moved the pedestal and statue and damaged other tombstones (the reason why one of them, still to be seen, is broken). When they failed to find what they were looking for, they left empty-handed. What the looters didn't realise was that Conrad's remains were *dentro* (inside) the pedestal, rather than *dietro*.

MONTESANTO, DANTE, CAVOUR, DECUMANI

QUARTIERE INTELLIGENTE ❶

3 Scala Montesanto
• Metro: Line 1 Dante, Line 2 Montesanto
• Funicular Montesanto (Montesanto)
• Tel: 327 0407003 • quartiereintelligente@gmail.com

> *"Green intelligence" in a built-up area*

Looking down from Scala Montesanto, the monumental flight of steps (built in 1869 by Gaetano Filangieri, Prince of Satriano) that connects the Montesanto neighbourhood with Corso Vittorio Emanuele, you may be surprised to see an amazing place known as the Quartiere Intelligente ("Smart Neighbourhood"), set up on a derelict site that had until the 1980s been home to a bus garage and a glove factory.

Since June 2013, following major rehabilitation work on one person's initiative, you can stroll through a lovely park, part garden and part vegetable plot, and relax sitting in the "Nest", a work by the artist Michele Iodice (see p. 335) entitled *Migrazioni*.

As yet little known, largely because it's tucked away in overcrowded Montesanto, the Q.I. association, which campaigns for environmental compatibility, uses the large white wall of an adjoining building as a screen to project videos by contemporary artists on ecological solidarity and the relationship between man and nature. The association also organises various activities: cultural events, shows, markets for organic and recycled products, gardening courses for schools, and creative workshops.

THE "HOLY LAND"
OF THE ARCHCONFRATERNITY OF PILGRIMS

❷

41 Via Portamedina alla Pignasecca
• Metro: Line 2 Montesanto • Funicular Montesanto (Montesanto)
• Visits 9am–2pm on reservation: 081 5518957
• museo@arciconfraternitapellegrini.net

A "holy
land"
in the heart
of the historic
centre

I n the crypt of the church of the Santissima Trinità (rebuilt in the 18th century) in the courtyard of Pellegrini hospital (another entrance at 44 Via Ninni), the plots of land enclosed by fencing are known as the "holy land" where deceased members of the Archconfraternity Augustissima Trinità dei Pellegrini (pilgrims) were buried. Until the 17th century, the bodies of the most prominent were dried, dressed in their red serge garments and stood upright in niches coloured red to symbolise the blood Christ shed for humanity, and thus for the charity. The modern confreres still wear these garments during their ceremonies.

After the restoration work, to avoid the bodies decaying further, the niches all around the crypt were closed with panels of wood – except one, which is

fitted with a window so that people can see inside.

Today, Pellegrini hospital, in the Pignasecca district (see box), is a modern building standing on the remains of a religious and hospitaller complex, founded in the 16th century by the archconfraternity. The primary purpose of this association was, among other charitable works, to aid pilgrims to the Holy Land. Every year, from 1600 onwards, this hospital took in 80,000 pilgrims. Of the original complex two churches remain: the 16th-century Materdomini (entrance on Piazzetta Fabrizio Pignatelli) and the Santissima Trinità mentioned above.

LEGEND OF THE DESICCATED PINE

According to legend, a pine tree grew in this district outside the city wall. A great many magpies hid in its branches, constantly stealing things from the local residents.

The ecclesiastical authorities, however, believed that the thieves were human and excommunicated the alleged perpetrators. Notice of the sentence was displayed on a pine branch, which soon withered. The district has been known ever since as "Pignasecca", the desiccated pine.

ITALIAN CLOCK
OF SPIRITO SANTO CONSERVATORY

Faculty of Architecture, University of Naples Federico II
402 Via Toledo
• Metro: Line 1 Dante, Line 2 Montesanto • Funicular Montesanto
(Montesanto) or Centrale (Augusteo)

A clock displaying only six hours

A very fine clock with a so-called "Italian" face, divided into six sections, can be seen set high up on the façade of the new Faculty of Architecture of the University of Naples Federico II, housed in the Spirito Santo conservatory. (See opposite for the origin of these clocks.) The conservatory was one of the city's numerous charitable institutions, dedicated to the care and education of destitute young girls. It was built in 1563 on the initiative of the Illuminati dello Spirito Santo, who received the go-ahead from Pope Pius IV. Pietro di Giovanni was responsible for the project and Mario Goffredo was commissioned to enlarge the adjacent church whose dome is a fine piece of architecture.

In 1590 the Congregation of the Illuminati also opened a Monte di Pietà (charitable institution). Later, King Ferdinand IV of Bourbon abolished the religious orders and the Monti di Pietà. The building was then ceded to the Bank of Naples, which until 1856 continued to shelter young girls.

THE OTHER TWO ITALIAN CLOCKS IN THE CITY
There are two more clocks with six-hour faces in Naples: one in the large cloister of the Charterhouse of San Martino and the other on the left tower of the church of Gerolamini.

WHAT IS THE ORIGIN OF "ITALIAN" CLOCKS?

The subdivision of the day into hours goes back to antiquity and was probably introduced by the Chaldeans. Whereas the Babylonians and Chinese measured time in double hours, twelve *kaspars* a day for the former and twelve *tokis* for the latter, the Greeks and Romans divided the day into two equal parts of twelve hours each. As the time from sunrise to sunset varied with the season, daylight hours in summer were longer than the hours of darkness, while the reverse held true in winter.

The rigorous discipline of monastic orders, especially the Benedictines, led to a radical upheaval in ways of measuring time. The hour began to be calculated by sundials that did not show the hour, but the religious duty to be fulfilled at various moments of day and night (matins, vespers, etc.). At the end of the 13th century, mechanical clocks made their appearance in Europe. This was a true revolution, as from then on the hour had a fixed duration, to such an extent that by the end of the 14th century most towns had abandoned the solar hour indicated by a gnomon to organise themselves by the striking of the church tower clock.

The day began at sunset and was divided into twenty-four hours: consequently the clock faces were graduated from I to XXIV. However people soon got tired of counting twenty-four chimes, not to mention the innumerable errors that occurred.

So from the 15th century the system was modified so that the clock would strike only six times a day instead of twenty-four. Little time was wasted in applying this simplification and so clock faces began to be numbered I to VI. During the Napoleonic campaigns, "Italian" time was replaced by "French-style" time, where clocks were numbered I to XII and the day started at midnight.

"HOLY LAND"
OF THE ARCICONFRATERNITA DEI BIANCHI

❹

Vico dei Bianchi allo Spirito Santo
- Metro: Line 1 Dante, Line 2 Montesanto
- Funicular Montesanto (Montesanto)
- Visits on reservation (authorization required): 081 5524570

> *One
> of the most secret
> "holy lands"*

A sturdy double flight of steps, similar to Neapolitan palazzo staircases of the 16th century, leads to underground rooms of the Reale Compagnia e Arciconfraternita dei Bianchi ("the Whites"), where the funeral rites of confreres were celebrated. On each side of the altar more steps lead to the "holy land" (see opposite), where the bodies were interred. The very fine 18th-century floor

tiles and the three paintings attributed to Francesco Solimena make the place less austere.

The church can only be reached through the archconfraternity offices. On the ground floor, you can admire altars of precious marble and paintings by 17th-century masters. In the adjoining assembly hall is a striking demi-lune painting, *The Washing of Feet*, attributed to Belisario Corenzio (around 1630).

The archconfraternity is the successor to an earlier charity, the Compagnia dello Spirito Santo, which dates back to 1555.

CHURCH "HOLY LANDS"
The "holy land" is an enclosed plot in the crypt of certain churches, where the dead used to be buried before their remains were exhumed and placed in ossuaries.

ARCHIVIO FOTOGRAFICO CARBONE

Associazione Riccardo Carbone
406 Via Toledo
• Visits on reservation
• Tel: 081 2514023 / 333 6436258 / 342 9750701
• www.archiviofotograficocarbone.org/
• associazionericcardocarbone@gmail.com

An exceptional photographic archive

Step back in time, to the era from the 1920s to the post-war economic boom, and meet Ernest Hemingway and US President John F. Kennedy, the young Sophia Loren and the *Principe della risata* ("Prince of Laughter") Totò, smiling among the crowds of Via Chiaia. Not to mention other internationally known names such as philosopher and historian Benedetto Croce, actor and playwright Eduardo de Filippo, Clark Gable, Charlie Chaplin, Orson Welles … Catch the eye of street urchins jumping into the sea from the Via Caracciolo docks, and of fishermen repairing their nets at Mergellina.

You can relive all these moments by visiting the wonderful archive of photographs taken by Riccardo Carbone during his fifty-year career.

Carbone, born in Naples in 1897, recorded the city through the pages of the local newspaper, *Il Mattino*. The first photographer to be accredited as a journalist, he convinced the director at the time, Edoardo Scarfoglio, to devote more space to images in the paper. This marked the birth of photojournalism in Italy … and in Europe.

Today the archive contains nearly 500,000 negatives, as well as thousands of engravings and glass photographic plates. Some of the oldest photos show Benito Mussolini's visit to Naples and Ischia in 1924, and sculptor Vincenzo Gemito at work on the bust of author Raffaele Viviani in 1926.

There are also views of 1930s Naples during Hitler's visit, the city ravaged by war, and the post-war period. Daily life and great events, famous and ordinary people, are recorded up until 1973. All this is preserved and archived in 1,000 cartons, each containing a dozen photographic reports.

This unique image bank was in danger of being lost: it was saved from oblivion by the Riccardo Carbone Association, whose mission is to protect and enhance the vast photographic collection.

A small permanent exhibition and another "virtual" display are always available. You can also buy engravings, volumes of photos and collections of postcards: the association invests the proceeds in the archive cataloguing project.

PALAZZO DORIA D'ANGRI

❻

28 Piazza 7 Settembre
• Metro: Line 1 Dante
• Montesanto funicular: Montesanto
• napolisegreta@gmail.com
• Only authorized

> *An elegant elliptical gallery and the "Garibaldi balcony"*

Palazzo Doria d'Angri is a magnificent trapezoidal-plan residence overlooking Piazza 7 Settembre. The balcony on its main façade is known for a significant historical event: it was from here, on 7 September 1860, that Giuseppe Garibaldi greeted the crowds and proclaimed the annexation of the Kingdom of the Two Sicilies to form the Kingdom of Italy.

But the interior of this aristocratic palazzo is much less well known. It was commissioned by Marcantonio Doria, Prince of Angri and member of a large Genoese family (which also owned Villa Doria d'Angri in Posillipo – see p. 25). The skilful Neapolitan painter Fedele Fischetti (1732–1792), in collaboration with Alessandro Fischetti and Costantino Desiderio, was responsible for all the interior decoration, as well as the spectacular frescoes of allegorical scenes.

Today, only the *sala degli specchi* (Hall of Mirrors) and the elliptical first-floor gallery, used as a ballroom, still have their original decorations. Along the gallery walls are portraits of the four doges of Genoa and Lamba Doria, capitano del popolo (captain of the people – a medieval administrative title), who led the naval ventures of the Genoese Republic. Fedele Fischetti's fresco in the entrance hall shows the *Triumph of Lamba Doria at the Battle of Curzola*. The magnificent ensemble has gilding, mirrors and stucco caryatids.

The building dates back to 1755, when Marcantonio Doria sought authorisation to build a palazzo for his family. Bureaucratic delays meant that it was his son, Giovan Carlo, who took over the project after Marcantonio's death in 1760. The designer was Italian engineer and architect Luigi Vanvitelli, who supplied the drawings in 1769, four years before his own death. The work continued thanks to Vanvitelli's son Carlo, Ferdinando Fuga and Mario Gioffredo. The residence had a chapel whose 18th-century altar can still be seen today.

More recently, the palazzo housed the education inspectorate, then a department of the Eleonora Pimentel Fonseca state school. It is now privately owned, but the owners are looking to sell.

FORMER OIL TANKS

❼

Boutique De Luca – 5a/5b Via Cisterna dell'Olio
• Metro: Line 1 Dante, Line 2 Montesanto
• Visits during shop opening hours (authorization required)
• Tel: 081 5520196, 081 5520642
• pasqualedelucasrl@virgilio.it

Stocks of oil below the city streets

In the basement of the De Luca fabric shop, you can visit two of the five refractory-brick tanks where, in the 18th century, the oil produced in the Kingdom of Naples and the Two Sicilies was stored.

Contrary to general belief, the oil was for consumption rather than for lighting – streetlights weren't introduced until fifty years later. An elevator takes visitors, accompanied by an employee, down to 15 m below ground level.

In these premises, now used as a warehouse, you can clearly see the large openings for pouring the oil into the tanks, the mouth of the hole blackened by contact with the oil. Other smaller openings were used to draw off buckets of oil for sale.

Also in the shop, two contemporary plaques indicate the capacity of each tank in *stara* (1 *stara* was equivalent to about 10.5 litres): the largest could hold 125,000 litres of oil.

On the shop floor you can see two openings covered by a glass plate for checking the condition of the oil.

This storage system allowed the precious commodity to be taken off the market or rapidly "fed back" when the commodity price fluctuated as it tended to do in the Kingdom of Naples.

The disused tanks ended up as storage space, as here, or even entertainment venues like the Modernissimo cinema nearby.

CLOCK IN PIAZZA DANTE

14 Piazza Dante
• Metro: Line 1 Dante, Line 2 Montesanto

> *A rare mechanism that follows the equation of time*

On the façade of the Convitto Nazionale Vittorio Emanuele II tower (formerly a monument commemorating the Bourbon King Charles III), there are two clocks, one large and the other small, bearing the inscription *EQUAZIONE DEL TEMPO*. The face, with its single hand, displays on each side the same series of three numbers: 5, 10, 15. The clock's extremely sophisticated mechanism always shows the discrepancy between apparent solar time (as measured by observation of the Sun or a sundial) and local mean solar time (as kept by conventional timepieces), expressed as a correction never exceeding 16 minutes. When the

hand indicates a negative value, the Sun is in the west, so a sundial will appear "fast"; whereas positive values indicate that the Sun is in the east and therefore "slow". This clock, which is the only one in Europe, came into operation in 1853. It was out of action for years until an astronomical geography teacher from Convitto, Daniela Salvatore, wrote a short treatise on the subject. Thanks to this publication, a senior official at the Banco di Napoli (Bank of Naples), Egidio Mitidieri, decided to fund the clock repairs and it has been in working order since 2008.

WHAT IS THE EQUATION OF TIME?

The equation of time is the difference between apparent solar time and conventional local time. This difference arises from the inclination of the Earth's axis and variations in the speed of its orbit around the Sun.

Since antiquity, astronomers have studied this phenomenon by measuring sidereal time and solar time, but it was only from the 17th century that a mathematical method was invented to calculate these variations. Dutch mathematician Christiaan Huygens was responsible for drawing up the first tables of equation of time values for each day of the year, published in his 1658 work *Horologium Oscillatorium*.

CLOISTER OF THE FORMER CONVENT OF SAN SEBASTIANO

⑨

41 Piazza Dante Alighieri
• Metro: Line 1 Dante
• Tel: 081 5491740

A well-hidden gem

Inside Convitto Nazionale Vittorio Emanuele II there is still a charming medieval cloister which formed part of San Sebastian convent. The church, dating from the time of Constantine, was destroyed in 1941. The small cloister, spanning two centuries (13th and 14th) during the Angevin domination, is surrounded by twenty-five columns built from recovered materials dating from the time of the "Low Empire" (the Dominate) to the Roman era. In the vaults, there are still some frescoes with naturalistic motifs of flowers and birds.

Today the cloister has two storeys, but the second is more recent. A half-moon relief decorates the upper section of one of the entrances. This work, carried out in the 15th century and attributed to Tommaso Malvito, probably belonged to a funerary monument that no longer exists.

ARCICONFRATERNITA DEI VERDI NEL PALAZZO RUFFO DI BAGNARA
Piazza Dante

Between the two churches of San Domenico Soriano and Santa Maria di Caravaggio, in Palazzo Ruffo di Bagnara, is the 17th-century chapel of Saint Ruffo. Today it belongs to the archconfraternity of the "Verdi" (Greens), formerly housed in the Complesso dello Spirito Santo, in Via Toledo. The archconfraternity takes its name from the green homespun cloth worn by members, who used to raise money for the dowries of young girls in need. The altarpiece representing Saint Ruffo is the work of Francesco Solimena, a major figure in Neapolitan Baroque.

LA CONIGLIERA ⑪
7 Vico Luperano
• Visits on request (knock at main entrance)

On request, in Palazzo Leporano (or Luperano) you can visit the remains of the 15th-century Palazzo della Conigliera, the extramural residence of King Alfonso II of Aragon. On his death in 1495, the building was inhabited by the Luperano family who renovated it, keeping some elements of the original building, to the design of the renowned architect Giuliano da Maiano.

HOTEL CORRERA AQUEDUCT

241 Via Francesco Saverio Correra
• Metro: Line 1 Dante
• Admission free
• Ask at reception for a guide
• Tel: 081 19562842 • info@correra.it • www.correra.it

A Roman aqueduct integrated into a hotel

Hotel Correra, a short distance from Piazza Dante, backs up against a wall of tuff. Inside, remains of the Graeco-Roman city walls have been incorporated in the décor and stones have even been left exposed in some of the rooms.

From the lobby, there is access to a 10 m long underground gallery where, during construction of the hotel in 2003, other remains were found – from a Roman aqueduct, according to some archaeologists. Although this little tunnel has even been used as a carpenter's storeroom, exhibitions are currently organised there. The gallery is assumed to be longer than 10 m, but for the moment no further excavations have been carried out.

Also in the lobby, a "cocktail corner" has been set up in a cave left just as it was found.

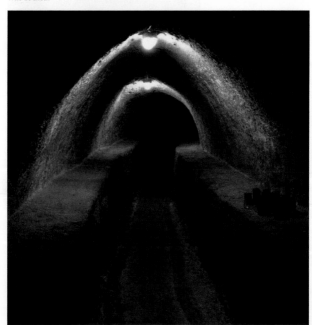

PASQUALE CATALANO, A SPECIALIST IN NATIVITY SCENES

5 Via Francesco Saverio Correra
• Metro: Line 1 Dante
• Visits December to June on reservation
• Tel: 081 5495593, 338 1156884
• pasqualecat@libero.it

> ## Just like an authentic 18th-century crib

Pasquale Catalano is a master of the art of nativity scenes (known as *presepiale* art from *presepe*, Italian for crib). Every year at his home, he spends forty days building a new nativity 4.5 m long, respecting a tradition born at the court of Naples in the 18th century.

While the décor varies from year to year, the essentials remain the same: the scene is always set in a hovel or the ruins of a temple; the cave immediately below the ground, the home of disturbing presences to be repelled (originally the devil was placed there to symbolise the subterranean Evil defeated by Good); the inn and the innkeeper, those too an incarnation of Evil (see p. 252); the three washerwomen, an allegory of Purification.

Signor Catalano explains that a crib in this style must pinpoint the moment of the birth of Christ; therefore anything that moves, like water flowing from a fountain or animated figurines, is banned.

These variations, he adds, belong to a commercial trend departing from the tradition whose origins date back to King Charles of Bourbon. Charles did in fact like to collect the figurines that were not only made by

renowned sculptors, but were dressed in costumes of pure silk and adorned with real jewellery.

The taste for figurines and cribs spread first among the aristocracy then through all social strata, handed down to us today in various interpretations.

WHERE CAN YOU SEE SOME EXTRAORDINARY FIGURINES?
"Le voci di dentro" by Alessandro Flaminio
111 Via San Biagio dei Librai • Metro: Line 1 Dante, Line 2 Montesanto
La scarabattola
50 Via dei Tribunali • Metro: Line 1 Dante
"Presepiando e non solo" by Aldo Caliro
85/c Via San Biagio dei Librai • Metro: Line 1 Dante, Line 2 Montesanto
(Aldo Caliro is in the Guinness Book of Records for his cribs that fit on a pinhead or an optical fibre.)

CHURCH OF SAN GIUSEPPE DELLE SCALZE 🔟

65 Salita Pontecorvo
• Metro: Line 1 Dante, Line 2 Montesanto
• Visits by appointment only
• Contact any of the following associations: Archintorno, Forum
Tarsia (posta@forumtarsia.it), Mammamà, Medici senza Frontiere,
Duomimatto, Ramblas, Altra Definizione

A forgotten gem

At first sight the church of San Giuseppe delle Scalze, surrounded as it is by imposing scaffolding, gives the impression of being under repair. But the scaffolding is just a simple precaution because the monument is so dilapidated. You can, however, visit it by appointment.

The entire church was built for the monastic Order of Discalced Carmelites by the Bergamo architect and sculptor Cosimo Fanzago, who worked mainly in Naples.

This gem of a building, with its very unusual stucco interior embellished with grand arches presided over by statues of Saint Joseph, Saint Peter of Alcantara and Saint Theresa, is considered one of the best examples of Neapolitan Baroque. The impressive central nave is as remarkable as the three sculptures. The church (which was closed after suffering serious damage in the 1980 earthquake) was built in 1660 on the site of a palazzo that the nuns had bought from Marquis Spinelli for 16,000 ducats. As Fanzago the architect had failed to find a suitable plot to build the convent as the Carmelites wished, he was obliged to make use of the structure of the existing palazzo. The order was suppressed from 1808, and in 1820 the building was taken over by the Barnabite Fathers. It was later converted into a boarding school and finally a day school. Although the church is closed for worship, it has never been formally deconsecrated.

The ceiling, destroyed in 1980, was decorated with frescoes by Luca Giordano and Francesco De Maria. They are now on display in the gallery of the Museo Nazionale (National Museum) at Capodimonte.

MUSEO HERMANN NITSCH

29/d Vico Lungo Pontecorvo
• Metro: Line 1 Dante
• Tel: 081 5641655
• Open Monday to Friday 10am–7pm, Saturday 10am–2pm
• Closed 3 August to 1 September
• Admission €10, concessions €5

A stunning contemporary art venue

The museum founded by Giuseppe Morra (also owner of the San Martino vineyard, see p. 105) opened in 2008 in a power station that had been shut down since the beginning of the 20th century. There are large-format photos of the idiosyncratic performances of contemporary Austrian artist Hermann Nitsch with whom Morra worked from 1974. Also displayed in the various rooms, covering an area of 2,000 m², are objects used by Nitsch for his street theatre performances in several cities around the world, including Naples.

Be warned that these images, aimed precisely at shocking spectators, might upset sensitive souls!

The plant was built in 1885 (the date can still be seen on some of the original pillars that have been preserved) by the engineer Paolo Boubée, who also designed the beautiful dome of Galleria Umberto I in Naples.

Hermann Nitsch (Vienna 1938) is the co-founder of the Viennese Actionism movement and the inventor of the Theatre of Orgies and Mysteries, which included all artforms. Among these, the most contentious performances involved public participation, witnessing the actual slaughter of animals whose blood was spread on huge canvases. The horror and disgust raised by this bloody spectacle, according to Nitsch, would initiate a counter-reaction of catharsis and purification.

INSTALLATION SEEN THROUGH A PEEPHOLE

Several spaces on the first floor of the Nitsch Museum were loaned to artists in order to create a work. The most original of these is a secret library called *Scriptorium dell'adepto*, an installation that you can only see as a whole by looking through a peephole.

The conceptual artist responsible for it, Luca Maria Patella, who was already active in the 1960s, wanted to pay tribute to Marcel Duchamp's last work, *Étant donné eau et gaz*.

The door of the room is in four colours, corresponding to Jung's four psychological functions. In the library you can consult Patella's writings on aesthetics, psychology and artistic avant-garde movements.

CASTS OF PARTHENON SCULPTURES

Accademia di Belle arti
6 Via Bellini and 107 Via Santa Maria di Costantinopoli
• Metro: Line 1 Dante, Museo • Metro: Line 2 Cavour
• Visits on reservation: 081 441900, 081 441887

Casts of Phidias' masterpiece in Naples since 1820

On the walls of the lecture hall of the Academy of Fine Arts (founded in 1752 by Charles of Bourbon) are displayed beautiful casts of the sculptural decoration of the Parthenon in Athens. All but three sections of the frieze, and the metopes and tympanum sculptures, belong to the series of casts executed on the spot by British diplomat Lord Elgin (1766–1841) before they were taken to London. The Neapolitan casts were offered to the Bourbon King Ferdinand I by the British King George IV in 1820.

NEARBY

GYPSOTHEQUE OF THE ACADEMY OF FINE ARTS

• Free admission 10am–1pm, Tuesday to Saturday

The large gypsotheque (museum of plaster sculpture and casts) of the Academy of Fine Arts has dozens of reproductions of major works from several eras. Among the colossal sculptures is the bust of Jupiter of Otricoli (the original is in the Vatican Museum) and the Antinous from Villa Mondragone (one of the twelve papal residences of the 16th century). The oldest sculptures date back to 1807.

A BEAUTIFUL STAINED GLASS WINDOW IN ART NOUVEAU

Just a few steps away, at number 104 of Via Costantinopoli, stands the villa Spinelli Barrile, built at the end of the 19th century by the homonymous marquis. Visitors are greeted by a grand stained glass window in Art Nouveau style, polychrome lead glasses, one of the few examples of this type that have survived in town. The annexed garden turns the place into a haven of peace. Today, a charming residence is situated there.

HOLY STEPS
OF SANTA MARIA DELLA SAPIENZA

(18)

Convento delle Ancelle del Sacro Cuore di Santa Caterina Volpicelli
47 Via Sapienza
• Metro: Line 1 Dante, Museo • Metro: Line 2 Cavour
• Visits by appointment (authorization required)
• Tel: 081 459362

*Little-known
Holy Steps*

You can book a visit to the monastery of Santa Maria della Sapienza, founded in the 16th century by Maria Carafa. This building contains virtually unknown wonders: the Holy Steps and a splendid church, considered one of the temples to Neapolitan Baroque. The church was remodelled and decorated in the 17th century by two great artists, Francesco Grimaldi and Cosimo Fanzago. Although badly damaged, it is now being restored.

The Holy Steps, twenty-eight of them, are in a vaulted corridor frescoed by a pupil of Francesco Solimena, Andrea D'Aste. The pictorial decoration, commissioned by Mother Marie-Thérèse Carafa, consists of a fresco in the vault depicting the Resurrection, a Crucifixion altarpiece at the top of the steps, and six oval paintings (now missing) representing the Passion of Christ.

To the right of the main altar, the original access to the Holy Steps is now closed off.

ORIGIN AND MEANING OF THE HOLY STEPS

In Christian tradition the Holy Steps led to the tribunal where Christ was taken for interrogation by Pontius Pilate before being crucified. In AD 326 Saint Helena, mother of Emperor Constantine, is thought to have brought the stone steps to Rome, where they were placed in the Santuario della Scala Santa near the basilica of Saint John Lateran. After the Council of Trent (1545–1563), called by Pope Paul III in response to Protestant reforms and to suppress the worldly excesses of the clergy, the Church tightened up ecclesiastical discipline by encouraging penitential practices. These included the dissemination of Holy Steps, reproductions of Rome's Scala Santa, of which there are still a couple of dozen around the world. Besides those in Naples (see opposite), there are stairs in Jerusalem (part of the original flight), Bastia and Lourdes in France, and in Italy at Prato, Turin, Mantua, Varallo … Traditionally, in order to gain indulgences or forgiveness, worshippers had to climb the steps on their knees while reciting prayers in order to reach an altar or a simple crucifix at the top.

HOLY STEPS IN NAPLES

- Santa Maria della Sapienza (see opposite).
- San Gregorio Armeno (p. 248).
- Arciconfraternita dell'Ecce Homo al Cerriglio. The Holy Steps connect the small chapel in the monastery of Santa Maria la Nova (12 Via del Cerriglio – Metro: Line 1 Università).
- Arciconfraternita dei Bianchi dei Santi Francesco e Matteo della Scala Santa. Founded in 1606, by concession of Pope Paul V (20 Vico Giardinetto – Metro: Line 1 Toledo).
- Former monastery of Santi Marcellino e Festo, where part of a 17th-century Holy Stair is preserved, restored by Luigi Vanvitelli in 1772, near the demolished oratory (10 Largo San Marcellino – Metro: Line 1 Università).

UNDERGROUND GALLERIES OF PIETRASANTA ⑲

Piazzetta Pietrasanta
• Metro: Line 1 Dante
• www.polopietrasanta.com

> *A 10,000 m² network of underground galleries*

To the right of the entrance to the Pietrasanta (Holy Stone) church, a hatch gives access to the early Christian chapel built in AD 533. In the 1960s a landslide caused the collapse of the right aisle, revealing the earlier building and the underground galleries.

In the course of restoration, the chapel has been converted into an exhibition space for objects found during the excavations: a Roman house and remains of the Greek city walls. From this first level about 5 m deep, you can descend another 30 m to take a trip through the bowels of the ancient city, on tracks dug into the rock wall by the *pozzari* (the men who maintained the wells and tanks). The total surface area of this intricate network of tunnels, part of which was used as a bomb shelter during the Second World War, is over 10,000 m². Of particular note is the jaw-dropping, strangely convoluted section where the wall forms "waves", which is why it's called ONDE M. A. (WAVE M. A.) by the cavers, who think this route could be 2,000 years old.

At a fork in the tunnels, on the wall at the entrance to the right-hand gallery, an engraved cross is followed by twelve groups of linked or intersecting crosses spread over several hundred metres. The twisting path runs along the axis of the palace of Raimondo di Sangro, Prince of Sansevero (see p. 234) and then straightens out to end under the altar of the church. The twelve groups of crosses seem to correspond to another sign carved on a white marble plaque set in the wall of the church bell tower on Piazza Miraglia side: a Greek cross with arms terminating in fleurs-de-lis, the emblem of the Military Order of Calatrava (the Castilian city where the order was founded). Experts calculate that the underground route marked out by the crosses is a link to the bell tower.

CLOISTER OF SANT'ANDREA DELLE DAME

Sant'Andrea delle Dame university campus - 7 Via Luigi De Crecchio
- Metro: Line 1 Dante, Line 2 Montesanto
- Funicular Montesanto (Montesanto)
- Open weekdays 9am–4pm

A
spectacular
double row
of palm trees

The cloister of Sant'Andrea delle Dame ("of the Ladies"), home of the Second University of Naples medical school, is all that remains of a monastic complex for young girls from upper-class families founded in 1583 by Giulia, Lucrezia, Laura and Claudia Parascandolo, the four daughters of a wealthy lawyer.

Initially known as Sant'Andrea delle Monache ("of the Nuns"), the convent was renamed for the "Ladies" in honour of its founders. Its religious vocation

was suppressed during the Napoleonic period and the building was later converted into a medical school.

The bright and spacious cloister, bordered by tall pillars of grey stone and embellished by a magnificent double row of palms, was decorated by the Flemish painter Pietro Mennes. This place, although open to all, is pretty well unknown except by university students.

SEVENTH HEAVEN LANE

Via De Crecchio, named in honour of an eminent 19th-century rector of the University of Naples Federico II, was formerly called Vico Settimo Cielo (Seventh Heaven Lane), probably derived from *Settimio Celio* Gaudioso, an African bishop of the 5th century who founded the monastery of Saint Gaudioso in this district. There is, however, a legend that the seven heavens refer to those of the Iris that appeared as a blinding light on 13 December 596, while they celebrated the funeral rites of the future Saint Agnello in the church of Santa Maria Intercede.

PRIVATE TOUR
OF MONASTERO DELLE TRENTATRÉ

21

8 Via Pisanelli
• Metro: Line 1 Museo, Line 2 Cavour
• Tel: 081 299963 • francesco33i@alice.it
• Visits on reservation for groups, one Saturday per month for individuals

A true rarity

The long history of the Trentatré (Thirty-three), founded in 1535, has made this convent quite a rarity. Although the site has always been closed to the public due to the strict Rule observed by the nuns, guided tours have been allowed for a decade or so, but only on certain dates. Many Neapolitans are even unaware of its existence.

Thirteen nuns still live there at present, supported by charity, and the founder Maria Lorenza Longo is on the way to beatification.

The building stands on the ancient Greek acropolis of the city, close to the remains of the Roman theatre. Besides the church, the tour takes in the refectory (where you can admire the fine *Supper at Emmaus* painted by Giuseppe Bonito in the 16th century), the cellars, the very pretty cloister and the parlour with its grille still in place where a few believers still come to ask the nuns to pray for them. Another curiosity is a small exhibition of baby Jesus waxworks, quantities of which have been made by the nuns since the 18th century. The figurines, which are offered to benefactors as Christmas gifts, differ from the Neapolitan artisan use of mainly plaster, terracotta and papier-mâché.

The adjacent church of Santa Maria di Gerusalemme, rebuilt in the 17th century, also complies with the Rule that imposes austerity and poverty: the decorative elements are basically stucco and wood, humble materials.

In 1518, the noblewoman Maria Lorenza Longo, after experiencing a miracle, founded the Ospedale degli Incurabili (Hospital for Incurables) for patients with syphilis. She designated some rooms in this building for the use of a small number of Capuchin Poor Clares, who observed strict cloistering.

In 1538, Paul III limited the number of nuns to thirty-three, as many as the years of Christ's life, hence the popular name of the convent. Another notable feature was that these nuns were all poor girls, including rehabilitated prostitutes. The reputation of holiness of the Thirty-three spread throughout Europe and led to the founding of numerous convents on the same model. There were 200 of them in the 18th century.

WHY IS THE NUMBER 33 GENERALLY ASSOCIATED WITH NUNS IN THE NEAPOLITAN LOTTERY?

Over the centuries, the popularity of this convent has become so rooted in the city's culture that number 33 in the Neapolitan Book of Dreams, the Smorfia (where each number has one or more meanings – see next pages), is associated, among other things, with nuns in general. Furthermore, the expression "like one of the thirty-three nuns" is used of people who are constantly asking the time: it seems that the nuns of the convent passed their time counting the quarter hours. The invention of the delicious sfogliatelle, a local pastry speciality, is also attributed to these nuns.

NEAPOLITAN LOTTO: A HISTORY OF DIVINATION

In Naples, the lottery has always been a kind of esoteric practice where Christian faith and paganism intermingle. The choice of numbers calls on cabalistic laws or numerology derived from Pythagorean theories.

So the numbers you play must always be inferred from a dream, an exceptional event or a news story.

To achieve this you have to consult the *Smorfia* (Book of Dreams), which lists all the things that correspond to the numbers 1 to 90, in words and images, so that even non-readers can use it. This numerological interpretation is sometimes very complex, especially as winning combinations range from one to five numbers.

Neapolitans, particularly residents of the *centro storico* (historic centre), then sometimes turn to an *assistito* (helped by [God]): those whom it is believed communicate with the dead, who in turn are supposed to intercede with the Almighty to change their family's fortune by making them rich.

If there have been no dreams or significant events, the "assisted", a veritable soothsayer, always guided by the souls of the dead, generates words or actions – necessarily ambiguous – to which the punter will attach a meaning by consulting the *Smorfia* at home. The delusional nature of these predictions has given rise to a common way of describing someone who rambles on: in the Neapolitan dialect, they're "dishing out numbers".

Generally, the "assisted", who don't have the right to play on their own account, are only paid with a percentage of the sum collected for a successful prediction.

Having procured the "good numbers", to increase your chances you must invoke the Madonna, a patron saint, souls in Purgatory (see p. 288) or an imp called the *munaciello* (little monk). God is never directly responsible. Prayers may be spontaneous or follow a model such as this: "Today it's the Moon / tomorrow it'll be Mars / and my chance will come / it'll come by sea / it'll come by land / come into my dream without scaring me / three beautiful numbers make me dream."

Stories abound relating to the Neapolitans' unbridled love of the lottery, for example:

Charles Dickens describes how in 1845 he witnessed a rider fall from his horse. As the hapless victim lay in a pool of blood, a passer-by asked his age before even offering to help, as he needed a third number to play – the other two being 56 (a fall) and 18 (blood).

On 29 April 1994, when John Paul II slipped in the bathroom and broke his hip, the *ricevitorie* (lottery offices) were taken by storm. Everyone played 56 (a fall), 32 (the pope), 90 (broken hip) and 29 (date of the accident). According to the *Corriere della Sera* reporter who wrote up this incident, if all the numbers had come up, the state would have gone bankrupt.

The celebrated Neapolitan author Matilde Serao has written: "The

Neapolitans are sober, they aren't corrupted by spirits, they don't die of delirium tremens, they're corrupted and die of lotto."

When a law was passed in 1734 to ban gambling over Christmas, Neapolitans invented the family game of *tombola*. This custom, which still thrives around Christmastime, involves all levels of society. To play, the numbers 1 to 90 (engraved on small wooden cylinders) are extracted from a conical basket with a hole at the top.

The players buy one or more cards with fifteen numbers printed on each. The money collected makes up the pot, which is then divided into five prizes. As each number is drawn, if it appears on their card(s), the players cover it with a bean from the pile in front of them. The winner is the first to cover two, three, four or five numbers in the same row. The jackpot is won by completing a whole card. Each number is traditionally called along with its meaning. In the old neighbourhoods, where the traditional culture hasn't yet broken down, a transsexual, or an elderly woman, is always responsible for the draw.

SMORFIA: THE REAL MEANING OF THE NUMBERS

The complete version of the *Smorfia* (a word derived from Morpheus, the god of sleep and therefore of dreams) is a veritable key to dreams in which each number has several meanings, and each meaning can be applied to many situations. There nevertheless is a classic popular version – the one used in the "family" lotto mentioned on the previous page – where each number refers to traditional beliefs, local culture, and life itself. Sexual allegories are common because many ancient rites were dedicated to the gods of fertility. Some topics need an explanation, while others are self-explanatory. The origin of these meanings is not always known. Note that women feature far more than men, traditional society in Campania being matriarchal.

1: Italy Before the unification of Italy (1861), 1 corresponded to the Sun, which was the subject of a primitive cult in antiquity.

2: little girl

3: cat In Neapolitan dialect, *gatta* (cat) is feminine and has a clear sexual connotation.

4: pig This was the sacred animal of Demeter, one of the main deities once worshipped in Naples. With the arrival of Christianity, Saint Anthony the Hermit took over from Demeter, so the pig was dedicated to him (see p. 345).

5: hand The number 5 refers to the five fingers. A magical symbol for thousands of years (hands are depicted in several prehistoric caves).

6: her that always looks down (female genitals).

7: vase An essential object that featured, like weapons, among the first "creations" of *Homo sapiens*.

8: Madonna The Virgin has replaced almost all pagan deities. Her feast days are 8 May, 8 October and 8 December.

9: offspring

10: dried beans They symbolise immortality because they "come back to life" in water after drying. Roman women wore bean-shaped pendants for luck. Beans are used to cover the drawn numbers when playing lotto with the family.

11: mice By running back and forth at high speed from the light to the shadows, they symbolically ensure the uninterrupted link between these two worlds, and therefore between spirit and matter, Good and Evil.

12: soldiers

13: Saint Anthony (of Padua). A particularly well-loved saint in Naples, whose feast day falls on 13 June.

14: drunkard In the Dionysian rites of old, very common in Graeco-Roman Naples, drunkenness, synonymous with loss of consciousness, was a way of communicating with God.

15: little boy

16: buttocks "To have buttocks" means to be lucky.

17: misfortune Although in Naples as elsewhere there shouldn't be 13 seated at table, it is Friday the 17th the Neapolitans dread. The number 17 is however associated with happiness in the Kabbalah, and some say that its bad reputation comes from the Roman numeral XVII, of which the anagram VIXI (I lived) means "I'm (now) dead."

18: blood - 19: laughter - 20: festival - 21: naked woman

22: madman - 23: idiot - 24: Carabinieri

25: Christmas The date marking the rebirth of the Sun (winter solstice) was already celebrated in Graeco-Roman Naples.

26: *Nanninella* Diminutive of Anna, the mother of Mary and patron of all female occupations, whose feast day is 26 July.

27: *càntaro* (chamber pot). This is a very common insult, equivalent to "asshole". The term is used in many colourful phrases, e.g. "*scassà 'o càntaro*", meaning "to shit in somebody's boots".

28: women's breasts

29: father of all children (male genitals). In Naples the phallus is still a widespread talisman, as it was in Roman times. Faced with a bad omen, men touch their crotch to ward off their fate, whereas women touch a red horn (see p. 78), the Christian version of the Roman phallus.

30: lieutenant's bullets Metaphor for "testicles". The only purpose of the lieutenant, *tenente*, is to rhyme with *trenta*, given that in Neapolitan the final vowel is not pronounced.

31: owner (real estate). Because the 31st is the day you pay the rent.

32: *capitone* (big eel). The indispensable Christmas Eve meal. This fish is very similar to the serpent, the embodiment of Evil. So to ward off Evil, it is cut up alive.

33: age of Christ This number is also associated with the nun, because in Old Naples there is a convent called the "Thirty-three" (see p. 204).

34: *capa* (head). But also the *glans penis*. In Neapolitan, *capa 'e cazzo* (literally dickhead) is a insult commonly aimed at airheads.

35: bird In many civilisations, birds represent the means of communicating with celestial bodies.

36: castanets Ancient instrument played in ritual dances during religious festivals in antiquity as today.

37: monk In the Campanian popular imagination, monks always have one foot in the world of magic. Some of them, it is believed, had the power to know the winning numbers in advance. *'O munaciello*, the little monk, is the notorious imp who, according to legend, appears in Neapolitan homes to bring happiness or misery, depending on how it is treated.

38: blows (beating up) - **39: hangman's rope**

40: *paposcia* (scrotal hernia). Several Neapolitan words and phrases associated with this condition are a source of ribald jokes. For example, if a man takes a chance by predicting rain, he is laughingly asked if he's got a hernia because, seemingly, it's painful when the weather changes.

41: knife (weapon). This is the weapon used by "men of honour" because it requires more courage than the gun.

42: coffee Neapolitans so love their coffee that, in the bars of the historic centre, regulars pay for two coffees, their own and one for the next customer who mightn't have any money on them.

43: "slut" on the balcony. Equivalent of "easy woman" because in bygone days if a woman lingered on the balcony it was to attract attention or wait for her lover.

44: bars (prison windows).

45: good wine Sacred drink in both the pagan and Christian eras, when it becomes the blood of Christ.

46: money - 47: death - 48: talking dead (in dreams)

49: piece of meat - 50: bread

51: garden Implying the female pubis.

52: mother Key character in Neapolitan culture in which the Great Mother was one of the main deities.

53: old man He personifies wisdom.

54: hat Historically, headgear has always been a distinctive mark of social class.

55: music A fundamental element of Campanian culture (see p. 78). Here, the two 5s represent the ten fingers needed to play an instrument.

56: a fall

57: hunchback Among Neapolitans, who are very superstitious, a hunchback (men only!) brings good luck and, to increase your chances, you even have to caress his hump.

58: parcel Synonymous with the gift that is used to cement social ties, seal pacts, finalise a marriage contract.

59: hairs   60: complaint (lamentation).

61: hunter The hunter always features in the Neapolitan nativity scene (see p. 252), where all the major magico-religious symbols of Campanian culture are found. As the oldest method of getting food, hunting is also often represented in the funerary paintings of antiquity.

62: murder victim   63: bride

64: *sciammeria* (formal dress – frock coat). This word is used to ironise about someone dressed in their Sunday best. A *sciammeria*, being a long jacket "cover-up", is also a synonym for the sex act.

65: tears Especially those of women beating their breast.

66: two single girls The allusion to the two 6s is obvious. The two marriageable girls, one beautiful and the other ugly, is also a recurring theme in Campanian folktales.

67: squid in the guitar A very suggestive phrase to describe the sex act.

68: *zuppa 'e carnacotta*, literally "cooked meat soup". This is traditionally a soup for the poor, made from a few green vegetables, aromatic herbs and thin slices of veal offal. It is served very hot over a layer of traditional *freselle* crackers.

69: upside down A number whose sexual meaning is blindingly obvious.

70: residential building

71: *ommo 'e merda* (manure). A very common insult.

72: wonder Here the meaning is rather that of another state of being as possessed by the divine light. In the nativity scene, in front of the cave of the Baby Jesus, there must be a *pastore d' 'a meraviglia*, an open-mouthed and open-armed shepherd struck by the divine event. In common parlance, the "amazed shepherd" signifies a blissful innocent.

73: hospital

74: cave Natural caves are imbued with a profound religious meaning in many civilisations, particularly in Campania. A number of rites did in fact take place in caves (see Crypta Neapolitana, p. 31). The cave also alludes to the ultimate "cavity", that of the woman who gives life.

75: Pulcinella (Punch, see p. 386).

76: fountain Fountains embody a magical value: apparitions and lovers' trysts take place near them. The fountain is also an essential element of the nativity scene, as it was near a fountain that the angel Gabriel announced to Mary that she was carrying the Baby Jesus.

77: devils This number is also associated with women's thighs, as the supreme temptation, to be resisted by saints and initiates to pagan religions preaching purity (such as Isis worshippers).

78: *bella figliola* (pretty girl). A euphemism to avoid explicitly saying *zoccola* (literally female rat), whore.

79: thief

80: mouth Of all the parts of the human body, the mouth has been chosen for its many essential functions: breathing, eating, talking, laughing, sensuality.

81: flowers They are associated with two critical phases of human life: marriage, from which life is born, and death.

82: set table For Neapolitans, a hearty meal is synonymous with a religious festival, family unity, pleasure, and needless to say an eternal dream for the poor. Tavern tables overflowing with food are never left out of the crib scene.

83: bad weather In the land of Sun-worshippers, bad weather is a poor omen. The Neapolitans make signs to ward off the fates if they wake to see an overcast sky. The number 83 is probably connected with the year 1783, when a downpour followed by a powerful earthquake devastated Calabria (formerly part of the Kingdom of Naples).

84: church - 85: souls in Purgatory (see p. 288).

86: corner shop Another vital place as it contains everything essential to life, not to mention embodying a basic human activity. An authentic Neapolitan nativity scene is always dotted with little shops.

87: *perucchie* (lice). This is one of sixty slang expressions for money. However to Neapolitans *quatte perucchie* (four lice) means something very cheap – *perucchiuso* signifies "miserly".

88: *casecavallo* Euphemism for someone that's a "pain in the neck", as you might say to them in English: "You get on my tits" or "You piss me off". Not only is *casecavallo* (a typical cheese from the Campania region; in Italian, *caciocavallo*) shaped like a distended testicle, but these cheeses are hung up in pairs in shops.

89: little old lady The very old woman is the one who performs the ancient rites: the relatives of Saint Januarius (see p. 399), the Sibyls, the *Befana* who brings gifts to children on 6 January, are all old women.

90: fear and the people If Neapolitans laugh at anything and everything, it's to relieve their angst: worry over the eruptions, earthquakes and endless wars that have raged through this beautiful country. This explains the double meaning of this last *Smorfia* number.

OFFICINA D'ARTI GRAFICHE
DI CARMINE CERVONE

㉒

12 Via Anticaglia
• Open Monday to Friday, 10am–6pm
• Tel: 081 295483
• carmine.cervone@libero.it

> **The smallest-ever museum of typography**

It would be an understatement to say that this is only a printing works (with a small museum attached) – the graphic arts workshop of Carmine Cervone, friendly expert in the art of printmaking, is a window into a lost world. Such is the happy outcome of a rich history of tradition and typically Neapolitan creativity. Three generations of typographers have worked here. In 2001, Carmine decided to restore the old printing equipment and revive traditional typography. He resurrected machines from the late 19th and early 20th centuries, from Germany, Italy, the UK (Heidelberg, Mandelli, Italtype), all now in good working order. Later on, he added printing presses dating from the mid-19th century. These impressive machines are entirely manual: that's why all the books produced here are unique, as copies are never identical. "With digital printing," explains Carmine, "the paper is actually 'cooked', whereas craft printing makes it possible to practise the very old art of leaving a mark, of indenting the paper. My aim is to keep alive an ancient and recognised tradition that made Naples famous around the world." Into the bargain, the cost to the customer remains the same as for a work printed using modern technology. At the centre of the workshop stands a Linotype

machine for mechanical composition. Each letter of a text is patiently and meticulously set in place by hand, whenever it appears, line after line. With his mobile chair, Carmine can easily move around the machines. The smell of ink and paper pervades the air, evoking the atmosphere of an age when time was not dictated by the speed of standardised production methods. These machines produce minor masterpieces such as art books, elegant notebooks, refined frontispieces and artistic prints. If you ask, Carmine will be happy to take you round the small but perfectly formed typography museum, next to the workshop. Here you'll see a press dating from 1840, printing instruments, vintage machines, precious sheets of paper and compositor's tools, as well as individual metal characters in all sizes and typefaces.

PALAZZO CARACCIOLO DI AVELLINO

Fondazione Morra Greco
17 Largo Proprio di Avellino
• Metro: Line 1 Museo, Line 2 Cavour
• Visits by appointment: email or follow links on website
• www.fondazionemorragreco.com
• info@fondazionemorragreco.com

A breathtaking series of frescoes

A visit to Palazzo Caracciolo di Avellino will blow you away – on the first floor is a spectacular series of rooms with frescoes by Baroque artist Giacomo Del Pó (1654–1726). As if by magic, you'll be transported to a fantasy land populated with human and animal and geometrical shapes. Although the frescoes suggest an open and deceptively deep space, the rooms are decorated from the walls to the vaulted ceiling, achieving an extraordinary and timeless effect. Collections of works by contemporary artists add to the charm.

The building's foundations date back to the 15th century. It was the seat of the Benedictine nuns of San Potito Sannitico before being purchased by Camillo Caracciolo (1563–1617), who enlarged and redeveloped the old convent.

Palazzo Caracciolo di Avellino, as it came to be known much later, was built at the beginning of the 16th century. It is one of the most important residential buildings in the historic centre, with many additions right up to the 18th century. First it belonged to the Gambacorta family, then to Caracciolo de' Rossi, before passing to the Princes of Avellino – a collateral branch of the Caracciolo family.

Italian Renaissance poet Torquato Tasso lived here from 1550 to 1554, as recorded by a marble plaque on the main façade. Having moved to Naples, Torquato's father Bernardo acquired an apartment in this palazzo, which belonged to the parents of his wife, Porzia de' Rossi. The wing where the Tassos lived no longer exists, destroyed in the heavy bombardment of the Second World War. The surviving section of the building now covers an area of some 2,000 m2 over five floors.

More recently, Neapolitan doctor and collector Maurizio Morra Greco bought the palazzo for the headquarters of the Morra Greco Foundation. Since 2015, the building has been extensively restored and restructured to convert it into a museum and exhibition centre.

INCURABILI PHARMACY

(24)

50 Largo Maria Longo
- Metro: Line 1 Museo, Line 2 Cavour
- Visits by small groups on reservation
- Tel: 081 440647
- info@ilfarodippocrate.it

> *A pharmacy of unequalled magnificence*

Built in the 16th century, then enlarged and refurbished (as seen today) between 1740 and 1760, the pharmacy in the Ospedale degli Incurabili (Hospital of the Incurables) is a genuine masterpiece. According to contemporary thinking, the beauty of the many works of art in the pharmacy was aimed at treating patients more effectively.

This marvellous little place is the last of the hundreds of such pharmacies that used to fill the city. The only proof of their existence is the many ceramic vases dispersed in public and private collections around the world. The two-room pharmacy, closed for over thirty years, was reopened to the public in 2011.

A monumental grey stone staircase takes you to the main salon with its tiled floor made by the prestigious Massa brothers' workshop (also responsible for the majolica work in the celebration cloister of Santa Chiara). At the entrance, two golden sculptures face one another: allegories of the "virgin uterus" and the "post-operative uterus" respectively. In the centre stands a rare walnut table, 5 m long, carved from a single massive trunk. All around the walls is a dazzling display of 420 multicoloured ceramic vases, also by Massa, decorated with scenes from the Old Testament and in a perfect state of conservation: the largest contained ointments, the smaller ones syrups – remedies mainly reserved for hospital patients.

The walls of the salon are covered from top to bottom with beautiful carved walnut cabinets with inlaid shelves, the work of cabinetmaker Agostino Fucito. The ceiling fresco by Pietro Bardellino features scenes from the Trojan War, but with a nod to medicine, as the hero Menelaus (or Achilles) is being cared for by Machaon, a warrior well-versed in the physician's art.

ELECTRICITY AS THERAPY IN THE 18TH CENTURY

At the four corners of the ceiling of the large salon are the portraits of four characters, all with connections to medicine except Italian physicist Alessandro Volta (1745–1827), who earned his place there because certain conditions were already being treated in the late 18th century using heat generated by electricity.

NAPLES, THE LAST BASTION OF *TERIACA*

Note also a large marble vase in which was kept a remedy long considered infallible against poisoning: *Teriaca* (Greek *thériaké*, antidote to poisonous animal bites). Naples was the last Italian city to cease production in 1906. (For more information, see *Secret Venice* in this series of guides.)

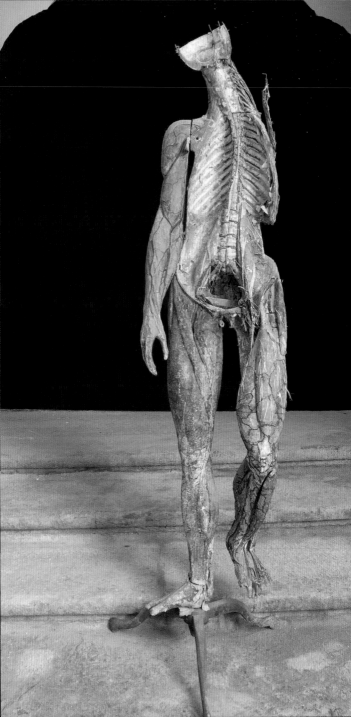

MUSEO DELLE ARTI SANITARIE
DEGLI INCURABILI

㉕

50 Largo Maria Longo
• Metro: Line 1 Museo, Line 2 Cavour
• Visits on reservation by phone or e-mail
• Tel: 081 440647
• info@ilfarodippocrate.it

A unique anatomical model

I n the Hospital for Incurables, besides the pharmacy (see previous double-page spread), a very interesting museum is housed in the premises of the former Convento delle Convertite (convent for reformed prostitutes). It bears testimony to the advanced level of modernity achieved by medicine in 16th-century Naples (the founding of the hospital by Maria Lorenza Longo dates back to 1518 – see p. 204).

The highlight of the Museum of the History of Medicine and Health is an anatomical papier-mâché model built in 1730/1740. This unique educational tool – complete with perfectly represented veins, backbone and muscles, which can be dismantled and articulated – was used in the centre's school of medicine. Among the many artefacts are rare surgical instruments, a portable pharmacy from the 18th century, one of the first glass feeding bottles in history and an anaesthetic mask, an all-time first.

The hospital, which has been operational since 1518, was one of the largest in Europe, with 1,600 beds when it opened.

In the courtyard, the marble basins can still be seen where, before they were admitted, the sick were washed then dressed in a long white shirt. The doctors washed their hands at the fountains on either side of the courtyard.

WHEN UNHEALTHY AIR WAS BELIEVED TO CAUSE SYPHILIS

The place where the hospital was built, Caponapoli hill, was purposely chosen for its particularly clean air as it was thought to cure syphilis. When the real cause of this terrible condition was discovered, the names of aristocrats and prelates disappeared as if by magic from the hospital records.

NEARBY

In the largest cloister of the Incurabili monastery complex, over a hundred species of medicinal herbs formerly grown here have recently been replanted. In the centre of the garden stands a beautiful camphor tree, planted in 1525, which is the oldest in Italy. The rooms used as a maternity ward give onto the adjacent cloister, referred to as the "cloister of the pregnant women", as indicated by an old plaque.

CHAPEL OF THE "CONDEMNED PRISONERS"

Cortile degli Incurabili
50 Largo Maria Longo
• Metro: Line 1 Museo, Line 2 Cavour
• Tel: 081 440647
• Visits on reservation, by email: info@ilfarodippocrate.it

The remarkable setting of Santa Maria Succurre Miseris

The chapel of Santa Maria Succurre Miseris della Compagnia dei Bianchi della Giustizia (Confraternity of the Whites of Justice), little known to Neapolitans, has strikingly rich decoration and original artwork by Giovan Battista Benaschi, Paolo De Matteis, Giovanni Balducci, Dionisio Lazzari and Andrea Merliano, among others. Other unmissable curiosities are the oil-painted pectoral plates worn by members of the confraternity, a number of relics, and the skull of an executed Spanish soldier with a hole clearly pierced in his forehead.

One of the biggest attractions, however, is a small wax model known as *La Scandalosa* (The Scandalous One), a terrifying image of a young woman whose delicate features are covered with ulcers, while worms, parasites and other creatures gnaw at her flesh. She has the characteristic signs of syphilis, considered a scourge of God. The disease was widespread at the time, and syphilitics were cared for at the Ospedale degli Incurabili (Hospital for Incurables). According to a tradition perpetuated by Neapolitan dialect poet Salvatore Di Giacomo, this ancient waxwork is a reminder of the rotten body of a courtesan, displayed to sinners as a warning, in the hope that such a dreadful vision would persuade them to change their ways.

CONFRATERNITY OF THE WHITES OF JUSTICE

The main mission of this white-hooded confraternity was assistance to condemned prisoners, whose last wishes they recorded in the registers they provided. Founded in 1430 by Salvatore La Marca, the confreres based at the chapel of Santa Maria Succurre Miseris counted among their members Saint Cajetan (Gaetano di Thiene, founder of the Theatine Order), Saint Alphonsus Liguori (author of the prayer "Tu scendi dalle stelle" / "You descend from the stars") and Francesco Caracciolo (known as the "hunter of souls"), as well as aristocrats and leading Naples merchants.

In 1583, fearing an anti-Spanish conspiracy, King Philip II ordered the dissolution of the confraternity. A few years later, however, their activity was allowed to resume, on condition that only ecclesiastics took part. Their assistance to convicts ceased in 1862, the year of the last execution, with a 20-year-old soldier as victim.

MUSEO DI ANATOMIA UMANA

Seconda Università degli Studi
5 Via Luciano Armanni
• Metro: Line 1 Museo, Line 2 Cavour
• Tel: 081 5667747
• http://musa.orpheogroup.com/it/
• Admission free Tuesday, Thursday and Friday, 10-13
• Reservation required

> *Human monstrosities*

The Human Anatomy Museum, founded in 1819 and completely unknown to the general public, figures among the top three in the world for the richness and importance of its collections, put together by eminent anatomists and later bequeathed to the university. They are kept in very elegant 19th-century cabinets in the monastery of Saint Patricia, now closed down.

Among the most impressive pieces is a calcified foetus 10 cm long that remained in the body of the mother for twenty-eight years and was discovered only after her death – an incident recounted in a scientific text of 1658.

There is no lack of eccentricities in these rooms, where you can see "artwork" in macabre taste, to say the least: a low table made from human blood, bile, brains and lungs, on which a female hand is laid, all preserved through a process called "petrifaction".

The many examples of deformities include a number of malformed foetuses preserved in formaldehyde and a skeleton of a woman who died at the age of 90 with severe arthritis.

In the section on anatomical dissection (417 dried samples dating back to the 18th century), two bodies are on display: their vascular system is revealed following injection with coloured dyes. The rarest exhibit is a humerus attributed in the archives to a skeleton prepared by Andreas Vesalius, the father of modern anatomy, in 1544 at Basle. As far as is known, this is unique in the world.

Note also the giant anatomical plates (70 × 100 cm), dated 1823, by the Siena anatomist Paolo Mascagni. There are only two sets in the world, the others (1825) being in Pisa.

Other curiosities include the skulls of four criminals known as the "Vicaria four". They were the protagonists of an incident that made headlines in the early 19th century: with the help of her lover, her father and a young surgeon who had fallen for her, Giuditta Guastamacchia planned her husband's murder. The four culprits were executed on Via dei Tribunali on 19 April 1800. Note the marks drawn on their skulls by criminology physiognomists.

Thanks to the work of the director of the institute, Professor Vincenzo Esposito, the museum was reopened to the public in 1997.

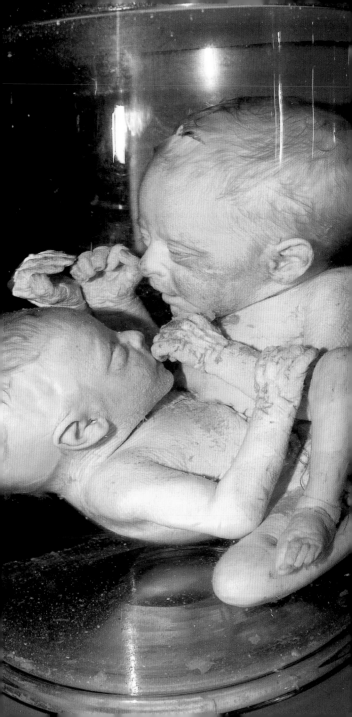

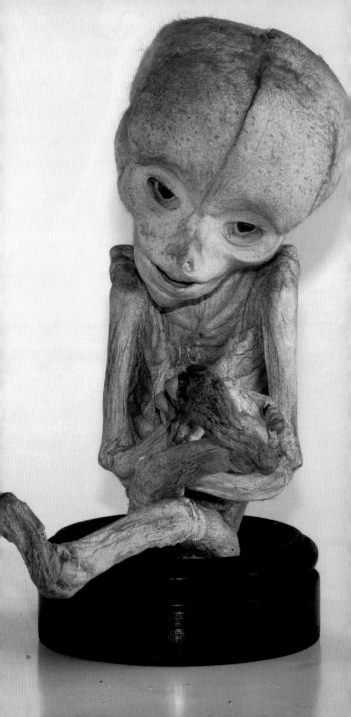

CASA ZEVOLA

3 Via Atri
• Metro: Line 1 Dante or Università, Line 2 Montesanto
• Funicular Montesanto (Montesanto)
• Further information www.giuseppezevola.it

> *The incredible apartment/ museum of a modern "disciple" of Giordano Bruno*

The large apartment of Giuseppe Zevola, Neapolitan painter, poet and philosopher, is a clever extravaganza: family furniture, Baroque mirrors and other unique objects hang from the ceiling, such as the "Lady Philosophy", made entirely from mirrors and round mosaics on a golden background swaying back and forth. All the doors and windows are painted in bright colours, as are the chairs, tables, tablecloths and plates. There is an abundance of chandeliers and rotating centrepieces on the tables, while on the walls the heroes of Indian mythology rub shoulders with saints and heretics. Zevola considers his amazing

residence, which he calls *Muta domus*, to be his personal theatre. As an unconditional admirer of the great philosopher Giordano Bruno, Zevola commits to memory and publishes extracts from his works. Having worked for ten years in the Historical Archive of the Banco di Napoli (see p. 279), the artist managed to assemble a collection of drawings, poems, puns, even doodles, left in the margins of their ledgers by former employees of the "*Banchi pubblici*" (old-time banks) from 1538 to 1861. The collection was published under the title *Piaceri di noia* (Pleasures of Boredom).

Since 2002, one of Giuseppe Zevola's works has been on display at Rione Alto (Line 1 of the metro), known as the "art" station.

COMMEMORATIVE PLAQUES
AT PALAZZO FILANGIERI

㉙

23 Via Atri
• Metro: Line 1 Museo, Line 2 Cavour

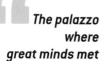

The palazzo
where
great minds met

The façade of Palazzo Filangieri, built in the 18th century by the Filangieri family of Arianiello, is studded with commemorative plaques dedicated to personalities who lived here between the 18th and 20th centuries: the one above on the right concerns the jurist and philosopher Gaetano Filangieri, born in 1752 (see below); the one below states that the celebrated philosopher Benedetto Croce (1866–1952) had an apartment there from 1900 to 1912.

The bottom-left plaque records that Goethe was a guest of the Filangieri family. In his *Italian Journey*, Goethe had indeed written that Gaetano Filangieri, whom he met on 5 March 1787, was worthy of the highest consideration and aspired to man's happiness without losing sight of the concept of freedom. Still on the left, the inscription above commemorates physicist and mathematician Nicola Trudi, professor of infinitesimal calculus at the University of Naples, who was well known for his treatises on "determinants" (the Trudi determinants).

GAETANO FILANGIERI: A NEAPOLITAN WHO INSPIRED THE AMERICAN CONSTITUTION

GAETANO FILANGIERI

Gaetano Filangieri is omnipresent in Naples: a beautiful street, a museum, a school and a lavish salon in the State Archives (see p. 156) all bear his name. However, the scope of this great philosopher has not been fully recognised – a leading figure of the Enlightenment in its specifically Neapolitan aspect, Filangieri was one of the most eminent jurists of his time. He was an enthusiastic reformer and advocated education for all, and the equitable redistribution of land and taxation based solely on income, revolutionary concepts at the time. His major work, *La Scienza della legislazione* (The Science of Legislation), was translated into several languages and was a major influence on the fathers of the American Constitution. Benjamin Franklin regularly consulted the Neapolitan thinker and highly esteemed his advice. Filangieri died in 1788 at Vico Equense on the Sorrento coast, where he had retired. He was only 36 years old.

REMAINS OF A DIOSCURI TEMPLE

"Limonè" limoncello factory
Piazza San Gaetano 72
• Metro: Line 1 Museo, Line 2 Cavour
• Tel: 081 299429
• limoncellodinapoli@yahoo.it
• Visits during normal shop opening hours

> *Reminders of the 1st century in the back shop*

Below the church of San Paolo Maggiore (Saint Paul the Greater), corresponding to the left nave, the "back shop" of the Limonè *limoncello* (a local lemon liqueur) manufacturers is a narrow corridor 6 m long with some vestiges of a Dioscuri temple: large blocks of yellow tuff from the foundations, a water tank and a well about 20 m deep in which you can still see the water mark, and a wall built in *opus reticulatum* (diamond-shaped brickwork). The site of the temple, dating from the 1st century AD, had probably already been used by the Greeks in the 5th century BC and it was near the Graeco-Roman forum of Neapolis – today Piazza San Gaetano. The present church was built in around the 8th century over the ruins of the pagan temple.

In Greek and Roman mythology, the twins Castor and Pollux were known as the Dioscuri, i.e. Sons of Zeus. They were both the sons of Leda and the brothers of Clytemnestra and Helen: Castor was the son of Tyndareus, a Spartan king, whereas Pollux was the son of Zeus, king of the gods.

CONGREGATION DEL CROCIFISSO DELLA SCIABICA

31

76 Via dei Tribunali
• Metro: Line 1 Museo or Dante, Line 2 Montesanto or Cavour
• Tel: 338 3647883
• Visits Wednesday 3pm–5pm, Sunday 9am–12pm
• Admission free

Body socks

A green door on the landing of the steps leading to the church of San Paolo Maggiore forecourt gives access to the Congregation del Crocefisso della Sciabica, founded in 1623 for pauper burials.

This charitable institution houses a chapel and small church built in the *cella* (inner chamber) of the Roman temple of the Dioscuri (see p. 229) where the remains of bodies that had been buried nearby in consecrated ground, now disused and inaccessible, are laid to rest.

Inside a glass case you can see a skeleton whose skull (never recovered) was replaced by a plaster mask. This body, dressed in a wedding gown, is that of

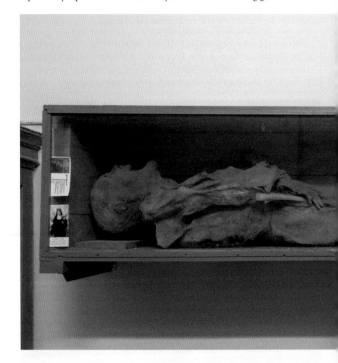

Maria Felice, last descendant of the Ricciardi family, who in 1833 was felled by a heart attack during her wedding in this very church. In another case lies the withered corpse of a priest who officiated for the congregation at an unknown date. The body was found intact except for the feet. Some kind soul has covered the stumps with socks so that he wouldn't look like an amputee.

ORIGIN OF THE WORD *"SCIABICA"*

The *sciabica* is a fishing net with very fine mesh used to catch any small fry. By using that name, the founders of the Crocefisso congregation intended to metaphorically save even those souls who had fallen through the usual "net".

In front of the church of San Paolo Maggiore, apart from the two columns at the entrance from the Dioscuri temple, there are also the remains of three large sections of marble pavement (stylobate). Two of these have been placed at the entrance to the church, while the third seems to have been used as a base for the statue of Saint Cajetan, second patron saint of Naples, to be found in the square named after him, Piazza San Gaetano.

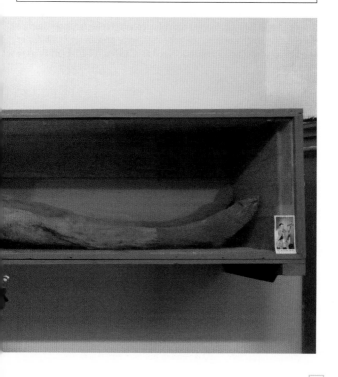

ARTWORKS BY NATHALIE DE SAINT PHALLE 32

Palazzo Spinelli di Laurino
362 Via dei Tribunali
• Metro: Line 1 Museo, Line 2 Cavour or Montesanto
• Visits on reservation by phone or e-mail
• Tel: 081 299579 • nhsp@aol.com

Dedicated to art

The large top-floor apartment of Palazzo Spinelli di Laurino has been dedicated to art thanks to Nathalie de Saint Phalle, a writer of French origin who has lived in Naples since 1993. Canvases, books, catalogues, musical instruments and other creations of great originality form a pot-pourri of works of art enhanced by the shimmering colours of the carpets.

Many artists, several of whom are very well known, have displayed their work in this large open space. Some have deposited their works, thus contributing to the atmosphere of cosmopolitan "cultural contagion". These artists include Neapolitan painter Giuseppe Zevola (see p. 227), American poet John Giorno and Neapolitan photographer/sculptor Beatrice Caracciolo. Other works in the collection were previously exhibited in another apartment (Il Purgatorio, used as a B&B until 2011) of Palazzo Marigliano.

A lovely room in the Palazzo Spinelli apartment can be booked for the night.

COURTYARD OF PALAZZO SPINELLI DI LAURINO

Although all Neapolitans know where to find Palazzo Spinelli (as they often queue outside one of the city's most famous pizzerias), only insiders are aware that that through the carriage door of the palazzo is a detail that you won't find in any of the city's other old palazzi: a superb elliptical courtyard. The owner of the building, Troiano Spinelli, the last Duke of Laurino, whose commemorative plaque can be found between the two flights of stairs, had his palazzo restored by the celebrated architect Ferdinando Sanfelice (see p. 317). A true original, Sanfelice turned the square courtyard into an ellipse, a tribute to Romanness particularly appreciated by Duke Troiano, true humanist that he was.

THE GHOST OF BIANCA

The legend goes that a ghostly woman wandered around near the staircase at Palazzo Spinelli. This would have been Bianca, the young lady companion of Lorenza Spinelli, Troiano's wife. Bianca was taken in as an orphan by the duke, but as she grew up her beauty aroused Lorenza's jealousy.

To be rid of her rival, the duchess spread the rumour that Bianca was trying to seduce her husband so had to be sent away. One night, with the complicity of a deaf-mute servant, she gagged and bound the girl before walling her up alive in one of the niches of the entrance hall. The unfortunate girl managed to untie her bonds and remove the gag, cursing her torturer thus: *"This wall is not enough to make me disappear. I will return, and when you see me, you will know what to expect. When you see me, you or someone else."*

HIDDEN SYMBOLISM OF CAPPELLA SANSEVERO

33

Chapel of Sansevero - 19/21 Via Francesco De Sanctis
• Metro: Line 1 Dante, Università
• Tel: 081 5518470
• info@museosansevero.it • www.museosansevero.it
• Open Monday to Saturday 10am–17.40pm, Sundays and holidays 10am–1.10pm • Closed Tuesday

Veiled hermetism of Raimondo di Sangro

The Sansevero chapel, built in 1590, was enlarged and embellished by Raimondo di Sangro in 1744 with an extensive collection of statues all dedicated to Mary, mother of Jesus. Beyond the religious orthodoxy of the statuary, there are a series of symbols of the hermetic heterodoxy that characterised the esoteric thinking of di Sangro, one of the founders of Freemasonry in Naples and an avowed practitioner of alchemy.

On the left side of the chapel is the statue of *Decoro* (Decorum), a young man with a lion's skin thrown over his shoulders in an allegory of Hercules, which symbolises Strength, intellectual Power. Opposite, *Amor divino* (Divine Love), holding up a flaming heart, symbolises the Power of the Spirit and the Heart that makes it possible to achieve chemical Marriage and Divinity, here embodied by the Divine Mother, patron of alchemists. A little further along is *Liberalità* (Liberality): the coin (*moneda*) and compass represent the Monad, Spirit of Man and the circle of the action of the Divine Will where its presence is diffused.

On the opposite side is *Educazione* (Education), which transmits

to the child, the neophyte, the elemental assumptions of hermetic Initiation – respect for freedom of thought and feelings of our fellow beings, with decorum and love in the service of Divine Wisdom symbolised by the Virgin. These principles are reinforced by the presence of other statues, those of *Sincerità* (Sincerity), *Soavità del giogo coniugale* (Sweetness of the Marital Yoke), *Zelo della religione* (Religious Zeal) and *Dominio di se stessi* (Self-control). Whoever does not possess these qualities will inevitably fail the Initiation that the symbolism evokes.

Sincerity, a caduceus in his right

hand and a heart in the left, represents spiritual introspection, the request for hermetic Illumination by the Initiate seeking to unite with the God within, in an act of absolute sincerity. *Sweetness of the Marital Yoke*, helmet on head and yoke in hand, indicates that gently but firmly, like a sacred warrior, he must gradually transform the life-energy into life-consciousness in the yoke of real life. *Religious Zeal* carries a torch evoking acquired knowledge and the duty to preserve it, without adulterating it with foreign elements, while respecting the freedom of thought which conforms to free will in general. *Self-control* (of one's baser tendencies) is the greatest and most sublime of battles that a man can fight, which is why this statue features a warrior holding a chained lion at his feet and an inverted torch, expressing the Love that emanates from the tamed beast (exterior and interior). This is the allegory of the triumph of Love and Wisdom over brute force, the ultimate transformation of the profane to the Initiate.

The abandonment of ordinary life for a spiritual existence is symbolised by the *Disinganno* (Disillusionment) statue, which represents a man releasing himself from the mesh of a net with the help of a winged genie, allegory of the divine Spirit. This is represented below by a bas-relief of Christ giving sight to the blind, transmitting the Light of Truth to those who live in the darkness of ignorance, the greatest blindness of all.

Finally, *Pudicizia* (Modesty) brings together all initiatory Wisdom, whose Light is sought by the neophyte wishing to become an Enlightened One.

WHY ARE TWO MEDALLIONS FACELESS?

Some of the statues in the chapel have associated medallions representing characters linked with the allegory. The medallions of Raimondo di Sangro's daughter-in-law and his wife, Carlotta Gaetani, nevertheless bear no images – at the time, it was considered bad luck to physically represent those who were still alive.

The statue of *Disillusionment* has also been interpreted by some as a reference to Masonic initiation in the 18th century: the neophyte did indeed go into the initiation ceremony blindfolded. He rang at the Lodge door, saying he was a blind man who wanted to see the light again. Once inside, the blindfold was removed. The ritual required that he should also have one shoulder bared in the same way as the statue.

The monument to Cecco di Sangro emerging armed from a sarcophagus commemorates the incident when, feigning death during the siege of Amiens in 1597, Cecco was locked in a crate that was then brought into the city. He climbed out during the night and opened the gates for his comrades in arms, who could then seize the city.

The statue of *Modesty* by Antonio Corradini represents Cecilia Gaetani d'Aragona, mother of Raimondo di Sangro, who died at the age of 20 (26 December 1710), when he was just 11 months old: the broken marble slab symbolises life cut short.
The statue also alludes to the goddess Isis (veiled), deity of the initiatory sciences: according to tradition, in Greek Neapolis *Modesty* was usually placed in the same setting as Isis.

SANSEVERO'S *VEILED CHRIST*: FROM LEGEND TO THE REALITY OF SUDATION AND MYSTICAL INTERNAL FIRE

The *Veiled Christ* statue in the Sansevero chapel, carved from a single block of marble by the Neapolitan Giuseppe Sanmartino (1720–1793), is considered the great masterpiece of 18th-century European sculpture.

It is said that Raimondo di Sangro (1710–1771), an avowed alchemist who had commissioned the sculpture, knew how to turn materials into stone and he was thought to have taught the sculptor how to calcify cloth into marble crystals.

This supposed secret seduced the artists of the day, including Antonio Canova, who tried to get to the bottom of it, saying he was ready to give ten years of his life in exchange for the mysterious procedure so he could create this strikingly unusual masterpiece.

The legend of the petrifaction of cloth is above all linked to the deeper significance, not of the shroud, but of *sudation* (perspiration), which arises from proximity to the heat of the Mystic Fire coiling up within the human organism (the Hindu *kundalini*).

The link between sudation and petrifaction is understood as follows: the internal heat is so intense that the body perspires and its crystals calcify or petrify.

The ancient alchemists explained this phenomenon by the biblical story of Lot's wife fleeing Sodom, who was turned into a pillar of salt when she looked back. The word "sudation", the consequence of which is that materials or bodies turn to stone, is derived from Sodom or Sod.

The steam bath is one of the basic techniques for increasing this mystical heat, with the result that sweating is occasionally given an ultimately "Creationist" value.

In many religious and mythological traditions, the first man was created by God following an intensive sudation. This idea of divine creation was eventually popularised by the use of steam baths, which held the same significance for the peoples of northern Asia and of Europe.

The realm of fire, of insensitivity to heat and hence to mystic heat, which makes extreme cold or glowing embers bearable, constitutes a magico-mystical virtue, which along with other no less miraculous qualities (ascension, levitation, etc.), translates in terms of the senses the fact that the mystic is already part of the spiritual world and its immaterial inhabitants. This is perhaps why the steam bath and sudation had a sacrificial meaning for the classical civilisations of antiquity – the believer offered his sweat to the Supreme Sun God, a gesture of purifying and merciful value that allowed him to enter that invisible world bodily and with no qualms and to evolve there, leaving behind the "dormition" of the physical senses by a definitive spiritual awakening, like a Christ or an Enlightened One throwing off the shackles of the flesh and the rule of death.

SINE ANTIQUA ARTE NON EST NOVA ARS

TRIPTYCH OF *CHRIST UNVEILED* OR *HIDDEN LIGHT*

㉞

Church of Monte Manso di Scala Foundation
34 Via Nilo
• Metro: Line 1 Dante
• Visits by appointment (phone)
• www.realmontemanso.it
• realmontemansodiscala@gmail.com

> *Christ*
> *unveiled and*
> *Christ veiled*

The lovely church of the Monte Manso di Scala Foundation, where you can book a visit, is incongruously sited on the third floor of a very elegant palazzo in the historic centre, just above the famous Sansevero chapel whose owner, alchemist Prince Raimondo di Sangro, let the Jesuits use the space.

In agreement with Pope Benedict XIV, they wished to counteract the prince's openly Masonic tastes by building a church exalting the Christian faith. The contemporary sculpture by Giuseppe Corcione, a triptych entitled *Christ Unveiled or Hidden Light* set three floors above the famous *Veiled Christ*, was another way of opposing the unorthodox ideas of the sulphurous Prince of Sansevero.

The institution of Monte Manso di Scala, founded in 1608 by Giovanni Battista Manso, was originally dedicated to charitable works, but later became a seminary for young nobles whose religious education was entrusted to the Jesuits. To this day the foundation, true to its spirit of solidarity, awards scholarships to young Neapolitans from impoverished aristocratic families.

The elliptical and light-flooded church, closed since 1959, was seriously damaged by the earthquake of 1980. It reopened in 2009 after lengthy restoration work funded by the foundation.

The Rococo altarpiece of the main altar, *Madonna in gloria con santi gesuiti*, representing the Virgin in glory with Jesuit saints, was painted by Francesco de Mura (1696–1782).

PLAQUE OF THE CHURCH OF SAN DOMENICO MAGGIORE

18 Vico San Domenico
• Metro: Line 1 Dante, Line 2 Montesanto

A mysterious plaque and hermetic verses

On the wall to the left of the main entrance of the church of San Domenico Maggiore (the most used access is in Piazza San Domenico, opposite) is a marble plaque inscribed with Latin verses whose meaning has totally baffled even the most eminent researchers from the 17th century to this day. The plaque itself is also a mystery as nobody knows its provenance, author or exact date. In the 17th century, Giovanni Antonio Summonte wrote in his *Historia di Napoli* (History of Naples) that in 1560, while the Dominican owners of the convent were having restoration work done on the church, this inscription was found below the marble slabs covering the floor. Also featured at the bottom left is a man wearing a sort of homespun robe, kneeling and with his hands clasped in prayer. As the monks thought it had something to do with water, they placed the plaque near the cloister's well. In 1605 it was moved to its present site.

Here is a literal translation:

"*The bringer of storms begrudged me the Sun, dear to God, and with the rain he carried far away the human bodies submerged in the sea. Now we suffer less cruel calamities; and beware the sinister Trojan line scattered under the sky. With my voice I beg the spirits and the guiding lights above, who with sin purged can pave the way to heaven. As the radiant Sun shines again, penetrating the water, the ice melts with the heat.*"

The lettering is in mid-15th century style, but some words suggest that this could be copied from a 13th-century inscription.

Philosophers and historians of different periods have put forward a number of hypotheses. Some went for the simplest explanation: a mischievous soul wanted posterity to rack its brains. Others saw in it the story of a shipwreck by a survivor who, perhaps for superstitious reasons, didn't want to be understood. Philologist A. S. Mazzocchi (18th century) went so far as to assign the four couplets to Petrarch, who reportedly described the terrible storm of 1345 during the reign of Joan I of Anjou.

For his part, historian S. Volpicella (19th century) interpreted it as a denunciation of the supposed poisoning of Saint Thomas Aquinas by Charles I of Anjou (*the bringer of storms*), of the Capetian line (*sinister Trojan line*). The Dominican C. Di Gregorio (17th century), careless of anachronism, claimed it was probably directions written by his confreres to find extremely valuable sacred objects hidden during the siege of Naples by Marshal Lautrec's troops in 1528. The list of alternative versions goes on …

The sumptuously decorated complex of San Domenico Maggiore, whose construction began in 1283, is of major historical interest. This Dominican monastery, where Thomas Aquinas, Giordano Bruno and Tommaso Campanella all spoke from the pulpit, was a peerless centre of philosophical study for centuries.

NEARBY

TOMB OF THE FIRST BISHOP OF NEW YORK

In the Treasure Room (access through the vestry) of San Domenico Maggiore is the striking tomb of Richard Luke Concanen. This Dominican priest (born in Ireland in 1747) was appointed first Bishop of New York in 1808 by Pope Pius VII while he was prior of the Dominican monastery in Rome. But he never managed to leave for the United States because he was held prisoner in Naples by the Napoleonic troops occupying the city, and had to administer his diocese by correspondence. He died two years later and was buried in the Dominican church of San Domenico Maggiore. Don't miss the mural on the Treasure Room ceiling, one of the most impressive works of Francesco Solimena, depicting the triumph of faith over heresy thanks to the Dominicans.

BIBLIOTHÈQUE MAURIZIO TADDEI ③⑦

Università degli Studi di Napoli "L'Orientale"
Palazzo Saluzzo di Corigliano
12 Piazza San Domenico Maggiore
• Metro: Line 1 Dante or Università, Line 2 Montesanto
• Funicular Montesanto (Montesanto)
• www.unior.it
• Visits on reservation

Gilded mythology

In the 17th-century palazzo that once belonged to the Duke of Corigliano and is now occupied by the University of Naples "L'Orientale", the Maurizio Taddei library

has been set up on the fourth floor, in a 1,000 m² space with a superb gallery known as the *galleria grande*. This example of pure Rococo has beautiful gilded stucco and frescoes depicting a battle between gods and giants (gigantomachy) and scenes from the *Aeneid*. The walls are also decorated with mythological themes, the four seasons, together with allegories of the works and virtues of the duke. The bibliographic heritage includes some 230,000 volumes, as well as newspapers, manuscripts and rare 16th-century editions in Chinese.

A HOTLY DISPUTED AMPUTATION

Built in the second half of the 18th century by Mario Gioffredo, Palazzo Casacalenda (17 Piazza San Domenico Maggiore), which belonged to the Dukes of Sangro Casacalenda e Campolieto, was restored by the renowned architect Luigi Vanvitelli. At the end of the 19th century, during the urban renewal project known as the Risanamento, it was decided to demolish two wings of the palazzo. Neapolitan historians, led by philosopher Benedetto Croce, firmly opposed this amputation that would have destroyed magnificent frescoes and an early Christian chapel, built on the ruins of a circular Greek temple dedicated to Eumelus of Corinth and incorporated in the building. Nevertheless one wing was demolished and part of the temple converted into a shop. So today on Via Mezzocannone you can see a strange barber's shop topped by a small circular tower in early 20th-century style.

THE DUKE'S STUDY

Palazzo Saluzzo di Corigliano
12 Piazza San Domenico Maggiore
• Metro: Line 1 Dante or Università, Line 2 Montesanto
• Funicular Montesanto (Montesanto)
• www.unior.it
• Visits on reservation

Rococo marvel

On the second floor of Palazzo Saluzzo di Corigliano, home of the University of Naples "L'Orientale", the "duke's study" is a pure Rococo marvel: the walls of the 5 × 5 m room are totally covered by gilded mirrors, a veritable set-piece created by architect and designer Filippo Buonocore. The room, which is miraculously still intact with its gilded wood carvings by Bartolomeo Granucci, was the private study of the former owner, the Duke of Corigliano.

The palazzo originally belonged to Duke Giovanni di Sangro Vietri, who commissioned it from the architect Giovanni Donadio, known as Mormando. The building was badly damaged by the 1688 earthquake. It was purchased in 1727 by Agostino Saluzzo, Duke of Corigliano, who completely renovated it. After a period of neglect (1935 to 1977), the palazzo was given a new lease of life when the university moved in.

Capello Miracoloso
di
DIEGO ARMANDO MARADONA

MADONNA
DI
BUENOS
AIRES
PROTEGGICI

NUESTRA SEÑORA DE LUJAN

'O Napoli è campione

Fm 88.7
la Tribu

📷 *Hai fatto la foto? E mo' te' vuo' piglià nu cafè?*
ATTENZIONE:
Se fai la foto e non prendi il caffè, la tua macchina fotografica potrebbe
caderti di mano (sarebbe un vero peccato)... *capisc'a me!*

📷 *Foto gemacht? Und jetzt einen Espresso?*
ACHTUNG:
Wenn sie das foto machen und dann keinen espresso nehmen,dann könnte ihnen
der fotoapparat runtetfallen (und das ware ja wirklinch schade)... *sie verstehen!*

📷 *T'as pris une photo? Eh, dis donc! Tu prends un café maintenant?*
FAIS GAFFE:
Car si tu prends une photo et meme pas un café, ton appareil photo
pourrait te glisser des mains (et cet serait vraiment dommage)... *t'as pigé!*

📷 *Sacaste la foto? Bueno attora tenes que tomarte un café?*
ATENCION:
Si sacas la foto y no te tomas un café, tu maquina de fotos
se te puede caer de la mano... *entendiste!*

MARADONA'S HAIR

Altar of the Nilo bar – 129 Via San Biagio dei Librai
- Metro: Line 1 Dante, Università, Line 2 Montesanto
- Funicular Montesanto (Montesanto)
- Tel: 081 5517029

*A footballer
venerated like
a saint*

Just in front of the Nile statue in the district known as the "Corpo di Napoli" (Body of Naples), Signor Bruno Alcidi, owner of the Nilo bar, built an altar in 1987 dedicated to Diego Armando Maradona: among other "relics" kept in a glass box is a hair from the football idol of Neapolitan *tifosi* (supporters). It was plucked directly from Maradona's head twenty-five years ago, when Signor Alcidi found himself on the same plane as the Naples team returning from a game in Como.

On the altar at the entrance to the Nilo bar, other than the hair, there are pennants, pictures, a vial containing real Neapolitans' tears of joy as a lucky charm, a prayer to San Gennaro (Saint Januarius) in the local dialect …

According to Signor Alcidi, setting up the little shrine did some good because Napoli won the first cup in its history just afterwards, and three years later the second.

The altar was recently redesigned after the fulfilment of a vow that the entire Alcidi family made when Maradona fell ill in 2000. Once the vow was made, says Signor Alcidi, the health of the *Pibe de Oro* (Golden Boy) improved and he was fully recovered by 2004.

Signor Alcidi has also posted an invitation on the altar, translated into several languages, to come and have a drink in the Nilo bar where other mementoes of the Argentine footballer are on display: posters, pictures, badges … all set off by the warm welcome from the bar's owner, who's always happy to tell the story of his altar.

SKULL IN SANTA LUCIELLA AI LIBRAI CHURCH ⓴

Vico Santa Luciella
• Metro: Line 1 Dante
• Associazione Respiriamo Arte: www.respiriamoarte.it
• Tel: 331 4209045

> **A frightening skull with ears**

In an alley of the historic centre of Naples, a mystery lies hidden in the vaults of Santa Luciella ai Librai church.

In the ancient ritual of double burial, after a brief first interment, bodies were exhumed to allow fluids to disperse and the corpse to be reduced to a skeleton.

Once the decomposition process was complete, the skulls were displayed around the edges of the underground vault, as at Santa Luciella.

But one of these skulls is different – it has protuberances that look like parts of the ear.

Nobody knows whether pieces of cartilage have survived decomposition, but the effect is no less frightening.

According to some authorities on the subject, these "ears" could be the result of a technique of mummifying flesh, a very old esoteric ritual (a hypothesis borne out by a Roman mosaic in the Archaeological Museum of Naples,

where a grimacing skull with bony
ears is surrounded by symbols and
mysterious figures).

For believers, on the other hand,
these ears represent a link between
the realms of the living and the
dead. Even if the practice is now
forgotten, as the Church became less
approachable people used to turn
to this skull with their supplications
and prayers, their hopes and
fears, convinced that they could
communicate with the hereafter
through its ears.

This little church, records of which
exist from 1327, underwent major restoration in 1724, when it took on its
typically Baroque appearance. It was dedicated to Santa Lucia (Saint Lucy,
patron saint of the blind) by the miners of the piperno volcanic rock, who were
constantly in danger of being blinded by flying splinters.

For this reason it's also known as the church of the Arciconfraternita
dell'Immacolata Concezione, San Gioacchino e San Carlo Borromeo dei
Piperneri (Archconfraternity of the Immaculate Conception, Saint Joachim
and Saint Charles Borromeo of the piperno miners).

THE HOLY STEPS
OF SAN GREGORIO ARMENO CONVENT

41

1 Via San Gregorio Armeno
• Metro: Line 1 Museo, Università or Line 2 Cavour
• Tel: 081 5520186 • sspsae-na.santelmo@beniculturali.it
• Church open Monday to Thursday 9am–12 noon, Saturday and
Sunday 9am–1pm, closed Friday • Cloister: daily 9.30am–12 noon
• Visits to some parts of the convent on request. Visits to the church
ambulatory and adjacent premises on 25 August only

*Memories
of cloistered
nuns*

Following the Council of Trent (1545–1563), the convent of San Gregorio Armeno, like many other convents, underwent far-reaching reforms such as the institution of mandatory penances. Among these was the construction of "Holy Steps" that the nuns of San Gregorio Armeno had to climb on their knees every Friday in March (a custom that lasted until the 19th century).

The lower section of the staircase, built in 1692, is decorated with paintings of angels and there are symbols of the Passion of Christ in a small room to the left of the altar, reached through the presbytery of the eponymous church (one of the most extraordinary examples of Neapolitan Baroque). The so-called "treasure room", where many sacred relics and objects are on display, is worth a visit.

OTHER CURIOSITIES OF SAN GREGORIO ARMENO

In a long room known as the "nuns' corridor" (access through the presbytery), between the grilles that allowed them to attend Mass without being seen, note the wooden altars with various objects set on them: clothed statues of saints, a Madonna wearing shoes and a silk dress in the fashion of the 18th century, Baby Jesuses with period wigs, opaline vases with flowers made from coloured beads and miniature furniture belonging to the young novices condemned to live cut off from the world.

In the cloister of San Gregorio Armeno convent, a plaque indicates that from the second week of December, Advent, the large and small ovens were for the exclusive use of the abbess, as she was not called to fasting like the other nuns.

The left wall of the staircase leading to the convent is decorated with frescoes featuring views and windows with dogs and cats sitting on the sill, probably an abbess's nod to her lost freedom.

At the top of the steps, on both sides of the main entrance, you'll notice two small doors: hidden behind them are the "wheels" (a kind of dumb waiter) to receive deliveries of food, clothes and other objects, the nuns' only means of communication with the outside world.

The convent was founded in the 8th century by Basilian nuns who'd fled Constantinople because of the war between iconoclasts and iconodules (those in favour of religious images). It was dedicated to Saint Gregory, to whom we owe the birth of the world's first Christian state, Armenia, which in AD 301, well before the Edict of Constantine (Edict of Milan, AD 313), adopted Christianity as its official religion.

FORGOTTEN FIGURINES OF THE FERRIGNO WORKSHOP

Giuseppe and Marco Ferrigno
8 Via San Gregorio Armeno
• Metro: Line 1 Museo, Università, Line 2 Cavour
• Tel: 081 5523148 • info@arteferrigno.it

Figurines as they used to be

The Ferrigno artisanal workshop (*bottega*), founded in 1836, is unusual in that it still produces the type of figurine forgotten even by most Neapolitans. Often they have delightful popular legends attached. Some of the most endearing forgotten characters are described here.

THE FIGURE WITH NO GIFT

There is one character in the nativity scene whose only gift is his wonder at the extraordinary event taking place before his eyes: the birth of Christ. The legend goes that the *pastore della meraviglia* (shepherd full of wonder), as the Neapolitans call him, was reprimanded by all the other characters for daring to appear empty-handed before the Virgin. But Mary had only kind words for him: "The world will remain beautiful as long as there are men and women who are capable of wonder."

Stefania

According to the Apocrypha, only married women who'd had children were allowed to visit the Virgin Mary. Stefania, a childless widow, still wanted at all costs to honour Mary, who was also her friend. So she decided to wrap a stone the size of a child in a blanket. Mary noticed this ploy, but took pity on the widow who longed for a child and told her that she'd soon have her wish. When Stefania went back home, the stone sneezed and turned into a baby. This is why Saint Stephen (Santo Stefano in Italian) is celebrated on Boxing Day.

The woman without hands

The poor woman, it is said, would have liked to help Mary give birth, but she couldn't as she had no hands. The Madonna gave her two new hands to thank her.

The wife of the black Magus

In the nativity scenes of yesteryear, notably those of nobles and the affluent classes, the black Magus on horseback was followed by a small group of four pages bearing a chair on which the king's wife was seated with a little dog. Over time, because this set was expensive to make, it was less and less in demand until it disappeared from the traditional crib. But you can see a beautiful example in the Ferrigno shop.

The perfect crib scene

Another character that is never missing from even the simplest crib scene is Benino the shepherd, sleeping on a hillside made of cork. Traditionally, Benino is said to dream forever of a wonderful manger with twelve sheep as white as snow (an allusion to pure souls) grazing around him. The shepherd's dream come true is precisely what you can see at Ferrigno's. Another fine rarity.

For the symbolism of the Neapolitan crib, see following double-page spread.

SYMBOLISM OF OBJECTS AND CHARACTERS FROM THE NEAPOLITAN NATIVITY SCENE

"Christmas is a time outwith History, a time in suspension where good and evil coexist," writes Roberto De Simone, the ultimate specialist in Campanian popular traditions.

In Naples, where the boundary between sacred and profane is blurred and flexible, there are different kinds of nativity scene.

There are those of the nobles and wealthy bourgeois, spectacularly rich in detail with figurines carved by recognised artists, which include some traditional themes without transgressing Christian dogma. And then there are the cribs for ordinary people, featuring a crowd of jostling figurines with rather rudimentary features, but so touching with their limbs glued back on over the years.

This kind of scene is packed with myths, superstitions and even symbols that are an outlet for collective fears (the devil, for example).

The landscape of the Neapolitan nativity scene says it all: made from cork, it is mountainous and full of winding roads dotted with figurines on their way down to the cave, always at the bottom in the foreground. Because you must first descend into the darkness (the tortuous paths) before reaching the light, or rebirth (represented by the Baby Jesus).

The well represents the link between the surface and the underground waters from which malefic spirits may emerge during Christmas night, because that's the time when Evil wanders abroad before the birth of Good. In the countryside, children are kept away from wells and no water is drawn on that night. The presence of "Madonnas of the Well" in many places around the city of Naples and throughout Campania shows the concern to protect this disturbing place.

The fountain with the woman. According to the Apocrypha, the angel Gabriel announced the birth of Christ to the Virgin near a fountain. In Campanian folktales, lovers' trysts and fantastic apparitions always take place close to fountains.

The bridge is a passage that leads to the "other side", and therefore also into the beyond, into the unknown. On Christmas night, it's said, terrifying encounters happen there: a nun displaying the head of her beheaded lover, werewolves, ghosts of suicides or hanged men … Throughout Europe there are legends about bridges built in one night by the devil or other evil spirits (e.g. at Cahors in France).

The windmill has arms that turn round like time, the time that's reborn on Christmas morning. It produces flour, which is as white as death but also life-giving as it's used to make bread, the universal food.

The river carries water which is life, but it can also be underground like the Styx, the river of Hades.

The inn is overflowing with food eaten at the Christmas feast. This banquet is actually funereal, burying time that dies before its renewal.

The inn also symbolises the risks of travel. In folk tales, ogres disguised as innkeepers chop up children to eat them, but Saint Nicholas puts a stop to that by sticking together the pieces of the innocent victims and resurrecting them.

The Magi ride horses of different colours, white like the rising Sun, chestnut like the sunset and black as the night. They symbolise the journey of the star which, like the Magi, starts out from the East. At the end of the night, the three kings are led before the Christ, who is the Sun reborn. In older nativity scenes there was also a queen (see p. 251), personification of the Moon, which follows the path of the Sun.

The washerwomen stand for the midwives who rush to help the Virgin. They spread out white linen, symbol of Mary's virginity.

The gypsy is an allegory of the prophecy embodied in the sacred representations of the past by the Sibyls. According to legend, a Sibyl foretold the birth of Christ. But the gypsy in the crib has iron tools in her hand, foreseeing the Passion of Christ.

The hunter and the fisherman embody, among other features, the two most ancient of human activities.

The food sellers always number twelve, because they stand for the twelve months of the year. For example, the tomato seller represents July, the watermelon seller August, and the roasted chestnut seller November ...

EMBLEMS OF NAPLES *SEDILI*

Piazza San Gaetano
• Metro: Line 1 Museo, Università, Line 2 Cavour

> *Historical*
> *symbols*
> *of the oldest*
> *neighbourhoods*
> *in Naples*

Above the entrance to the Opera di San Lorenzo Maggiore Museum (not to be missed) are the crests of the seven *sedili* (municipal districts, also called *seggi*) of the city of Naples. Each of these institutions brought together representatives of the noble families who lived in the corresponding neighbourhood. These were derived from the very old *fratries* (brotherhoods) that governed the city in Graeco-Roman times and which, according to historian Filippo Pagano, became *sedili* in the 9th century. The *sedili* were abolished in 1800 by Ferdinand IV of Bourbon. It was in 1808, during the Napoleonic era, that the first town hall was established.

The "Y", a millennial symbol of great complexity, corresponded to the *sedile* of Forcella ("little fork") where there was a Pythagorean school using this letter as its insignia. The letter could also be an allusion to the gallows, because it was at Forcella that condemned men were executed by hanging (see also p. 147).

The "P" represented the one and only *sedile* of the people; the "door" crest symbolised Portanova (created when a new gate was cut in the city walls at the seafront); the "mountain" was the crest of Montagna, so called because of its elevated location; the "hairy man" was linked to the Porto (port) area; the "white horse" to Capuana (called after the powerful Capuano family); and the black rearing horse was the emblem of Nilo (or Nido) *sedile*, where many Alexandrians lived in Roman times. The colour of the two horses is strictly related to the geographical position of these two districts.

The *sedile* was also the building where the elected representatives met. It was squarely built and consisted of two rooms, one small and the other large, for important occasions.

At the beginning of Vico Sedil Capuano stands a column surmounted by an arch (now incorporated into a modern building) that used to be part of Capuano *sedile*. A wall plaque in Piazza Portanova commemorates the *sedile* of that name.

BANKSY'S *SAINT WITH A PISTOL* GRAFFITI

112 Piazza Girolamini
• Metro: Line 1 Dante or Museo, Line 2 Cavour

> **Street art
> in the historic
> centre**

A t the base of the wall to the right of the church and convent of the Gerolamini, the celebrated artist Banksy has painted a figure inspired by Saint Agnes (whose church is in Piazza Navona in Rome). The image is surmounted by a pistol with a gear-wheel halo. This artist, who has become very well known and sought after in the art world, has left work on the walls of many cities around the world. In Italy he chose Naples, where apart from Saint Agnes he painted Saint Teresa lying near a pile of fast-food packaging. This image, unfortunately covered by the graffiti of a rival artist (not by vandals), is on the wall opposite the church of Santa Chiara in Via Benedetto Croce.

Banksy, about whom little is known, not even his real name, was born in Bristol in 1974 or 1975. The artist's anti-establishment and provocative graffiti express his rebellion against consumerism and corruption.

NEARBY

RELIQUARY CABINET AT THE CHURCH OF THE GEROLAMINI

142/144 Via Duomo
• Metro: Line 2 Cavour, Line 1 Museo, Università, Dante

In the monastery church of the Gerolamini, the reliquary cabinet in the so-called martyrs' chapel (right side of the transept) is an absolute rarity. The cabinet, built into the altar, is fitted with a mechanism of weights and counter-weights by which the altarpiece can be moved to reveal polychrome wooden busts of the martyrs. The sculptures containing their relics are invaluable as the decoration was carried out using a very specialised technique common in Spain in the 17th and 18th centuries, *estofado de oro*, which involved imitating the richness of inlaid garments by means of pure gold leaf and red, emerald green and azure blue lacquers. The mechanism is currently out of use, but funds are being raised to repair it. Two of the busts are on display in a chapel in the left nave and the others are being restored.

Note that the name of the square is spelled differently on two nameplates – Gerolomini and Gerolamini – because so far nobody has been able to decide which is correct.

DISCOVER THE SPECTACULAR STREET ART OF NAPLES

In addition to the city's immense historical wealth, urban art also flourishes, both in the historic centre and in the suburbs, often with input from local residents. Here are some examples.

Adriana Caccioppoli, *Il Bacio* (The Kiss), painting on paper (stencil), San Pietro a Maiella

Naples-born artist Adriana Caccioppoli uses the stencil technique and her paintings are displayed throughout the city. You can see this particular couple kissing in Via San Pietro a Maiella, near the entrance to Naples Conservatory of Music. The reference to Robert Doisneau's famous photograph *Le baiser de l'hôtel de ville* (The Kiss by the Hôtel de Ville) is obvious. This isn't an isolated image, but part of a cycle of works entitled *Ritroviamo la strada* (Back to the Streets). The artist's goal is to portray simple, genuine feelings, as if she was inviting us to return to spontaneity and free ourselves from constraints.

Francisco Bosoletti, *Parthenope*, frescoes, Salita San Raffaele

Strolling around the streets of Materdei, you might happen across this fascinating female figure. *Parthenope* is a 15 m painting by Argentine artist Francisco Bosoletti, commissioned by the Materdei R_esiste committee as part of the R_estate festival. The crowdfunding project was led by the residents, without whose determination this huge mural would never have been created. The Siren Parthenope is a mythological figure, half-fish, half-bird, ethereal but imposing, enveloped in feathers and plant motifs, with a human face that expresses pride and a magnetic attraction.

Roxy in the Box, *Mission Possible*, painting on paper (stencil), Piazza Sisto Riario Sforza

In *Mission Possible*, two friends (Saint Januarius and Caravaggio) meet for a chat, comparing the front pages of the international press

that, not without irony, recall the city's problems through references to Andy Warhol, the 1980 earthquake and even the art of Roxy in the Box. Two icons are central to the Neapolitan imagination: Saint Januarius of Benevento, whose miracles, especially the liquefaction of his blood, are a source of grace and hope; and Caravaggio, rebel artist par excellence. These characters fit naturally into

Via dei Tribunali (which crosses the piazza), personified as two locals, one with a foot braced against the wall, the other with a foot on a Super Santos ball, as if celebrating the insouciance and stubborn will to live of the Parthenopean people.

Žilda, *Il vento pesa quanto le catene* (The Wind Weighs as Much as the Chains), painting on paper (stencil), Palazzo Sanfelice, 6 Via Sanità
The spectacular architecture of Palazzo Sanfelice, with its maze of staircases, courtyards, doorways and washing draped over balconies, is home to a work that is both melancholic and intimately linked to the city of Naples and its origins, lost in the sea, myth and the light of the moon. Inspired by a piece of music by her compatriot Arnaud Michniak, French street artist Žilda's back view of a naked man, his wrists in chains, faces a sky heralding a storm and a blackly raging sea, Vesuvius glowing in the distance. The image fits perfectly into the architectural context, creating an illusion of opening to the outside, an effect at once poignant and distressing that seems to symbolise the helplessness of man in the face of nature.

OTHER WORKS OF URBAN ART
- On the Ex-Opg façade (http://jesopazzo.org/), a creation by internationally recognised Italian street artist Blu. In 2011, *The Guardian* ranked him among the top ten in the world.
- In the Vergini-Sanità district works by Bosoletti, Tono Cruz and Mono Gonzalez.
- In the Quartieri Spagnoli (Spanish Quarter), featuring kaf&cyop and Mario Filardi (large portrait of football legend Maradona in 1990, restored by Salvatore Iodice).
- Down the Salita della Pedamentina, one of Naple's oldest stairways (works by Zolta).
- In the northern suburb of Scampia, works by Felice Pignataro (died 2004), an artist who dedicated his life to the neighbourhood by founding the GRIDAS cultural association and Scampia Carnival.
- In the Vomero district, frescoes by Orticanoodles in memory of crime reporter Giancarlo Siani, murdered by the Camorra in 1985.
- In Forcella, Jorit Agoch's Gennaro, a spectacular mural of Saint Januarius; and his portrait of actor and playwright Eduardo De Filippo at the San Ferdinando theatre (Agoch's work can be seen all over the city).
- In the historic centre, original images by Exit Enter.

A regularly updated map of these artworks is available on the Instagram page on Neapolitan urban art (napolistreetart@gmail.com). The Napoli Paint Stories association organises guided street art and graffiti-themed tours (333 6290673, napolipaintstories@gmail.com).

PALAZZO CARAFA

46

121 Via San Biagio dei Librai
• Bus: 149 or 24 (Sant'Anna dei Lombardi stop)
• Metro: Line 1 Dante

The head of Virgil's horse

The fine Renaissance Palazzo Carafa holds a copy of the horse's head originally exhibited in Naples National Archaeological Museum in the 18th century. Considered as the symbol of the city (see below), the provenance of the head has always been disputed: some have seen it as a Greek original while others (including 16th-century art historian Giorgio Vasari) attributed it to Donatello. Since 2012, archival documents have confirmed the second hypothesis.

Before it was deleted, this inscription could be read on the base on which the sculpture now rests:

This head shows
All the nobility and immensity of his body,
A barbarian forced the bit on me
Superstition and greed put me to death,
The regrets of the good increased my value
Here you see my head,
The cathedral bells keep my body
The symbol of the city perished with me ...

There is a rumour that on some days a horse is heard whinnying when the cathedral bells ring out. Be that as it may, this horse is legendary.

Until the 14th century, in a square near the cathedral stood a huge bronze horse that had the power to heal sick animals, give immunity to healthy ones and increase the fertility of males. This bronze was thought to have been carved by Virgil, who later placed it on this site.

For centuries, Neapolitans would bring along their beasts, harnesses hung with little crescent loaves and garlands of flowers, to have them walk three times around the monument. According to Virgil's biographer Donatus, the loaves evoked the symbolic bread that the Emperor Augustus gave Virgil when the poet cured several of his horses of a mysterious ailment.

This ritual lasted until 1322, the year when the body of the statue was destroyed, in line with the Angevin monarchs' determination to eradicate all traces of pagan beliefs.

The legend goes that it was a cardinal, annoyed by this horse that was more popular than Saint Januarius, who had the bronze melted down to make the cathedral bells. Another version blames the blacksmiths, who were envious of the horse's powers that stopped them making a living.

The free and unrestrained horse is one of the most significant and persistent symbols in Neapolitan mythology. The people saw themselves in this untamed bronze horse, as borne out when two of the city's conquerors, Conrad of Swabia (1253) and Charles of Anjou (1266), had a bit fitted to the horse to ratify their conquest and point out to the Neapolitan rebels that they had to submit to Christianity.

Once the horse was gone, the cult moved to the church of Sant'Eligio Maggiore (Saint Eligius, protector of blacksmiths). On 1 December, unshod horses were brought in and their shoes hung on doors. Gradually, Saint Eloi was replaced by Saint Anthony the Abbot, whose church was built in the district named after him during the Angevin period (see p. 345). This saint has the power to heal all animals and on 17 January, his feast day, a number are brought to the priest to be blessed. Until some forty years ago, the animals were dressed up in the kind of finery worn at the time of the bronze horse and, as before, they turned three times around the church …

The blessing of the horses also exorcises the dangers of travel: once horses were no longer used as a means of transport, all kinds of vehicles continued to be blessed. This ritual is still practised today but in a very low-key fashion.

Until the 18th century, the horse was the emblem of two neighbourhoods: Nilo and Porto Capuana. The first was black, the second white. They symbolised the darkness and the light, black on the left and white on the right (facing the city, back to the sea), exactly as the Moon and the Sun frame the Madonna of Piedigrotta (see p. 32).

For more on the Neapolitan horse, see following double-page spread.

THE NEAPOLITAN HORSE: AN EXCEPTIONAL ANIMAL

If riding reached new heights in Naples, it was thanks to the Neapolitan horse, an exceptional animal of majestic grace, both lightweight and powerful. The finest mounts were raised on the plains of Capua, where the extraordinary fertility of the land led the Romans to call this region "Campania Felix".

These ideal geographical conditions were complemented by the expertise of farmers who for thousands of years had carried out felicitous crosses between the robust local horses and the elegant oriental animals imported by the Etruscans (who had settled in the Campanian hinterlands).

The Romans added the finishing touches when they crossed these horses with the Barb breed, famous for its stamina and power, which they bought in North Africa. Incidentally it was among these horses of Capua that Roman senators chose their mounts for triumphal parades.

In the 14th century, the reputation of Neapolitan breeders was confirmed by Boccaccio in *The Decameron* (Andreuccio da Perugia, day II, story V). In this story, the horse dealer comes to Naples seeking a bargain among these valuable animals, as his purse contains the tidy sum of 500 gold florins (by way of comparison, the queen of Naples, Joan of Anjou, sold Provence to the papacy for 80,000 florins a few decades later). Chroniclers down the ages have subsequently celebrated these magnificent animals coveted by all the kings of Naples to the extent that they severely punished anyone who took them out of the kingdom. And the prices people were willing to pay for a "Neapolitan" were often exorbitant.

Even today, this horse is legendary for all lovers of dressage, particularly in other countries, and even more so because the breed was thought to have died out in the early 20th century.

Then, in the 1990s, a miracle occurred. A coffee importer from Piano di Sorrento, Giuseppe Maresca, launched a wild challenge to revive the glorious Neapolitan horse. Against all odds, despite the many sceptics, overcoming huge numbers of difficulties and with no public or private funding, he managed to replace this missing piece in the mosaic of Neapolitan history.

Deep in Serbia, just as the country was about to be plunged into the horrors of war, Maresca located a direct descendant of a Neapolitan stallion. His name was Neapolitano and he was 20 years old. After surmounting the bureaucratic red tape, in 1990 Neapolitano "Il Vecchio" returned to the country of his ancestors, which had left for Austria 200 years earlier.

Waiting for the old stallion were a few mares, amazingly saved from extinction by Capuan peasants. Before he died, the stallion sired Neapolitano I di Vicalvano and a lovely mare, Cianciosa di Vicalvano. The miracle had come to pass.

Today the Neapolitan has its studbook like any other officially recognised breed. The precious horses of the Maresca breeders, who seem to have stepped by magic out of an old engraving, live in classy stables on Vicalvano hill, a paradisiacal site between Sorrento and Amalfi.

The only thing left to do now is to set up a Neapolitan academy that can compete with those of Vienna, Versailles and Jerez, as Maresca has dreamed of for years. At present the "Federico Grisone" academy exists only on paper, but to put this remarkable project into practice what place would be better suited than the former Bianchini barracks at 178 Via Amerigo Vespucci?

The 16th-century building, today partly occupied by Treasury offices (after being converted into barracks), was intended as a site for training the thousands of horses from the kingdom's many breeders. Not many people know that the first covered riding school in Europe (and probably in the world) was built at this *"Cavallerizza"* so that horses could be trained even in bad weather.

It was also in 16th-century Naples that the equestrian Federico Grisone wrote the first riding treatise in history since Xenophon (4th century BC). Signor Maresca is pleased to show visitors around his horses (at Piano di Sorrento, 45 km from Naples): maresca.giuseppema@tiscali.it.

SHIELD OF THE CITY OF NAPLES

Cappella del Tesoro di San Gennaro
147 Via Duomo
• Metro: Line 1 Museo or Università, Line 2 Cavour
• Tel: 081 449065
• Open 9am–12pm and 4.30pm–7pm

**A place
of worship
that doesn't belong
to the church**

A t the entrance to the Treasury chapel, the shield of the city engraved on the floor marks the boundary between the secular and the ecclesiastical. The chapel has in fact always belonged to the city, represented by a "Deputation", which originally consisted of twelve members, two for each area of Naples (formerly called *sedili* – see p. 255). Since 1601, this city institution has watched over the relics of Saint Januarius, including a vial containing his blood, and manages everything relating to the worship and treasure of the patron saint of Naples.

1526 was a terrible year: the French were besieging Naples and the plague was resurgent. So the Neapolitans pledged to erect a magnificent chapel dedicated to San Gennaro if he liberated them from these scourges. As calmer times returned, on 13 January 1527 funds were collected and the promise was formalised in a notarised document. But construction work on the chapel didn't start until 1608 under the direction of the Deputation. The treasure, formerly preserved in one of the bell towers, wasn't installed in the chapel until 13 December 1646.

IS THAT DOMENICHINO'S TOMB AT THE CHAPEL ENTRANCE?

When the elected members of the Deputation decided to entrust the paintings that decorate the chapel to non-Neapolitans, local artists felt gravely insulted. It seems that they exerted strong pressure on their "foreign" competitors. The less experienced of these soon abandoned the idea of accepting the commission, as in the case of Il Giuseppino (Cavaliere d'Arpino), and Guido Reni, who left Naples in haste after one of his collaborators was attacked with a knife. Although Domenico Zampieri, known as Il Domenichino, complained that he had received a threatening letter, he was persuaded by the Deputation, who promised him close protection. Yet Domenichino, the Baroque master of the Bolognese School, died suddenly on 6 April 1641, poisoned, it is said. He is thought to have been buried somewhere in the chapel, but exactly where isn't known. But just before the entrance door you can see a tombstone without a name, apparently untouched, fitted with four metal rings to open it ...

BARS OF THE TREASURY CHAPEL'S MONUMENTAL PORTAL

48

Cappella del Tesoro di San Gennaro
147 Via Duomo
• Metro: Line 1 Museo or Università, Line 2 Cavour
• Tel: 081 449065
• Open 9am–12pm and 4.30pm–7pm

> ### *A door that resonates like a xylophone*

The Treasury chapel of San Gennaro was also one of the Neapolitan temples of music where the teachers were none other than Scarlatti, Cimarosa, Paisiello (author of the concert for the coronation of Napoleon Bonaparte), Provenzale …

The entrance to the chapel is a masterpiece by the famous architect Cosimo Fanzago, who wanted to blow away his contemporaries with a feature as unusual as it was surprising: when struck with a metal object, the bars emit a sound like a xylophone, and each bar corresponds to a different note. Although this extraordinary instrument was probably never used, it still achieved its designer's aim of astounding visitors.

STATUE OF THE VIRGIN THAT TERRIFIED WORSHIPPERS

Of the 54 solid silver busts stored in the Treasury chapel, two represent the Virgin Mary.

On one of these busts only the head was originally in silver, the body being pasteboard covered with a layer of silver. But this "economical" ploy didn't work, as during processions the heavier head would fall off the body and sow panic among the worshippers. So the Deputation commissioned a headless torso, which was completed by Tommaso Treglia in 1717.

"IL RE DI POGGIOREALE", A TRAFFICKER WHO BROUGHT THE TREASURE OF SAINT JANUARIUS BACK TO NAPLES

According to the latest valuation, dating back to 2010, the treasure of Saint Januarius is thought to be the most valuable in the world, even exceeding that of the British Crown Jewels or the Russian tsars.

Over the centuries, donations from eminent personalities and ordinary people have enriched the treasure chest, now consisting of 21,160 pieces. This vast heritage has remained intact since 1305, never stolen or used to pay for wars (Museum of Treasure of San Gennaro, www.museosangennaro. it, 081294980, every day 9am-5pm). There are endless anecdotes about Neapolitans' faith in their patron saint and the determining role of the Deputation. The least well known of these concerns a trafficker who was dubbed the "King of Poggioreale" (Royal Hill). During the Second World War, a German captain took the treasure to the Vatican for protection. Once the conflict had ended, despite the insistent demands of the Deputation and Cardinal Ascalesi to repatriate the Neapolitan heritage, the Vatican turned a deaf ear. One day, a certain Giuseppe Navarra, known to have grown rich on the black market (hence his nickname – the 1961 film on the subject

was internationally released as *Black City*) – offered to bring the treasure back to Naples. The Deputation and the cardinal agreed. A few days later it was discovered that the man, seemingly disguised as a bishop, had managed to get hold of the treasure. But there was no further news of him, which worried the citizens greatly. Then, completely unexpectedly, he suddenly resurfaced with great ceremony, his car at the head of a procession of truckloads of treasure. The "King of Poggioreale" explained that he'd had to travel by small mountain roads to avoid criminals and the Allied troops who could have confiscated the precious load. Giuseppe Navarra died in poverty, forgotten by all.

SELF-PORTRAITS
ON THE TREASURY CHAPEL ALTAR

⓭

Cappella del Tesoro di San Gennaro
147 Via Duomo
• Metro: Line 1 Museo or Università, Line 2 Cavour
• Tel: 081 449065 • Open 9am–12pm and 4.30pm–7pm

Hidden
self-portraits
by the artist

Gian Domenico Vinaccia, having worked for three years on the front of the solid silver altar, died in 1695 a few days before seeing his work in the Treasury chapel, and before he could enjoy the much anticipated celebrity. However, the talented sculptor and engraver managed to escape oblivion by theatrically appearing in his own masterpiece: the man in glasses with his head emerging in front of that of the horse ridden by Cardinal Alessandro Carafa (the main figure in the procession bringing the relics of Saint Januarius back to Naples) is a self-portrait. And that's also the artist with hat in hand, bowing to observers.

THE DOME: EACH FACE HAD ITS PRICE

After the death of Domenichino, the Deputation commissioned Giovanni Lanfranco to fresco the dome to represent Paradise. This work is populated by countless faces because, it seems, the celebrated painter had signed a lucrative contract stipulating that his fee would vary depending on the number of characters he painted.

THE "TESORO VECCHIO" CHAPEL OF SAN GENNARO

Duomo
147 Via Duomo
• Metro: Line 1 Museo or Università, Line 2 Cavour
• Tel: 081 449097
• Cathedral open daily 9am–1.30pm and 4pm–7.30pm
• Visits to the Tesoro Vecchio on request

> *The very first treasury chapel of San Gennaro*

U p on the wall of the cathedral's left nave you can see the shutters of a blocked-up window that formed part of an upper floor of the chapel known as the "Tesoro Vecchio". From here, before the construction of the present Treasury chapel, the cardinal showed the faithful the miraculous liquefaction of the blood of Saint Januarius.

Access to this floor is near the left tower, where a spiral staircase leads to the oratory of the Archconfraternity of Santa Restituta dei Neri (the "Blacks") whose members always wore black habits. The confreres' main occupation was to arrange the burial of those with no means of their own who had met with a sudden death. The interior of the oratory is decorated with Mannerist and Baroque paintings (including a canvas by Francesco Solimena), all beautifully framed in stucco; the altarpiece is a *Nativity* by Fabrizio Santafede. In the sacristy of the Archconfraternity is a fine portrait of the viceroy, the Duke of Alba, and his wife Maria.

NEARBY

MARBLE CALENDAR OF THE 9TH CENTURY

The door in the left aisle leads to the courtyard of the Archbishop's Palace, where a section of paved Roman road can be seen among other archaeological remains, as well as various pieces of architecture from antiquity. On one wall hangs a rare marble calendar of the 9th century, from the church of San Giorgio Maggiore. Fantastical animals are carved on one side of the calendar, while on the other the liturgical celebrations of the Neapolitan Church are given, notably those relating to the Greek rite. This artefact is a major historical document in that it gives information on the saints venerated at that time, as well as the death dates of twenty-three Bishops of Naples. In the inner rooms is a permanent exhibition of carriages that once belonged to cardinals.

THE *"PASSO DA TERRA"* OF THE DUOMO 🖲52

147 Via Duomo
- Metro: Line 1 Museo, Line 2 Cavour
- Tel: 081 449097
- Open daily from 9am—1.30pm and 4pm—7.30pm

> **Unit of measurement in Naples before the metric system**

In the last pillar of the cathedral's left nave, the metal bar that can be seen embedded along its length is an instrument of land measurement (see below), known as *passus ferreus* or *passo da terra*: since Roman times units of measurement had been installed in sacred places to deter fraud.

The use of the *passo* dates back to the Byzantine duchy (established in the 6th century, it gradually became autonomous and lasted five centuries), during which Naples adopted the provisions regarding weights and measures listed in the *Pragmatica Sanctio* (edict) of the Roman Emperor Justinian.

According to some archival documents, the *passus ferreus* was set in a column of the basilica of Santa Restituta that was later incorporated into the cathedral. The column was then moved into the Caracciolo Pisquizy chapel and finally to its present site in the 14th century, when construction work on the new cathedral was completed by Robert of Anjou.

In 1480, the King of Naples Don Ferrante of Aragon (Ferdinand I) restored some order to the different measurement systems and determined that from now on there would only be two measures: the *passo di terra* equivalent to

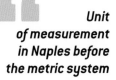

7.33 palms (1.85448 m) for dividing neighbouring land, and the *passo itinerario* corresponding to 7 palms (1.84569 m), used to define the limits of large properties.

The palm, in the Kingdom of Naples, was equivalent to 12 onces (26.36 cm), the average hand size of a man about 1.80 m tall.

The current metric system was devised in 1791 in France. For his part, the Bourbon King Ferdinand IV – exiled to Sicily during the Napoleonic period – launched the "Sicilian metric system" that was applied throughout the Kingdom of the Two Sicilies only to be abolished on the unification of Italy (see p. 412).

HOW IS A METRE DEFINED?

It is all too often forgotten that the metre is a French invention, being defined by the Paris Académie des Sciences in 1791 as one ten millionth of a quarter of a meridian of the earth.

By this definition, the circumference (that is, meridian) of the Earth was 40,000km.

After the establishment of the first standard metre, it was 1875 before seventeen other nations signed the "Convention du Mètre". In 1899, the Bureau of Weights and Measures had a standard metre cast in platinum-iridium alloy, which was held to be subject to only infinitesimal variations; that original bar can still be seen at the Pavillon de Breteuil in Sèvres (Hauts-de-Seine).

With the advent of laser technology, the Conférence Générale des Poids et Mesures (CGPM) in 1960 gave a definition of the metre that is rather less comprehensible to the layman: 1,650,763.73 wavelengths of orange-coloured radiation emitted by the krypton 86 atom.

In 1983 came an even more esoteric definition: the metre is the length of the path travelled by light in vacuum during a time interval of 1/299,792,458 of a second.

According to the theory of relativity, the speed of light in vacuum is the same at all points, so this definition is considered to be more accurate.

SALA DEL LAZZARETTO
OF THE FORMER DELLA PACE HOSPITAL ❺❸

226 Via dei Tribunali
• Metro: Line 1 Museo, Line 2 Cavour
• Tel: 081 7951321 / 081 7951996 • municipalita4@comune.napoli.it
• www.comune.napoli.it
• Visits during certain cultural events or on request

> *Lepers cared for in a luxurious city centre hall*

Behind the 15th-century palace that belonged to Sergianni Caracciolo, favourite of Queen Joan II of Anjou, the buildings currently occupied by the local municipal offices once belonged to the hospital of the Brothers Hospitallers (built in 1587), an impressive complex comprising two cloisters and a Baroque church, of which only a small section is open to the public. On request, you can visit the huge lazaretto, the only place in the city that accepted lepers and patients struck down by the plague and other infectious diseases. The impressive dimensions of the Sala del Lazzaretto, richly decorated with paintings depicting the Virgin and the saints of the Order of Saint John of God by Giacinto Diano and Andrea Viola, are 12 m high, 60 m long and 10 m wide. At the far end, a beautiful 18th-century marble altar used to conceal the surgery. The raised gallery that runs around the walls was used by the staff to distribute meals to avoid contagion.

"MAY THE LORD DELIVER ME FROM SAD NEIGHBOURS AND VIOLINISTS"

At the end of the courtyard of the former della Pace hospital, these words in the regional dialect of the 16th century can be read on a wall plaque: *"God deliver me from canine jealousy, bad neighbours, and the lies of a respectable man."* In the 17th century, the historian Carlo Celano wrote that these words were traditionally said to have been engraved by an honest man unjustly sentenced to death after false accusations. He is thought to have left all his property to the nearby hospital on condition that the brothers display the inscription on the wall outside their hospital (the present inscription is a copy of the original, which was moved inside the hospital in 1893) and ensure that it stayed there forever. He had even specified that if the plaque had to be destroyed, all his assets would pass to the Ospedale degli Incurabili. It is said that until the 19th century the administration of this institution regularly sent a courier to check if the inscription was still in place.

The historian Bartolomeo Capasso, however, thought that the condemned innocent had played the violin all day long, oblivious to the exasperation of his neighbours. One of them, a tailor who could no longer concentrate on his work, is thought to have taken advantage of a murder on the street to denounce the violinist and be rid of him for good. A story that seems to bear out perfectly the Neapolitan saying: "May the Lord deliver me from sad neighbours and violinists."

MUSEO ARCHIVIO STORICO DEL BANCO DI NAPOLI ⑤④

214 Via dei Tribunali
• Open Monday to Friday 10am–6pm, Sunday 10am–2pm, closed Wednesday
• Occasionally open in the evening
• Guided tours run by Associazione Culturale NarteA
• Tel: 081 450732
• info@ilcartastorie.it • www.ilcartastorie.it

> **The largest banking archives in the world**

The Banco di Napoli's Historical Archives are the largest in the world, filling 330 rooms in two monumental buildings (Palazzo Ricca and Palazzo Como or Cuomo). The countless files of the ancient Neapolitan public banks are preserved here. The immense rooms are lined with about 80 km of shelving, where 17 million names, and hundreds of thousands of payments and details of banking operations are classified, painting a fascinating picture of Naples and southern Italy from 1573 to the present day.

It is here that the archives of the eight banks, all but one of which were founded to prevent the scourge of moneylending, are stored. They merged to form the Banco delle Due Sicilie in 1809, before becoming the Banco di Napoli after Italian unification.

You can visit a number of these storerooms as part of an organised tour that is astonishing from beginning to end. The corridors and halls are lined with enormous shelves, where various types of documents from different banks have been classified. Among the most impressive are the "major registers", which contained the accounts registered in clients' names and divided between "debit" and "credit" columns. The *pandette* – massive tables with details of all the clients, classified by their first and last names and the corresponding number on the "major register" – also played a key role. In some of the rooms, high up on the shelves, there are *filze*, files composed of several *bancali* or copies of notes relating to payment orders, "threaded" (hence the term *filza*, or "string") onto one another.

Among the archives' most valuable treasures are the copybooks (*copiapolizze*) with listings of insurance bonds, as well as "registers" of payment orders. Thanks to these documents, details of historical characters and events can be accurately reconstructed.

Some of these stories are told in the ilCartastorie Museum's permanent multimedia exhibit, Kaleidos. The itinerary, on the first floor of the Archives, reveals some of the "hidden" presences in the pages of the ancient tomes. Find out about the vicissitudes of Philip of Bourbon, an Austrian lieutenant or an ordinary criminal through images, voices and sound effects.

ENIGMA OF THE FOURTH CARAVAGGIO

A payment order of the Banco di Sant'Eligio, hidden between the pages of a copybook in the Banco di Napoli's Historical Archives (see previous page), lies behind one of the unresolved enigmas of 17th-century art: "*Banco di Sant'Eligio 6 October 1606. To Nicolò Radolovich 200 ducats. And for this one, the reason for payment to Michel Angelo Caravaggio, for the price of an icon of painting that he must make and put in place next December, measuring 13 palms and a half high and 8 palms and a half wide, with the figures above, the image of the Virgin with the Child in her arms, surrounded by a choir of angels and below Saint Dominic and Saint Francis in the middle, both embraced by the right hand of Saint Nicholas and the left of Saint Vitus.*"

The mystery remains, even today: where is this "Radolovich" Altarpiece, named after the rich merchant who commissioned it? Was it completed or, indeed, ever painted? Was it destroyed during a popular uprising? Or divided into sections and sold?

An image of this painting, recreated from the above description by the Fondazione ilCartastorie, can now be seen at the museum.

The Radolovich Altarpiece isn't the only Caravaggio painting referred to in texts preserved in the Historical Archives: in 1607, the magnificent *Le sette opere di Misericordia (The Seven Acts of Mercy)*, which Caravaggio had just completed, made his name as an artist. This studied and complex painting, which earned him 400 ducats, was made for the church of Pio Monte della Misericordia in Naples and is still there. The records in the archives detail the moment when the young Lombard painter received his rich reward.

THE FOURTH CARAVAGGIO

The Radolovich Altarpiece has been called the "Fourth Caravaggio" because it would have been the fourth painting completed by Caravaggio during his Neapolitan stay, after *The Seven Acts of Mercy* (1606–1607, Pio Monte della Misericordia, 253 Via dei Tribunali); *The Flagellation of Christ* (1607–1608, Museo e Gallerie Nazionali di Capodimonte, 2 Via Miano); and *The Martyrdom of Saint Ursula* (1610, Palazzo Zevallos Stigliano, 185 Via Toledo).

BIBLIOTECA ALFREDO DE MARSICO

Castel Capuano
Piazza Enrico de Nicola, access by Castel Capuano
• Metro: Lines 1 and 2 Garibaldi
• Visits by appointment (by phone or e-mail)
• Tel: 081 269416
• bibliotecademarsico@tin.it
• www.bibliotecastoricadicastelcapuano.it

The essence of Neapolitan advocacy

Housed in Castel Capuano, the Norman royal palace (2nd century), which was converted into the Palace of Justice in the 16th century (itself transferred in 2000 to the business centre on the outskirts of the city), the exceptional Alfredo De Marsico library owes its name to the eminent jurist of that name (1888–1985).

The library, opened on 19 July 1986 in the beautiful hall of the Criminal Court where the Council of Queen Joan of Anjou sat in the 14th century, houses over 80,000 volumes dating from the 16th to the 20th centuries. Some rare editions are even cited by the British National Library as the only copies in the world. They are also invaluable for their precious bindings and refined typography.

This bibliographic heritage has been enriched over the centuries through donations from illustrious lawyers. Among them are the last memoirs of Giovanni Napolitano, father of Giorgio, current President of the Italian Republic.

Not only does the library contain legal works, it also has collections of authoritative philosophical and literary treatises, ancient codes of law, monographs, encyclopedias and four rare editions (1612, 1622, 1683, 1759) of John Calvin's writings.

The frescoed vaults of the two rooms at the entrance to the library, painted by Belisario Corenzio, represent the Judgment of Solomon, the Judgment of David, allegories of the virtues and coats of arms. In the 16th century, the so-called "small throne" room was designed for individuals attending the trial of those indicted for serious threats to social order. This "small throne" in red velvet with gold armrests, which had probably belonged to Francis II of Bourbon, was confiscated from a mob boss. The artefact was exhibited in June 2013 in the basement of Castel Capuano as part of a stunning display on various notorious news items. Among the most original were a life-sized wooden jaguar in whose belly had been hidden a large quantity of cocaine, counterfeit cigarettes, and a rubber mask with the face of actor Lino Banfi, used for a hold-up.

MATERDEI, SANITÀ, CAPODIMONTE

THE CAPTAIN'S SKULL ❶

Cimitero delle Fontanelle
80 Via Fontanelle
• Metro: Line 1 Museo or Materdei, Line 2 Cavour; Bus: C51
• Tel: 081 5573913
• Open 10am–5pm • Admission free

> *Neapolitan version of "Don Juan"*

Among the mass of skulls piled up in the central aisle of Fontanelle cemetery – known as the aisle of the *anime pezzentelle* (see opposite) – the skull of the captain, distinguished by the number of candles placed in front of its *scarabattola* (mini-chapel), is the subject of an amazing legend.

A feisty local youth, who was an incorrigible womaniser, used to meet his conquests in the cemetery. One evening, after that day's lover had left, he wanted to smoke a cigarette.

All of a suddenly the eye-sockets of the skulls around him lit up

like eyes of fire and stared at him as a sign of reprobation. The young man laughed and challenged death, inviting it to his coming wedding. On the wedding day, during the feast, a carabineer dressed in black arrived and sat at a table without speaking or eating. Asked who he was, he replied that he'd only reveal that in private to the married couple. So they went with the carabineer to a room away from the crowd and he asked the youth if he remembered the invitation he had issued in the cemetery. Once again the miscreant laughed at the stranger and even offered to shake his hand. The captain took off his uniform, revealing his skeleton, and struck the couple down on the spot (adapted from Roberto De Simone, *Novelle K666*, Einaudi, 2007).

THE FORGOTTEN HISTORY OF THE FONTANELLE

The 16th and 17th centuries were particularly disastrous for Naples: earthquakes, eruptions, famines and epidemics followed one another (the 1656 plague alone killed 250,000 out of 400,000 residents), with everything made worse by the negligence of the Spanish viceroys. As the church cemeteries were full to capacity, gravediggers exhumed bodies by night, without the knowledge of the families, and threw them into the mass grave in the old Fontanelle quarry (outside the city walls at the time). They were so numerous and so crudely buried that whenever there was a heavy storm, the torrents of silty water flowing down from Capodimonte hill washed out the corpses that the terrified residents then saw floating down the streets.

When in 1837 church burial grounds were demolished, according to Amedeo Colella (*Manuale di napoletanità*, 2010), Fontanelle cemetery is thought to have held 8 million skeletons.

In 1872, the ossuary was redesigned by Father Gaetano Barbati with the support of local women and divided into three sections. To the left, the "priests' aisle" houses all the bones from the churches and their congregations, with at the bottom a very evocative cave known as the "Tribunal". It is here that, for over a century, the Camorra (Neapolitan criminal organisation) godfathers would meet for their initiatory rites and oaths of allegiance in blood, as well as to issue death warrants. In the centre, the "plague aisle" takes in all the victims of epidemics. To the right, in the *"anime pezzentelle"* (poor little souls) aisle, a chapel is festooned with thousands of femurs, stacked like books, surmounted by skulls which are said to be arranged in male/female pairs. "This is the library of the dead who are engaged [to be married], not of dead fiancés", declared a young boy who showed Roberto De Simone round in the 1970s.

After its closure following the ban imposed by the Church in 1968, the ossuary was restored and it was reopened to the public in 2011.

THE WOMAN KILLED BY GNOCCHI AND OTHER FONTANELLE TALES

During the Second World War, an American soldier came to pray for the souls of the "library fiancés" (see above) to heal his daughter, who had an incurable disease. His prayers were answered and the daughter recovered. So the soldier hastened back to the cemetery to thank the "fiancés", but he suffered a heart attack and dropped dead in front of them. "He died of joy," exclaimed Michelino, Roberto De Simone's young guide, "and now you can see his picture here." There were indeed stacks of photos in the Fontanelle at the time (according to Roberto De Simone, *Novelle K666*, Einaudi, 2007). Although the corpses in Fontanelle cemetery are usually unnamed, those laid to rest in a glass coffin in the "priests' aisle" on the left are the Count of Cerreto, Filippo Carafa and his wife Margherita Petrucci, who died at the end of the 18th century. The mummified body of the woman with a gaping mouth, as if she was vomiting, fired people's imagination. They explained this oddity in their own way: the countess must have choked on her gnocchi …

For the cult of souls in Purgatory, see following double-page spread.

THE CULT OF SOULS IN PURGATORY: WHEN THE DEAD AND THE LIVING HELP EACH OTHER TO REACH PARADISE

Although the cult of the dead is practised in different ways in other regions of Italy and around the world, that of the souls in Purgatory exists only in Naples, the city where death cohabits particularly lightly with life. And Purgatory – middle Earth between Hell and Paradise – is the ideal point where the living and the dead are not too far removed.

In Neapolitan culture the dead have always been honoured as they were in life and "friendly" relations maintained with the deceased, but from the 17th century the souls in Purgatory came to the forefront in popular beliefs. At that time, survivors of the many plagues that befell Naples began to develop a symbiotic relationship with the dead: the living, thanks to their prayers and devotion, would help the dead to ascend to Heaven; once up there, the dead would intercede on behalf of their benefactor with the saints and the Virgin.

The souls in Purgatory would thus heal the sick, find good husbands for young women, bring back an unfaithful lover and even give out winning lotto numbers (see p. 206), the only way for the impoverished to aspire to a better life.

This cult is physically expressed in two ways: by mini-chapels still scattered around the streets of the historic centre, and specific signs of devotion that can be seen in the hypogea of some churches and in Fontanelle cemetery (see p. 287). In the mini-chapels, the statuettes or paintings of souls in Purgatory are all in a similar style: surrounded by flames with arms raised to the sky, where there is a holy image, each representing a trade or social situation (public writer, fisherman, priest, mother and daughter, married couple ...). In the ossuaries you can see skulls placed in mini-chapels with rosaries, embroidered handkerchiefs, flowers, candles and ex-votos set before them.

This ritual was practised by women, known as 'e maste (the bosses): every Monday (the day formerly devoted to lunar deities of darkness, such as Hecate or Diana) they would go into the ossuaries and after carefully cleaning their "chosen one", recite prayers to him or her until they reached a peak of histrionics, sometimes culminating in a trance. The pact between the masta and the deceased was only sealed under certain conditions: she began by choosing a skull from among the thousands piled up in the tomb, cleaned it with alcohol and covered it with a white cloth – preference being given to children, who, since antiquity, have been considered as intermediaries between the two worlds. If at night the masta dreamed of a stranger who revealed his

or her identity and life-story, the link with the "chosen one" was established: the following Monday, the white cloth was replaced with an embroidered handkerchief and the "contract" was signed.

Some of the "chosen" became famous after having accomplished many miracles (see below).

Following the Second Vatican Council (1962–1965), the ecclesiastical court banned the cult of the unknown dead in 1969, calling it "superstitious, arbitrary and therefore inadmissible", because "the holiness of the living person could not be demonstrated". So some ossuaries were closed. But the Neapolitans, used to the art of braving prohibitions that stifle their freedom and culture, have persevered, even if nowadays to a lesser extent.

WHAT IS "REFRISCO"?

The prayers and attention lavished on the dead are referred to as *refrisco* (freshness or coolness) in the Neapolitan dialect because they soothe the suffering caused by the flames of Purgatory. "*Refrisco*" is derived from the Latin *refrigerium*, a word used by the Romans to describe the funeral rituals designed to assist the deceased in their journey to the next world. The early Christians understood *refrigerium* as "comfort", either spiritual or material (a banquet or alms), to sooth the soul of the deceased. Incidentally, the typical phrase used by a true Neapolitan who wishes to warmly thank someone is: "*Frisco all'aneme 'e tutte 'e muorte tuoje*" (Comfort and peace to the souls of all your dear departed).

On the other hand, to curse someone, a Neapolitan will utter imprecations against the souls of the dead relatives of the "enemy".

SWEATING SKULLS

Some skulls that don't collect dust but droplets that look like sweat are thought to be miraculous (see, for example, the skull of Donna Concetta in Fontanelle cemetery). This phenomenon is due to the fact that in some places, particularly where there is high humidity, dust simply doesn't lie. As for the "sweat", it's only condensation.

There's a very unusual museum of souls in Purgatory in Rome – see *Secret Rome* in this series of guides.

ACQUAQUIGLIA DEL POZZARO

106 Via Fontanelle
• Note that there are several numbers 106 in this street – follow the sign
• Open daily 10am–5pm
• Check current opening hours before visiting
• Tel: 339 2239172
• acquaquiglia@gmail.com

> *Old wells dug out of the Fontanelle tuff*

I n Via Fontanelle, at number 106, most people never notice this small doorway. Unknown even to local residents, the Acquaquiglia del Pozzaro is a route dug out of the tuff, along which you'll find no less than five ancient wells (hence the name Pozzaro, *pozzo* meaning "well"). Historically, water was abundant in this part of the city, known as the Fontanelle (Fountains).

Once inside, you'll have the chance to explore galleries leading to several underground chambers on different levels. You'll see the historic stratification that characterises this district, where the tuff has been excavated by hand, as well as the remains of the staircase of a former convent, old cisterns and hydraulic galleries. At the foot of the descent is a kind of large cellar where dried cod used to be prepared.

Vincenzo, the host, is very hospitable. He says that over fifty years ago this place was probably a *basso* (typical Neapolitan one- or two-roomed ground-floor dwelling, opening directly onto the street): seven people lived here, including the grandfather *baccalaiuolo* ("codman"). Subsequently, it was closed for over twenty years. Only recently has Vincenzo taken the initiative to clean up the galleries to make them accessible: he has cleared piles of rubbish, installed lighting and displayed all the objects found there over the years: tools, candles, work appliances, ceramic bricks (*riggiole*), old sculptures, etc. On the edges of the wells, grooves (*grappiate*) can still be clearly distinguished in the walls at various levels, which the men who looked after the water supplies (*pozzari*) used as steps. As they wore a type of coverall resembling a monk's habit, in the collective imagination they gave rise to the legend of the "Monaciello" (literally, Little Monk), a mischievous "house spirit" who supposedly had access to every house by coming up through the subterranean wells.

WHY THE NAME ACQUAQUIGLIA?

This term, literally meaning "shell water" (*acqua della conchiglia*), derives from a shell-shaped 16th-century fountain that stood in the neighbourhood of Santa Maria La Nova, in the historic city centre.

LA SANITÀ BRIDGE

124 Via Sanità
• Metro: Line 1 Museo, Line 2 Cavour

Bridge in a cloister

The so-called "La Sanità" bridge was built in 1807 on the orders of Joseph Bonaparte to connect the city centre with the Royal Palace of Capodimonte, which was very difficult to reach. To achieve this new route that would span the valley of the densely populated La Sanità neighbourhood, architect Nicola Leandro, who was site manager, did not hesitate to "desecrate" the beautiful monastic complex of Santa Maria della Sanità: the grand cloister of the monastery was completely demolished while the smallest and most original cloister, which was oval-shaped, was partially vandalised and disfigured with a huge pillar as seen today.

The La Sanità bridge changed its name in 2011 and is now known as the "Maddalena Cerasuolo" bridge in homage to a member of the resistance who managed to stop the German troops who were preparing to blow it up to cut the city off from the Allies' northern advance.

MODEL OF BATTAGLINO CHARIOT ❹

Church of Sant'Agostino degli Scalzi
Salita San Raffaele, 6 Via Sant'Agostino degli Scalzi
• Metro: Line 1 Dante
• Visits: Saturday and Sunday, 10am—12pm

I n the sacristy of Sant'Agostino degli Scalzi is a wooden model of a chariot containing a variety of sacred representations dominated by the statue of the Immaculate Virgin. The sculpture dates from the mid-18th century and the artist is unknown. The model recalls the lavish floats used in the 17th

" An unexpected testimony of former ecclesiastical splendour

century for Easter Saturday processions, which were named after the gentleman

who introduced them: Pompeo Battaglino, who was also the sponsor of the great pomp of these celebrations.

The Easter procession took on such importance that the most eminent dignitaries from the viceroyalty, the militia of the three Knightly Orders of Spain, the royal guards, the yeomen of the guard, the most eminent prelates of the city and the archconfraternities all took part. Although the procession was abolished in 1749 because of its prohibitive cost, it had become so famous that Italian and European personalities made a special effort to be there.

Until the early 20th century, when a Neapolitan wanted to indicate something grandiose, he would say that "it looked like a Battaglino chariot".

CURIOSITIES OF SAN GENNARO CATACOMBS ❺

13 Via Tondo di Capodimonte
Basilica of Madre del Buon Consiglio
• Bus: R4, C63, 178 (Capodimonte stop)
• Metro: Line 1 Museo, Line 2 Cavour
• Tel: 081 7443714 • prenotazioni@catacombedinapoli.it
• Guided tours every hour Monday to Saturday, 10am–5pm, Sunday 10am–1pm
• Admission: €8, concessions €5

> **The strange stone phallus and the deaconess's fresco**

In the catacombs of San Gennaro (which are as vast and rich as Rome's), in the middle of a square room there sits a phallic stele that has intrigued experts ever since its discovery in the 18th century. From the name of the god Priapus cut into the stone to the seemingly meaningless inscription in a language resembling Hebrew, an air of mystery still hangs over the significance of this stele.

Since the Greek god of fertility, Priapus, is associated with orgiastic rites, researchers exclude any connection with the Christian religion and even less with Judaism – not known for its predilection for sexual rites. Professor Lacerenza, an academic expert in Hebrew language and culture, hypothesises that the stele doesn't date from antiquity but from the 18th century, when it was thought to have been taken into the catacombs by clever but naughty eccentrics to have some fun at the expense of posterity. If this is a hoax it has certainly been successful, given the amount of publicity surrounding it.

THE NOBLE CERULA AND A HITHERTO UNKNOWN SAINT PAUL

During restoration work in 2011, in an upper gallery to the left of the extraordinary fresco that adorns a deaconess's tomb, a magnificent fresco of Saint Paul has emerged from under a thick layer of plaster. The exceptionally well-preserved painting is distinctive as much for the brilliance of its colours as for its expressive features.

Cerula, the deaconess, holds two open Gospels – a very unusual occurrence according to the director of the catacombs, Father Antonio Loffredo, in the sense that open Gospels are a prerogative of images of bishops.

The veil covering the woman's head and chest is decorated with a purple border with dancing cupids printed (or embroidered) around it. Although this detail is a sign of wealth, it also reflects the Coptic or Eastern origins of Cerula, which at the same time testifies to the presence of Christians fleeing persecution by the Arian Vandals, following their leader Quodvultdeus, the Bishop of Carthage exiled to Naples whose tomb is in the bishops' crypt of these catacombs.

THE HISTORIC OMEGA WORKSHOP

12 Via Stella
• Metro: Line 1 Museo, Line 2 Cavour
• Visits on request by phone or email
• Tel: 081 299041; omegant@tin.it
• www.omegasrl.com/

> **Naples,
> glove capital
> of the world**

Places retaining that inimitable mixture of hospitality, tradition and class, encapsulating the true essence of Naples, have become increasingly rare. The Omega workshop is undoubtedly one of them. Crossing the threshold of this artisanal glovemaker, founded in 1923, is to experience a tradition that has indisputably contributed to the prestige of the city, now considered the glove capital of the world. The owner, Mauro, will be glad to regale you with anecdotes, secrets and stories about this ancient profession. Visitors have the opportunity to watch the "glovers" at work and hear explanations of the different stages of manufacture, the properties of the raw materials and current marketing trends (these gloves are especially sought-after in France).

The ground-floor warehouse is where all the skins from various suppliers are kept. The corridors and halls are filled with hundreds of supple gloves of assorted colours and shapes, laid out on large wooden tables. Everywhere is the pervasive, pleasant smell of hand-worked leather. Four generations of the founding (Squillace) family and their skilled craftworkers have succeeded each other in this workshop, where the know-how, techniques and traditions of aspiring glovemakers have been passed on. This is where some of the world's major fashion houses have sourced their products for years.

The glovemaker's craft, popular since the 18th century, really took off at the beginning of the following century. The presence of the Bourbon court gave a further boost to the production of this sought-after accessory. In the past, Naples was responsible for about 90 per cent of all Italy's glove exports: in the Sanità district whole families, sometimes twenty or thirty people, devoted their time to glovemaking. An 1888 document in Omega's possession records that there were forty-one glovemakers in Naples that year, providing work for a total of 6,800, so at the time this cottage industry was the city's biggest employer. A handcrafted pair of leather gloves is the result of at least 25 different operations, from cutting to finishing. All these stages, completed entirely by hand even today, are generally carried out by homeworkers, either within the neighbourhood or in the surrounding villages.

PALAZZO ALBERTINI DI CIMITILE STAIRCASE ❼

76 Via Santa Teresa degli Scalzi
• Opening hours: as caretaker's lodge

A spectacular staircase

The sumptuous palazzo of the Princes of Cimitile (formerly known as Palazzo Calabria and Palazzo Acquaviva d'Atri, after the previous owners), on the right going up Via Santa Teresa degli Scalzi, has a superb interior staircase that can be viewed by asking permission from the caretaker.

This square-plan staircase rises up with a single rampant enclosed between pillars, which in turn are linked to ogival cross vaults.

The palazzo, commissioned by the nineteenth Duke of Atri, Rodolfo, a member of the prominent 18th-century Neapolitan House of Acquaviva, was built on the site of earlier residences dating back to the first half of the 17th century. The design is attributed to Giuseppe Astarita, the family's trusted architect. In 1774, the building was purchased by Giovan Battista Albertini, Prince of Cimitile, who refurbished it in a different style. It was severely damaged during the construction of Via Santa Teresa in the first half of the 19th century, when a basement was added.

The palazzo, which has recently been converted into apartments, formerly housed the precious collection of books of another Prince of Cimitile, Fabio Albertini, as well as an extensive gallery of paintings. The aristocratic effigies of the original owners, the Marulli d'Ascoli family, and the Calabrias who inherited it, can still be seen on the top gate at the level of the roadway.

In the late 1970s, the staircase was restored under the supervision of the conservator and historian of Italian Renaissance and Baroque architecture, Roberto Pane.

NEARBY

On the first floor of the palazzo is the Dafna Home Gallery, a remarkable exhibition space dedicated to contemporary art, which opens onto the artist Danilo Ambrosino's studio house. With the help of architect Anna Fresa, Ambrosino has transformed his home into a gallery (see www.dafna.it).

BONELLI COLLECTION

8

Fondazione Casa dello Scugnizzo Onlus
3 Piazzetta San Gennaro a Materdei
• Visits on reservation, by phone or email
• Tel: 340 4844132
• g.bonelli72@gmail.com

10,000 memories of Naples from the last two centuries

A visit to Gaetano Bonelli's private collection of memorabilia, the fruit of thirty years' research, comes as quite a surprise. Some 10,000 items are preserved there: curiosities, relics, documents, all kinds of rare objects from many aspects of life – historical, cultural, social, economic. The only common thread is Naples' rich cultural heritage. This assorted heritage has been carefully laid out and categorised on shelves, in drawers or in boxes – a real cabinet of curiosities, reflecting the journalist owner's passionate enthusiasm for local history.

Among the wonders you'll discover are wooden printing blocks from an 1825 map of Naples, hand-painted lottery cards from the early 19th century, a little image printed on fabric from the first half of the 19th century representing Our Lady of China (with almond-shaped eyes!) in Naples, "Saint Januarius' hat" (from Benevento in Campania), and other relics from the same era.

Bonelli will no doubt add to the enjoyment of your visit with his descriptions of these treasures, laced with Neapolitan anecdotes and stories, as well as personal testimonies about the city's origins.

Regno delle Due Sicilie

Uniforme da
Primo Capitano
della
Gendarmeria Reale

1832 – 1861

Regno delle Due Sicilie

Uniforme da
Primo Capitano
di
Artiglieria

1832 – 1861

Regno delle Due Sicilie

Tenente di Galla
della Guardia d'Onore
11° Squadrone
"Terra d'Otranto"

1832 – 1861

FULVIO DE INNOCENTIIS COLLECTION

- Metro: Line 1 Materdei
- Collection under surveillance 24/7
- Visits for cultural associations or with authorisation (fulviodeinno@virgilio.it)

> **Uniforms from the Bourbon era, ceremonial dress, helmets, swords ...**

Royal Guard of Honour ceremonial dress from the Kingdom of the Two Sicilies, uniforms of the National Guard (from the Kingdom of Italy), very rare Garibaldian uniforms, around seventy Bourbon and Piedmontese sabres, helmets from many countries, fascinating military decorations, even German uniforms from the Second World War ...

Discovering the Fulvio de Innocentiis collection is a real trip back in time, whether this sort of thing is your hobby or you're just curious. One of the rooms in his house is devoted to these unexpected and authentic rarities. Each item, carefully placed in a display case or on a dummy, is accompanied by an explanatory panel.

De Innocentiis has been obsessed with the military since childhood. As well as being a skilled historian and photographer, he has been an international chess player for the past decade. He is also a first-rate performer of Neapolitan songs. His love of collecting things is largely inherited from his father, who specialised in stamps.

This little private museum is the result of over fifty years of diligent research around the world, from antique markets to second-hand dealers and collectors. Great patience is needed: reassembling an entire uniform and locating all the original pieces (each uniform has its own shoulder strap, belt, sword, etc.) can take twenty years. "Very few people, we're told, can tell one Bourbon button from another ...", says De Innocentiis.

His most treasured exhibit is a rare decoration embroidered with the Order of Francis I of Bourbon, for which a collector from Emilia-Romagna offered a considerable sum in the early 1980s. But his offer was declined.

In his long quest for acquisitions, De Innocentiis says he once met somebody, obviously not short of space or funds, who collected wartime armoured vehicles (tanks, vans). Some people even collect aircraft.

CASA MORRA

10

Fondazione Morra
29/d Vico Lungo Pontecorvo
• Metro: Line 1 Materdei
• Tel: 081 5641655
• Open Monday to Friday 10am–7pm, Saturday 10am–2pm
• info@fondazionemorra.org • www.fondazionemorra.org

> *An art collection in a palazzo with a Sanfelice staircase*

Casa Morra is a museum space created by Neapolitan gallerist Giuseppe Morra in the historic Palazzo Ayerbo d'Aragona Cassano: a 4,200 m2 complex designed to accommodate the extensive Morra Collection.

Over 2,000 artworks are waiting to be discovered, presented thematically as a journey through the history of contemporary art from core movements such as the Gutai group, Happening & Fluxus, Viennese Actionism, Living Theater and Visual Poetry to the most avant-garde Italian and foreign artists.

Casa Morra is reached via a spectacular central staircase: the first flight leads to a landing from which two symmetrical balustrades (separated by

another semi-circular landing) lead to the upper floor. The late Baroque architect and painter Ferdinando Sanfelice, designer of the most beautiful Neapolitan open staircases, created this splendid architectural feature.

This former hunting lodge is typical of the emerging suburbs of the city as it appeared in the 1566 "Atlases of Lafréry" (collection of maps). Between the end of the 17th and the beginning of the 18th centuries, the building was converted into a stately home.

Casa Morra is now a "living" contemporary art venue, encouraging reflection and research on society and its constant evolution.

EXHIBITIONS SCHEDULED UNTIL 2116

It's unusual for a calendar to list exhibitions as far ahead as 2116. Morra has indeed planned 100 years of events, designed through a game of snakes and ladders with multiple references and interconnections. Exhibition cycles are regulated by the alchemy of the numbers 3 and 7, which sometimes coincide with the number of artists presented, or the quantity or sequence of the works displayed. All this makes for a unique atmosphere where the charm of the "container" (the building) is transformed through contact with perpetual contemporary animation (the exhibitions are constantly changing).

MANN'S HIDDEN TREASURES ⓫

Museo Archeologico Nazionale di Napoli (MANN)
19 Piazza Museo
• Metro: Line 1 Museo, Line 2 Cavour
• Only open to the public on special occasions
• www.museoarcheologiconapoli.it • www.facebook.com/MANNapoli

> ***Secret depositories known as "Sing Sing"***

Like many other great collections, the National Archaeological Museum of Naples has a precious "secret" treasury. This is hidden in the museum's depositories where the artefacts – classified, inventoried and analysed by experts – are kept in strict order ready for new exhibitions. These storerooms, scattered throughout the building, hold an impressive volume of archaeological pieces that alone would fill another exceptional museum. Most of them are in the roof space or in large basement rooms known as cavaiole. These were carved out of the volcanic rock during construction of the building – originally a cavalry barracks and home to the University of Naples before the museum was established by the Bourbons in the late 18th century. The basement rooms, fitted out in the late 1970s, were

nicknamed "Sing Sing" in reference to the notorious maximum-security prison in New York State. Along the corridors is a succession of rooms closed off by grilles, which house Graeco-Roman artefacts classified by material. Several rooms are devoted to bronze objects, for example tableware, candelabras, oil lamps, heaters, locks, statuettes of divinities and vast quantities of everyday utensils found at Pompeii and Herculaneum.

Small vases, bowls, cups, bottles of various shapes and unguentaria (vials for storing perfumes or oils) are kept behind glass. Ordinary earthenware dishes, perhaps less attractive but no less important, are also held here.

The collection of vases – one of the largest in the world – has its own special charm. Many kinds of Greek painted ceramics are represented, as well as a great variety of iconographic subjects and pictorial styles from various sources (especially the sites of Magna Graecia – the ancient cities along the coast of southern Italy).

The museum prides itself on its extraordinary heritage of ancient works of art and artefacts, dating from prehistory to late antiquity, displayed over some 18,000 m2. All this material – more than 8,000 objects, many of great value – comes from excavations of Pompeii and Herculaneum, as well as important sources such as the Farnese Collection of classical art and several archaeological sites in southern Italy. An indispensable key to understanding the history and art of antiquity.

STATUE OF LAKSHMI

Gabinetto Segreto, Museo Archeologico Nazionale di Napoli (MANN)
19 Piazza Museo
• Metro: Line 1 Museo, Line 2 Cavour
• Open Wednesday to Monday 9am–7.30pm, closed Tuesday
• Closed 1 January, 1 May and 25 December
• If Tuesday is a public holiday, the museum closes Wednesday

> **One of the Secret Cabinet's surprises**

I n 1939, an ivory statuette of Lakshmi, Hindu goddess of wealth and good fortune, female beauty and fertility, was found in a modest house at Pompeii (since named after her). Now preserved at the National Archaeological Museum of Naples, in the Gabinetto Segreto (Secret Cabinet – the private rooms for the Bourbon monarchy's collection of ancient erotica), this sculpture shows the deity almost naked, dressed only in rich jewels that leave her breasts and genitals uncovered. She is flanked by two servants carrying items for the toilette.

The statuette is probably one of those *apophoreta* of which the Roman poet Martial speaks in his epigrams: these were rewards for the winners of the dice games held during banquets. Or perhaps it is meant for the toilette, as the little round hole at the top of the head would suggest. Whatever its function, this unusual little sculpture is clear evidence of the commercial relations that already existed in the 1st century AD between the Mediterranean countries and the East, centred on the seaport of Puteoli (now Pozzuoli).

NEARBY

VERY RARE CROCODILE MUMMY

In ancient Egypt, crocodiles were revered because they were associated with the god Sobek and the fertility of the Nile. Some specimens were mummified. Necropolises entirely dedicated to animal burials have been found at several Nile Valley sites. The crocodile exhibited in the MANN Egyptian section, 261 cm long and 60 cm wide, preserved with broad strips of cloth, palm leaves and ropes, has been dated to between 664 and 332 BC. Two small partially mummified young crocodiles lie next to the body of the adult specimen.

CRUCIFIX OF SAN CARLO ALL'ARENA CHURCH ⓭

70 Via Foria
• Metro: Line 1 Museo, Line 2 Cavour
• Visits 7.30am–11am and 5pm–7pm
• Tel: 081 441482

The wounded Christ

On 11 November 1923, the church of San Carlo all'Arena was badly affected by fire, which among other damage brought down a precious crucifix that shattered on the floor. The figure of Christ carved by Michelangelo Naccherino in 1599 from a single block of marble, which originally stood in Spirito Santo basilica, is so realistic that it has even been compared with the famous *Veiled Christ* statue in the Sansevero chapel. After extremely skilful restoration work, the statue was returned to its many devoted followers. The new and inevitable injuries "inflicted" on the statue have only accentuated its dramatic effect. The sculpture is in the fifth chapel, dedicated to Saint Charles Borromeo (16th-century Archbishop of Milan), whose shroud is said to have been kept in one of the other chapels.

The church was laid waste when it was occupied by the French troops, who used it as a barracks. It was was almost entirely rebuilt by Francesco De Cesare in 1837.

WHY "ALL'ARENA"?

The church of San Carlo all'Arena, so called to distinguish it from the church of San Carlo a Mortelle, was commissioned from Fra' Giuseppe Nuvolo in 1631 by the Carthusian monks. The name "all'Arena" (of the arena) alludes to the sandy clay on which the church was built – an alluvial sediment that slid down from the surrounding hills and was generally known as the "Lava of Vergini".

NEARBY

FATE PRESTO: REPRODUCTION IN THE METRO OF A "NEAPOLITAN" ⓮
WORK BY ANDY WARHOL

The hundreds of passengers who hurry every day along the corridor connecting Line 1 to Line 2 of the metro (between Museo and Cavour stations) don't take much notice of a large poster reproducing the front page of the local daily *Il Mattino*, which came out in the aftermath of the 1980 earthquake. Although most Neapolitans think it's a simple tribute to the many victims of the disaster, the poster is actually a reproduction of a work by Andy Warhol (the original is in the Royal Palace of Caserta).

The pop art celebrity was so touched by the simple yet meaningful title *Fate Presto* (Hurry Up) that he decided to immortalise this tragic event in the history of southern Italy. Warhol later made a series of eighteen paintings representing the Vesuvius eruption at different hours of the day, one of which is displayed at the Capodimonte gallery.

PIAZZA CAVOUR TUNNELS

15

La Macchina Del Tempo
Il Museo del Sottosuolo
140 Piazza Cavour
• Metro: Line 1 Museo, Line 2 Cavour
• booking@ilmuseodelsottosuolo.com
• Tel: 081 8631581

The underground museum

Nobody would think that the little door behind the two metro stations in Piazza Cavour leads to a extensive underground world, much less well-known than the other passages under the city streets. A long stairway leads down 20 m to an intricate network of tunnels, galleries and caverns hewn in the tuff, the largest of which covers 3,600 m².

Some of this space was used as an air-raid shelter during the Second World War, when over a thousand people took refuge there. The site has now become a museum, founded by Clemente Esposito, president of the Southern Speleological Society.

Glass cases display artefacts found during the excavations: an old gun, vials belonging to an ancient pharmacy that stored its goods in one of the underground quarries, as well as tools, oil lamps and crockery.

Further down, you end up in a quarry with walls 8 m high, around which benches have been dug out of the tuff walls to serve as makeshift beds during the war.

This is the only network of tunnels under the city where the modern aqueduct (Carmignano) runs over the remains of the aqueducts of antiquity. Another distinctive feature is that it's the only quarry outside the city walls, excavated in the 17th century when exploitation of the caverns under the city was banned for fear of subsidence.

BOMB SHELTER IN BABUK'S GARDEN

55 Via Giuseppe Piazzi
- Metro: Line 1 Museo, Line 2 Cavour
- Visits by reservation only: • Tel : 081 5499250
- www.amicidimarcelproust.it
- proustswann@gmail.com

*A shelter
for the elite*

Behind a 16th-century palace that belonged to the Caracciolo del Sole family there is a little garden, measuring about 1,000 m², full of lemon trees, flowers and beautiful fountains: a charming hideaway among the many modern buildings.

The restoration work was carried out by Professor Gennaro Oliviero, President of the "Friends of Marcel Proust" association, which since 2009 has organised visits and events. Professor Oliviero wished to name this garden after his cat, Babuk, to which he was very attached.

Among the greenery is the entrance to a 17th-century underground quarry, which was later converted to a 700,000 litre cistern. This was abandoned after the 1884 cholera epidemic, when the Serino aqueduct was built. In those days the steps were extended to reach the bottom of the tank at a depth of 14 m.

During the Second World War, the space was used as an air-raid shelter, as borne out by objects found during repair work. It was called the "elite" shelter because it was reserved for the wealthy of the neighbourhood. After the war, the old quarry was completely forgotten.

On the walls, still coated with waterproofing material, you can still see the marks left by the stonemasons and the outline of steps cut out by the cistern maintenance workers. There are also strange carvings in the tuff, such as crosses or salamanders. The main chamber led to galleries, some of which are still piled with old gravel. Only one of them has been cleared and leads to a small quarry that you can arrange to visit.

EVENTS ORGANISED BY THE "FRIENDS OF MARCEL PROUST"
The association occasionally organises very agreeable literary events or performances: www.amicidimarcelproust.it

LITTLE SECRETS OF PALAZZO DELLO SPAGNOLO

⑰

19 Via Vergini
• Metro: Line 1 Museo, Line 2 Cavour
• Admission free

To reach Capodimonte hill, where he had a palace built to display the works of art inherited from his mother, Elisabeth Farnese, Charles I of Bourbon had to travel along Via Vergini. This street with its silted-up surface was so steep that even the horses couldn't make it: only oxen could.

> *When the king changed horses for oxen to climb the Vergini slopes*

At the superb Palazzo dello Spagnolo (Palace of the Spaniard – don't miss the famous and strikingly original external staircase), at the beginning of the slope, the king stopped to exchange his beautiful horses for these humble bovines. For the residents of this house and the whole neighbourhood, it was the perfect opportunity to get a close look at the king.

But every good thing comes to an end: when Joachim Murat ascended the throne of the kingdom of Naples, he had a much more accessible new road built linking the city centre to Capodimonte. The palace where the oxen awaited the king, designed in 1738 by Ferdinando Sanfelice, is so named because it was occupied in the 19th century by a Spanish nobleman, Tommaso Atienza, known for his eccentricity.

NEARBY

SIRENS OF PALAZZO SANFELICE

⑱

2/6 Via Sanità

Ferdinando Sanfelice (1675–1748), born into a family of the old Neapolitan nobility and an enlightened Freemason with innovative and bold ideas, was known for the audacity of his projects, notably his staircases that were so outrageous that, fearing they would collapse at any moment, people nicknamed them: "*Sanfelì lievet' 'a sotto*" (Sanfelice, don't stay under there). He built the eponymous palazzo for his own family, or rather two palazzi with identical portals – one built from scratch and another restored next door. Some obscure details: the pediment of the two portals is flanked by two Sirens who are represented with wings and a fishtail, which is very rare because in iconography Sirens are usually either bird-women or mermaids (see p. 153). Also note in the vault of the entrance hall the eight-branched star, a symbol with multiple meanings familiar to both Templars and Freemasons.

PALAZZO DE' LIGUORO DI PRESICCE

12 Via Arena della Sanità
• Metro: Line 1 Museo, Line 2 Cavour
• pdeliguorodipresicce@gmail.com

> **Home of "the saintliest of Neapolitans and most Neapolitan of saints"**

At the heart of the Vergini district with its streets teeming with life and chaotic traffic, the Palazzo de' Liguoro di Presicce is not only a discovery, but a genuine experience, because you touch on the very essence of "*napoletanità*" (being, feeling a real Neapolitan).

This is entirely due to the owner, Princess Paola di' Liguoro di Presicce, who has restored this superb 16th-century residence and welcomes visitors with exquisite courtesy.

The princess is a direct descendant of Saint Alphonsus Maria de' Liguori, known as "the saintliest of Neapolitans and most Neapolitan of saints", who lived in this building. His statue still stands in a niche in the staircase wall.

Although only a few traces remain of the palace chapel, the first-floor rooms still have the elegant 17th-century decoration attributed to Domenico De Mare. The princess's own large apartment, part of which can be visited on request, is a treasure trove of huge mirrors, 17th-century inlaid furniture, imposing bookcases and sparkling chandeliers.

As for the ballroom with its frescoed vault, you'd think it had come straight out of Visconti's *The Leopard*.

Madame de' Liguoro, having lived in Rome for a number of years, chose to settle here, because, she says, "In Vergini we breathe the air of truth." She is devoted body and soul to the rehabilitation of the neighbourhood, weighed down as it was with far too many unfounded prejudices rooted in the minds

of Neapolitans themselves. To this end, she funds a number of cultural events such as putting on plays.

The princess also rents the other apartments in the palace to artists or writers, thus creating a fantastic reserve of culture and creativity without equal in the city.

STUDIO OF PAINTER MASSIMO D'ORTA

43a Vico Santa Maria del Pozzo
- Metro: Line 1 Museo, Line 2 Cavour
- Visits on request
- dorta.massimo@libero.it

An artist's studio in a predestined site

The painter Massimo D'Orta – brother of Marcello D'Orta, author of the 1990 bestseller *Io speriamo che me la cavo* [I'm hoping I get out of this], who died in 2013 – willingly welcomes visitors to his workshop, which he also calls home, in Palazzo de' Liguoro di Presicce (see previous double-page spread).

The artist works in the salon of the large apartment with a ceiling that retains traces of earlier frescoes. When Massimo D'Orta first visited the

apartment in 2000, he refused to live there because of the terrible state it was in. Then, after a few days, he returned to have a better look round. As he entered the salon, all of a sudden he distinctly heard a voice whispering: "I was expecting you." When he got over his bewilderment, he decided to buy and restore the apartment. Less than a week later, the representatives of a wealthy Texas businessman, having seen Massimo D'Orta paintings in an exhibition, commissioned a life-size copy (2 × 3 m) of Caravaggio's *Descent from the Cross*, a work that the artist had always dreamed of reproducing. What's more, the fee for this commission easily covered the significant cost of the restoration work. D'Orta later discovered that in this apartment had lived a disciple of Saint Alphonsus de' Liguoro, Saint Gerard Majella (1726–1755), much loved in the neighbourhood for his work helping the poor. His benevolent presence, they say, still protects this former palace.

From the painter's workshop, you can admire a beautiful magnolia around 500 years old and over 20 m high.

GREEK HYPOGEA IN NAPLES

126/129 Via Santa Maria Antesaecula
• Metro: Line 1 Museo, Line 2 Cavour
• Tel: 347 5597231
• Guided tours by appointment with the Celanapoli association
• celanapoli@libero.it

> **Greek tombs under buildings in the historic centre**

In the Vergini district, a steep flight of steps leads to the two hypogea in the care of the Celanapoli association. The underground tombs, discovered when checks were carried out after the 1980 earthquake, are part of a great Hellenistic necropolis (4th century BC) that was once in the open. It was in use until the 2nd century AD, then gradually covered by 10 m of sediment. In the 16th century, when building began in this area, the tuff layer was excavated and much of the necropolis was destroyed.

A number of these tombs, many of which were converted into cisterns by the inhabitants of the stately palazzi of the 18th century, had been known since at least 1649, when the historian Carlo Celano was already mentioning grave robbers being arrested by the authorities. So there are not many intact tombs left. Furthermore, although the water stored in these chambers preserved their decoration for a few centuries, the worst damage occurred after the cholera epidemic of 1884, when water storage was banned for reasons of hygiene.

From then on, these precious relics would become a dumping ground for

rubble, which also makes the current excavations extremely complex.

The tombs, all monumental and certainly belonging to notables, were dug into the tuff wall that stretched along the extramural perimeter from north to east of the ancient city of Neapolis (now Via dei Cristallini, Vico Traetta, Via Santa Maria Antesaecula). To imagine what this necropolis was like, think of the excavations at Petra in Jordan, whereas their decoration is reminiscent of Macedonian art. In fact, these structures have no equal to this day.

The first hypogeum is called "dei Togati" because of the extraordinary high relief depicting a lifesize man and woman, both draped in togas. The upper section is regrettably hidden by a supporting arch from the building above. On one side, you can make out a very poorly preserved panther, an allusion to the Dionysian cult. The burial chamber, measuring 15 m², is still filled with rubble.

The tomb known as the "Melograno" (pomegranate) is better preserved. In the burial chamber, once entirely covered with frescoes, you can still see a frieze of pomegranates, pine cones, lotus flowers and eggs, as well as an unidentified fruit, all evoking fertility.

In another inaccessible section are traces of the sarcophagi. Descending to a depth of about 20 m, you reach the place that until the early 20th century was used as a cold store for meat and charcuterie. Cattle bones can still be seen there.

Four tombs from the same Hellenistic necropolis are accessible at 133 Via dei Cristallini (see following double-page spread).

"CRISTALLINI" HYPOGEA

133 Via dei Cristallini
- Metro: Line 1 Museo, Line 2 Cavour
- Visits can be booked during the first and third Saturdays of May only
- napolisegreta@gmail.com

A unique tomb

Four exceptional tombs from the Hellenistic necropolis of Vergini district (see previous double-page spread) were discovered in perfect condition in 1888 when cleaning out the well underneath Baron Giovanni di Donato's palace. The site, 11 m below street level, is down a flight of steps in the courtyard of the building.

Like all the other tombs, these are constructed on two levels. The atrium chambers that once stood on the ground floor, intended for funeral rites, are connected to the burial chamber by a passageway (*dromos*). The first atrium was decorated with eight bas-reliefs, only one of which remains. The associated tomb has been almost completely destroyed by stone-masons. The second is stunning in its incredible state of conservation (funerary urns, frescoes and altars). In the third, covered by a pitched roof rather than a barrel vault, are superb bas-reliefs including one of a farewell scene (see below). Its unique tomb of incomparable beauty features bas-reliefs, sarcophagi with ornamental marble pillows, and paintings, including a magnificent Medusa, that seem freshly restored. The last vault is completely different, surrounded by the niches (columbaria) typical of Roman cemeteries, proof that they reused the site. Among the many objects found there are painted vases, statuettes, terracotta fruits and eggs, jars of ointment and inscriptions in honour of the deceased.

TOUCHING FAREWELL SCENES IN THE MUSEO ARCHEOLOGICO NAZIONALE

Metro: Line 1 Museo, Line 2 Cavour

The "Napoli antica" section of the Archaeological Museum of Naples (the world's most important repository of Graeco-Roman art), inaugurated in 1999, is still little known although of major interest. The most notable exhibits include the so-called "*de commiato*" (farewell) bas-reliefs from the tombs of Vergini and La Sanità. Most of these show two people shaking hands. The most touching scene is that of two men, with a woman caressing the cheek of one of them, most likely the deceased. Not to be missed.

CHURCH OF SANTA MARIA ANTESAECULA 〈23〉

Dispensaire Asl
48 Via Santa Maria Antesaecula
• Metro: Line 1 Museo, Line 2 Cavour
• Viviquartiere association
• Visits on reservation by phone or e-mail
• Tel: 339 6304072 • viviquartiere@libero.it

A
former church
in a health centre

Within a modern public building you'll be amazed to find the vestiges of a large 17th-century convent – the construction date of 1622 can still be read on the original gate. In that year, to escape the epidemics that were constantly breaking out in the city, the girls' boarding school in the Vicaria Vecchia district, founded in 1275 by Charles I of Anjou's chancellor Pierleone Sicola, was moved to the present location because of its reputation for hygiene.

The original name of this institution, Santa Maria a Sicola (after the founder), was changed to Santa Maria Antesaecula in memory of the Virgin Mary's words: "*ab inizio et ante saecula creata sum*" (At the beginning of time, before the world was, I was created). The property later became a Dominican monastery. There's not much of the old structure left.

The church (entrance in one of the offices), rebuilt on several occasions and closed for a long period, is used today for cultural events. Urbanisation has also spared part of the original garden. At the end of the Second World War, reconstruction work exposed the crypt that served as a burial ground, with its pierced seats used for drying out corpses (see also San Gaudioso catacombs, p. 331), which were left in place.

At 109 Via Santa Maria Antesaecula, a plaque marks the building where the famous comedian Totò lived.

THE FERTILITY CHAIR

Church of Santa Maria della Sanità
14 Piazza della Sanità
• Metro: Line 1 Museo, Line 2 Cavour
• Tel: 081 7443714 • info@catacombedinapoli.it
• Open daily, 10am–5pm

In the chapel dedicated to Saint Thomas
Aquinas at Santa Maria della Sanità
church is a chair made from volcanic
stone dating from the early Christian
period, originally an episcopal chair in the
catacombs beneath. The Dominicans moved
it to its current location in the 17th century.

Sit in this chair if you want to bear a child

According to legend, the chair has the
power to cure sterility in women who sit in it. This belief, which endured
until the last decade or so, is no longer so widespread. Nowadays the chair is
even behind a barrier.

OTHER FERTILITY CHAIRS IN NAPLES

In Vico Tre Re a Toledo in the Spanish quarter, women are commonly seen
queuing in front of the church of Santa Maria Francesca delle Cinque
Piaghe di Gesù to sit on a wooden chair that had belonged to Sister Maria
Francesca, the saint addressed by women wishing to bear a child. In
this church, the relics of a lock of hair and one of the saint's vertebrae
form part of the same ritual. For the miracle to happen, the vertebra
should brush against the belly of the would-be mother. The home of
Maria Francesca (also known as "Santarella" – little saint), next to the
church, is open to all those who wish to visit or pay homage to the saint
born on 25 March 1715. She is said to have received the stigmata. There
is no longer any trace of a third chair that used to be in Santa Maria della
Catena church.

SAN GAUDIOSO CATACOMBS

14 Piazza della Sanità
Entrance in Santa Maria della Sanità church
- Metro: Line 1 Museo, Line 2 Cavour
- Tel: 081 7443714 • info@catacombedinapoli.it
- Open 10am–1.30pm: last guided tour of catacombs 12.30pm
- Admission: €10 valid for one year, includes San Gennaro catacombs

> *Skeletons
> in fancy dress*

Access to San Gaudioso catacombs is by a flight of steps below the presbytery of Santa Maria della Sanità (17th century). In the early 16th century, these vast underground galleries were used to preserve the dead, using a Spanish method that had been adopted by the Dominican and Capuchin monks.

While the bodies of the poor were crammed into ossuaries, the aristocrats were carried into these underground tunnels to undergo a very special treatment: after sitting the corpse in a niche made for this purpose (which can still be seen today), it was pierced. Apparently the bodies were burst open to empty them of all fluids, hence the Neapolitan term *schiattamuorto* for undertaker (corpse-piercer) and a fairly common and unsavoury insult: *puozze schiattà* or *puozze sculà*, "go and bust a gut" or "go and drip".

As the Dominicans considered the soil as a gift from God that shouldn't be contaminated by sinful man, these bodily fluids were drained into a pot placed under the seated corpse. Once the body had dried out, the head (seat of the soul) was detached and inserted in the wall of a tunnel next to the main chamber. Then a life-size mural was painted of the deceased's fully clothed body under its own head and a few explanatory details were inscribed on the wall.

The first mural depicts Donna Sveva Gesualdo, Princess of Montesarchio, who paid 600 ducats to benefit from this treatment. Note also the spouses holding hands. There's a legend that these two saw a terrifying and unwelcome guest arrive at their wedding, the ghost of the captain whose head is preserved in the nearby Fontanelle cemetery (see p. 287). On the left is a magistrate, Diego Longobardo, with his robes and judge's gavel, dead in 1632; next come Marco Antonio d'Aponte, Scipione Brancaccio with his sword, Alessandro d'Afflitto and the painter Giovanni Balducci with his ruler and palette.

In 1637, this practice was abolished because of the Dominicans constantly knocking holes in the walls to insert the aristocrats' heads (which, incidentally, brought the monks a significant extra income) and threatening the stability of the whole district. Besides, the damp tunnels became a breeding ground for germs because of this method of treating corpses.

In 2002, the pastor of Santa Maria della Sanità church founded a cooperative, the Paranza, with the aim of training young people and raising funds with which to restore and reopen monuments. The cooperative also manages a B&B, Casa del Monacone – an exemplary start-up of a very useful business, regrettably little known.

PALAZZO DE' LIGUORO-SANTORO STAIRCASE 26

8/10 Salita Capodimonte
• Metro: Line 1 Museo, Line 2 Cavour
• Tel: 347 5597231 • celanapoli@libero.it
• Guided tour on reservation with the Celanapoli association

Extraordinary architecture carved out of the tuff

Built into the tuff hillside of Capodimonte, Palazzo de' Liguoro-Santoro (named after its successive owners) dates back to at least 1746, as indicated by the marble inscription at the entrance. You'll immediately realise that the building is totally different to its neighbours. In the entrance hall, entirely hollowed out of the tuff, a closed door on the left leads to the old cemeteries also dug into the hillside. A small altar stands in the centre, and to the right a few steps will take you to one of the most original and most spectacular stairwells in the city: a spiral staircase carved out of the tuff and covered with lava stone of unparalleled grace and perfection.

Another peculiarity is that on climbing to the top floor, instead of being plunged into darkness as in most buildings, you're bathed in the light streaming through the circular openings. The staircase leads to a private roof garden with a beautiful view over the city centre. During guided tours you can sometimes visit this garden.

MICHELE IODICE'S WORKSHOP

132 Salita Capodimonte
• Bus: C63, 2M, 178, R4
• Visits on reservation
• mic.iodice@gmail.com

Sculptures in a stable

A former quarry, first used as a stable and then a slaughterhouse and accessed through the entrance hall of a building, has been converted into a studio by a Neapolitan artist who displays hundreds of sculptures along the tuff walls. Michele Iodice, the sculptor, has also brightened up his studio with towering plants that add to its originality. Local people say that this was where the replacement oxen were stabled while they waited to be harnessed to the king's carriage whenever he and his family took the only road up to the Royal Palace of Capodimonte, which was too steep for the horses (see p. 317).

NEARBY

WINE TAX MARKER

Further along Salita Capodimonte you come to Via Sant'Antonio a Capodimonte where, between 1 Salita Capodimonte and 111 Via Sant'Antonio, a plaque marks the boundary of the "wine tax". Among the earliest collectors of this tax, which was payable on the sale of carafes and casks of wine in the City of Naples, was Gregorio Carafa di Stadera, an aristocrat who lived in the 12th century..

MUSEO DI CAPODIMONTE AND REAL BOSCO ㉙ DI CAPODIMONTE

2 Via Miano, mezzanine
• Visits on request, except Wednesday
• Tel: 081 7499130
• mu-cap.accoglienza.capodimonte@beniculturali.it

The private apartments of the Bourbon court

Since the palace of Capodimonte has been opened to the public (visits on request), the privately owned apartments of the Bourbon court (which then passed to the House of Savoy) have been recreated on the *"piano matto"* ("crazy floor"), a mezzanine below the piano nobile (main floor) reached by the monumental staircase designed by architect Ferdinando Sanfelice. This series of rooms overlooking the Royal Forest, the city and the Bay of Naples was once an elegant private residence. Seven rooms and over 200 works of art (paintings, sculptures, decorative objects including fabrics and curtains) recapture its refined ambience, whereas the writing room, bedrooms and maid's room strike a more intimate note, far from the majesty of the royal reception rooms on the main floor.

In 1816, this was the residence of Ferdinand I. Around 1850, Princess Maria Carolina of Bourbon-Two Sicilies, his granddaughter, stayed there while in Naples. When the House of Savoy took over from the Bourbons, the apartments were intended for the junior branch of the Dukes of Aosta.

A *MARGHERITA* FOR THE QUEEN

The Torre garden with its many fruit trees, to the south of the palace, was called the "French garden" or "Biancour garden" in the 18th century after the origins and name of the family of gardeners who tended it.

The Torre building, at the back of the palace, was the gardeners' residence. The house is typically rural, with its few rooms all on one floor. A water tower stands against the wall and below is a wood-fired oven.

In 1889 the *pizzaiolo* Raffaele Esposito cooked the margherita – a pizza garnished with mozzarella, tomato sauce and basil. It went on to become world-famous. Raffaele came from the Pietro e Basta Così (now the Brandi) pizzeria, and on this occasion was invited to Capodimonte by King Umberto I and Queen Margherita.

From the early 19th century (see Francesco de Bourcard, *Usi e costumi di Napoli*, Alberto Marotta, 1866), various types of pizza – *marinara, margherita* and the *calzone* (a pizza folded in half, with a filling) – were being made in Naples, using oil, salt, oregano, garlic, grated cheese, lard, basil and mozzarella.

TORRE DEL PALASCIANO

B&B La Torre di Rò
53 Salita Moiariello
• Metro: Line 1 Museo, then Bus C63
• Tel: 081 457711, 335 6957720
• www.latorrediro.com
• Reservation by e-mail: info@latorrediro.com

> ❝ *A strange tower inspired by Palazzo della Signoria*

Built to the plans of architect Antonio Cipolla for Ferdinando Palasciano (see below), the extraordinary Palumbo tower that flanks a palazzo dating from 1868 is clearly inspired by the medieval Palazzo della Signoria in Florence. The enchanting verdant garden all around the tower, with its beautiful trees – oaks, oranges and laurels – is just a short distance from the Royal Palace of Capodimonte. Although the tower stands out against the Neapolitan landscape and can be seen from afar, not many locals know that it is open to the public: it has recently been restored and converted into a B&B.

Through the entrance hall to the left, near the wall, stands a grey stone obelisk (1868) engraved with the names of famous people. The beautiful staircase leads to the three guest rooms (each located on a different floor and all with private bathrooms). At the top is a panoramic terrace with a parapet pierced with niches known as Ghibellines. From here, Palasciano's wife Olga de Wavilow could even see the monumental tomb of her beloved husband, located in the so-called "corner of illustrious men" in the city's main cemetery at Poggioreale. Indeed the statue of the deceased, on a pedestal 5 m high, is hard to miss.

FERDINANDO PALASCIANO, ARMY DOCTOR OF THE TWO SICILIES

Dr Ferdinando Palasciano (1815–1891), appointed army doctor of the Kingdom of the Two Sicilies, was in Sicily during the riots of 1848. He cared for the enemy wounded against the orders of General Carlo Filangieri and so found himself accused of insubordination. Condemned to be shot, he was rescued by King Ferdinand II, who commuted his sentence to a year in prison. This incident laid the foundations of the Geneva Convention of 1864, which in turn gave rise to the Red Cross.

The care that Dr Palasciano lavished on Garibaldi, after he was seriously injured fighting at Aspromonte, led to a growing friendship between the two men and they corresponded over a long period. Their letters are preserved in the San Martino Museum.

OSPEDALE LEONARDO BIANCHI   **31**

230 Calata Capodichino
• Bus 125 from Napoli Centrale station (Calata Capodichino stop)
• Tel: 081 2546118 / 081 2546147

A hospital theatre

For the past 15 years, Roberto De Simone has rehearsed his performances in the abandoned Leonardo Bianchi psychiatric hospital. The new life of this vast hospital complex (fifty-four buildings over 20 hectares) began in the 1990s with the abolition of asylums. Before the hospital was permanently decommissioned, its administrative rooms were opened up for artists to rehearse in front of the patients. This experiment was designed to help them make a smooth transition to the "outside world". De Simone was one of the first to accept the challenge. What was supposed to be a temporary experiment then became a ongoing palliative.

The asylum, built in 1902 and commissioned in 1909, was one of the most important in southern Italy. Its archives contain thousands of documents considered to be a valuable asset, essential to studying the history of psychiatry. After the patients had gone, some buildings were used by the social security services. The current director of this branch of public health, Dr Anna Sicolo, is striving to set up a museum to save these symbols of human incarceration from oblivion.

Two books have now been published on this site, which clearly fascinates artists: *Folia/Follia: Il patrimonio culturale dell'ex ospedale psichiatrico "Leonardo Bianchi" di Napoli,* by G. Villone and M. Sessa, published by Gaia; and *Libera Viva*, which documents a photographic/archival project by Italian artist Elisabeth Hölzl, published by Verlag für Moderne Kunst (in English).

ROBERTO DE SIMONE, BARD OF NAPLES

Composer and concert pianist, conductor and founder of vocal groups, musicologist, essayist and mythologist, playwright and director, Roberto De Simone turns everything he touches to gold. All his works cover the full range of performance arts: dramatic style and colourful language, song and dance, intellectual and popular culture, obscenity and refinement are all in harmony in the hands of such a prodigy. Roberto De Simone dares to try anything and succeeds in everything, which has prompted Giulio Baffi, Italy's most respected theatre critic, to say that "the theatre will be eternally indebted to Roberto De Simone".

De Simone has also safeguarded an invaluable cultural heritage that would otherwise have been lost for ever: in the 1960s, he tirelessly roamed around the region to record and transcribe tales and songs from the oral tradition. In addition to his discoveries in the countryside are the nuggets he unearthed in libraries and archives, real assets to leave to posterity. To make these forgotten treasures better known, he launched the Nuova Compagnia di Canto Popolare, an extraordinary group of singers. Success was global. In 1976, it was the turn of *La Gatta Cenerentola* (Cinderella), a musical in which De Simone wove a web of the most significant magico-religious symbols from the ancient culture of his homeland. In Naples, *La Gatta* became a rare phenomenon in that it appealed to intellectuals as much as to ordinary people. (It came to London's Sadler's Wells theatre in 1999.) Riccardo Muti hit the nail on the head in saying that De Simone is "the soul of his city".

De Simone, an artist of inexhaustible talent, constantly renews himself and success follows success. So far he has to his credit twenty musicals (composed and directed), a dozen concertos and an opera, not to mention the plethora of operatic productions for the most prestigious national and international theatres. The value placed on his many essays, among which *Il segno di Virgilio* (The Sign of Virgil) is a veritable bible of Neapolitan mythology, is such that they sell out as soon as they appear. His books are never reissued, like his shows, which are rarely repeated. He's keen to preserve the authenticity that might succumb to rampant commercialisation.

De Simone's love of folk traditions has inspired him to collect a mass of objects that he wants to make accessible to the public in a museum devoted to folk art. The Naples city hall had promised him a space in the historic centre, where he'd be able to fulfil another dream: setting up a music school. The promise is now dead in the water, as he's accepted an offer from the nearby municipality of Portici, site of the summer residence of the kings of Naples. The mayor of Portici has offered to make available a beautiful 18th-century villa because, he says, "Roberto De Simone forms part of the heritage of humanity." So Naples has missed a unique opportunity to embrace one of its exceptional sons, who has devoted his soul and his genius to the city.

CLOISTER OF THE FACOLTÀ DI VETERINARIA ㉜ (UNIVERSITÀ FEDERICO II)

1 Via Delpino
• Metro: Line 1 Museo or Garibaldi, Line 2 Cavour or Garibaldi
• Tel: 081 2531111
• Open Monday to Friday 8.30am—6.30pm

One of the city's best-preserved and least-known cloisters

At the former monastic complex of Santa Maria degli Angeli alle Croci, now home to the Faculty of Veterinary Science, you can visit one of the best-preserved cloisters in the city. Built in 1581, it was extended and embellished a century later by Cosimo Fanzago. The arches of the cloister, surrounded by a covered gallery with grey volcanic stone columns, are decorated with 17th-century frescoes attributed to Belisario Corenzio and depicting episodes from the

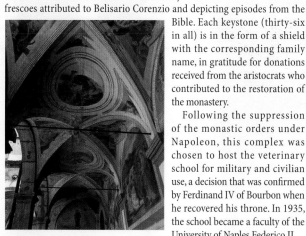

Bible. Each keystone (thirty-six in all) is in the form of a shield with the corresponding family name, in gratitude for donations received from the aristocrats who contributed to the restoration of the monastery.

Following the suppression of the monastic orders under Napoleon, this complex was chosen to host the veterinary school for military and civilian use, a decision that was confirmed by Ferdinand IV of Bourbon when he recovered his throne. In 1935, the school became a faculty of the University of Naples Federico II.

NEARBY

MUSEO DI ANATOMIA VETERINARIA ㉝
1 Via Delpino
• Tel: 081 5644238 • Visits on request
• Admission free

The Museum of Veterinary Anatomy, on the third floor of the building that houses the Faculty of Veterinary Science, preserves the bodies of various animal species that have been injected with plasticised liquids so that the arterial and vascular systems are revealed. The museum also has a collection of Mediterranean fauna, mainly marine, either dry or preserved in formalin.

SAINT ANTHONY THE HERMIT'S PIG 🟢34

Church of Sant'Antonio Abate – 302 Via Foria
• Metro: Line 1 Museo, Line 2 Cavour

*Fire
and pork fat*

The church of Sant'Antonio Abate (Saint Anthony the Hermit), built at the time of King Robert of Anjou (14th century) and refurbished in the Baroque style after a fire, became extremely popular after Virgil's bronze horse was banned (see p. 262). In order to heal their sick horses, people began to celebrate a ritual around this church identical to the one previously held around the statue attributed to Virgil. Although the animals' harnesses were originally decorated with little crescent loaves, these have morphed into biscuits coated with white icing that are sold on the steps of the church on 17 January, the saint's feast day. This is the same date when animals are taken there to be blessed. Despite this background, it's a pig, not a horse, that stands at the saint's feet –representing all the other animals. The healing power attributed to Saint Anthony is indeed strictly linked to the pig: the monks of Saint Anthony, to whom the Angevin king had assigned the religious complex with its hospital, were known for their ointment prepared from pork fat, with which they treated burns and shingles.

Interestingly, shingles is called "Saint Anthony's fire" in the Neapolitan dialect, because the other attribute of this saint is just that – fire. The legend goes that Saint Anthony the Hermit, in his desert retreat, struggled with the Devil tempting him in the guise of a pig. So Anthony descended to Hell to retrieve the souls taken by Lucifer and stole fire by lighting his *tau*-shaped staff (see next page), which explains his reputation as the Devil's worst enemy and healer of conditions associated with fire.

With their taste for esotericism, the Neapolitans couldn't help but be captivated by this charming myth. They raised pigs in the street and particularly appreciated those with distinctive marks on their coats, more so if they formed the letter *tau*.

On 17 January, the pigs were decked out with ribbons and offered to the monks. The same day, huge bonfires were lit to burn the evil, after the statue of the saint was paraded on a white horse (nowadays a great fire is still lit but under the strict control of firefighters, and a white horse is no longer used to carry the statue). Sacred pigs proliferated in the city and were only banned in 1663–1664 because of an accident: during the solemn procession in honour of Saint Januarius, a piglet slipped between the legs of a bishop who fell over with a great crash.

Gradually, the monks who took over from the early followers of Saint Anthony lost their predecessors' pharmaceutical knowledge. However, belief in the benefits of pork fat was so tenacious that until the end of the 19th century, every 17 January, a monk offered worshippers a small piece of bacon wrapped in a image of the saint folded into a cone.

SAINT ANTHONY'S MONKS AND THE TEMPLARS

The Knights of Saint Anthony belonged to an ecclesiastical and hospitaller order founded in 1095 at Vienne in the south of France. They were called to Naples by the Angevin kings but driven out by the Aragonese in the 15th century. Wearing a white cloak bearing a distinctive blue *tau* (known as Saint Anthony's Cross), the last letter of the Hebrew alphabet (modern *tav*), the main vocation of these noble laymen was to care for the sick – they founded some 370 hospitals throughout Europe.

It is possible that some Templars, after the suppression of their order, converted to monks of the Order of Hospitallers of Saint Anthony.

At Naples, the wounded brought back from the Holy Land were treated in the hospital opposite the church of Sant'Antonio Abate (Saint Anthony the Hermit). There seem to have been some Templars among them who, according to the local elders, are thought to have left traces of their passage in the underground tunnels criss-crossing Borgo Sant'Antonio Abate. So it could have been the Templars who revealed the secret of the miraculous ointment to the monks.

A STRANGE PROCESSION AND A BUNGLED THEFT

Neapolitans' devotion to this saint in whose honour they held the first winter festival was such that the procession lasted ten days! It began on 6 January and ended on the 16th, the eve of the feast itself.

On the first day, the gilded silver statue of Saint Anthony was brought from the cathedral and set on the right of Saint Janarius, then paraded in a carriage drawn by a white horse preceded by a band of trumpeters. The procession passed through all the city neighbourhoods where the merchants competed for the "visit of the saint", who was supposed to protect them from misfortune.

The luckiest ones welcomed the statue by showering it with gifts and money. In the evening, Saint Anthony was housed in the first convenient church along the route.

The crowd meanwhile jubilantly cheered the procession along by lighting fires. On the evening of the 16th, the statue was displayed in its home church; during this final part of the route, people were invited to throw out all their old wooden goods for burning in the grand closing bonfire, so as to destroy all the negative vibes from the previous year. On the 17th, the blessing of the animals took place.

In 1808, as the statue stood in the church of Sant'Antonio Abate, thieves stole the silver bust of Saint Blaise and then tried to make off with Saint Anthony, hauling the statue up with ropes they had slipped through one of the church windows.

But the ropes gave way and the thugs took to their heels. This incident gave rise to the proverb *"Saglia Antuono ca Biase è sagliuto"* (Let Anthony up because Blaise is up), which is repeated when an event or person is expected to follow another event or person.

BLESSING OF THE ANIMALS

Saint Anthony, who was supposed to have healed a dying piglet that a sow left at his feet, was soon attributed with the power to protect pigs and other animals. So in modern Italy and elsewhere, a number of priests conduct a blessing of the animals on 17 January, the saint's feast day (supposed date of his death around AD 340). Where once only farm animals were concerned as they represented a valuable source of income, nowadays all animals are welcome without exception: dogs, cats, rabbits, horses, even snakes, camels and other exotic animals that eccentric owners like to keep.

Throughout pre-war southern Italy, Naples included, the ritual was to have the animals turn three times in a circle around the church, the figure 3 and the circle being notorious magical symbols. In Naples, this only concerned horses: every Sunday from 17 January until the first day of Lent, the people celebrated the same ritual around this church as previously held around the statue of Virgil's horse.

Other relics of that time are in the form of biscuits coated with white icing sold in the streets around the church during the festival.

These are copies of the crescent loaves with which the horses used to be decorated.

Today, the festivities have been markedly toned down. As the benediction service has replaced the ancient ritual in Naples (as elsewhere), the ceremony takes place at early Mass and the animals are blessed in the church itself.

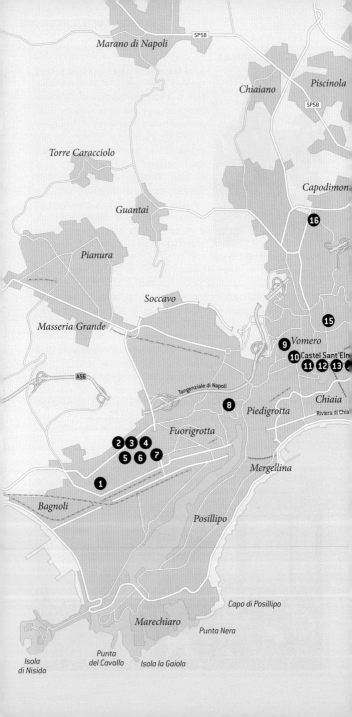

OUTSIDE THE CENTRE WEST

NEAPOLITAN RIDING ACADEMY ❶

Circolo "La Staffa"
37 Via Beccadelli (access by Viale della Liberazione)
• Metro: Line 2 Campi Flegrei; Rail: Ferrovia Cumana, from Montesanto (Mostra stop)
• Visits: contact Carla Travierso, Consigliere alla Casa
• Tel: 081 5703619

A park with splendid ancient pines, home to an elite club

The "U. De Carolis" Neapolitan riding academy, founded in 1937, is located in a 3 hectare park scattered with ancient pines and cypress-flanked avenues – totally unexpected in a heavily urbanised neighbourhood.

You can book a visit to the attractive premises of the prestigious La Staffa

club. Its large rooms, decorated in typical 19th-century Neapolitan style, are richly furnished with 18th-century pieces bequeathed by the city's most eminent aristocratic families, notably by the academy's founder, the Marquis Riccardo De Luca di Roseto.

You'll also appreciate the pieces made by the Giustiniani, the famous Neapolitan ceramicists. In the main salon, a wide bay window overlooks the large indoor arena where riding lessons and competitions are held.

The Neapolitan Riding Academy, near the Mostra d'Oltremare complex (see next page), was opened in 1940 by King Victor Emmanuel III. In the following years it was patronised by the most illustrious Neapolitan and Italian riders, including Prince Umberto of Savoy.

After the Second World War, thanks to its founder the Marquis De Luca (who was the academy's director for over thirty years), the indoor arena, the La Staffa club and the two swimming pools were rebuilt.

GOLDEN CUBE IN THE EXHIBITION PARK

Mostra d'Oltremare
54 Via John Fitzgerald Kennedy
• Metro: Line 2 Campi Flegrei; Rail: Ferrovia Cumana (Mostra stop)
• Tel: 081 7258000
• presidenza@mostradoltremare.it • www.mostradoltremare.it
• Visits from Tuesday to Saturday 6pm–midnight, Sunday and public
holidays 10am–midnight • Admission €1
(NB: access also by Piazzale Vincenzo Tecchio)

A corner of Africa

Some of the attractions in the huge exhibition and recreational park of the Mostra d'Oltremare (Exhibition of Overseas Territories) are still little known to Neapolitans. The "golden cube", for example, is one of the pavilions devoted to Italian East Africa built during the 1940 Triennial Art Exhibition. Inside, the walls were frescoed by Giovanni Brancaccio with depictions of Julius Caesar and Mussolini on horseback. The exterior of the pavilion is covered

with an ochre-coloured mosaic whose golden reflections in sunny weather earned the building its name. The work is inspired by the architecture of the Ethiopian city of Aksum.

A little further on, the "Fasilides baths" in the centre of a little lake recall the castle of the Emperor Fasilides at Gondar, also in Ethiopia. This monument commemorates the colonisation of the Mussolini era: the city of Gondar, whose castle was restored by Governor Mazzetti in 1938, became the symbol of Italy's occupation of Ethiopia.

Leaving behind the avenue of palm trees, you'll come across the Rhodes pavilion, which is Arabist in style; Giovanni Battista Ceas took the Order of Hospitallers' medieval inns as his model.

The Mostra d'Oltremare, originally known as the Mostra Triennale delle Terre Italiane d'Oltremare (Triennial Exhibition of the Italian Lands Overseas), inaugurated in 1940, is the very image of fascist propaganda. After suffering severe damage during the war, the park was rebuilt and renamed the Mostra Triennale del Lavoro Italiano all'Estero (Triennial Exhibition of Italian Work around the World), becoming an example of Mediterranean post-war rationalism.

TUNNELS BELOW FONTANA DELL'ESEDRA

Mostra d'Oltremare
54 Via John Fitzgerald Kennedy
• Metro: Line 2 Campi Flegrei; Rail: Ferrovia Cumana (Mostra stop)
• Tel: 081 7258000
• info@mostradoltremare.it • www.mostradoltremare.it
• Visits: authorization required
• Booking required by email: presidenza@mostradoltremare.it
(NB: access also by Piazzale Vincenzo Tecchio)

You can book a visit to the tunnels under the Esedra fountain at the Mostra d'Oltremare. The fountain, 230 m long and 20 m wide and covering 900 m², is one of the largest in the world. The highest water jet reaches 40 m. At certain evening events, when water jets and lights play to the rhythm of music, 140 projectors illuminate the scene.

Below one of the largest fountains in the world

NEARBY

A ROMAN ROAD BELOW THE EXHIBITION PARK ④

During construction work on the complex, some Roman remains were discovered – a road, a mausoleum and an aqueduct. The stretch of road, which is 200 m long and paved with lava stones, formed part of a highway from Naples to the large commercial port of Pozzuoli, which intersected a secondary route. The surface of the heavily used road is worn in places by chariot wheels. You can also see the remains of a pavement. After the damage caused by the Second World War, the small archaeological park was restored thanks to the renowned archaeologist, Professor Amedeo Maiuri. The mausoleum and chapel opposite were reconstructed following the original model.

RAI PRODUCTION CENTRE

5

9 Viale Guglielmo Marconi
• Metro: Line 2 Campi Flegrei; Rail: Ferrovia Cumana (Mostra stop)
• Visits can be arranged in May during the annual "Maggio dei Monumenti" event
• www.comune.napoli.it
• cpnarainapoli@rai.it

A "television factory"

Construction of the Naples headquarters of Rai (Radiotelevisione italiana, Italy's national broadcasting company), over an area of 18,000 m², began in 1958 and was completed in 1961, when

the first recording took place. If it's not in use, you can visit the TV1 studio (area 800 m², 12 m high), one of the largest in Europe, where such series are made as *Un Posto al sole* (A Place in the Sun), a huge hit since 1996. In the corridor leading to the studio, wall paintings show the main actors and "guest stars" of this TV soap. Among the other areas accessible to visitors is the studio hosting regional news programmes. Original pieces of equipment have been preserved here and there by way of souvenir.

Rai's sound archives of Neapolitan songs, with over 40,000 digitised pieces, also feature in the tour, as does the auditorium where you can admire the organ with 10,000 pipes, the largest in Europe.

ROMAN BATHS ON VIA TERRACINA ❻

Via Terracina junction with Viale Marconi
• Metro: Line 2 Campi Flegrei; Rail: Ferrovia Cumana (Mostra stop)
• Tel: 081 5529002
• rootsdiscoverycf@gmail.com
• Gruppo Archeologico Napoletano • info@ganapoletano.it
• Open on certain occasions or on reservation with Associazione
Culturale "Roots Discovery"

2,000-year old mod cons

A "rest area" of the Roman era on Via Terracina (2nd century AD) was discovered in 1939 about 2 m below street level during the construction of the Mostra d'Oltremare (see p. 352). These excavations, which had been forgotten for

decades, were recently reopened to the public – although only on certain occasions.

This installation on a busy road linking Naples to the commercial port of Pozzuoli was equipped with baths, latrines and other facilities for the comfort of passing travellers.

Black and white mosaics on marine themes can still be seen: in their bathhouses, the Romans generally avoided colourful mosaics that could be damaged by steam and moisture. The building was equipped with an ingenious system to recycle water: after being used for bathing, it poured into small channels used to clean the latrines.

NAVAL BASIN OF THE HYDRODYNAMIC LABORATORY

Faculty of Naval Engineering, University of Naples Federico II
21 Via Claudio
• Metro: Line 2 Campi Flegrei; Rail: Ferrovia Cumana (Mostra stop)
• Tel: 081 7683308 • miranda@unina.it • www.dii.unina.it
• Visits on reservation

*Europe's
largest university
naval engineering
facilities*

The Faculty of Naval Engineering's facilities are the largest in Europe. The huge pool, opened in 1980 and modernised a few years later, is 147 m long by 9 m wide and 4.20 m deep.

It is equipped with a device known as the "swell absorber", which is capable of reducing the impact of incidental swell by

95% on waves between 5 m and 7 m long. On the sides of the pool, two rails are used to activate a gantry that can take a load of 28 tonnes: a small-scale boat is attached to it and lowered into the water to be tested under various atmospheric conditions. These tests are for yachts as well as cruisers or merchant ships.

Two beeps warn technicians and visitors when a test is about to be launched: the gantry operates with sudden accelerations that in an instant can reach 7 m per second.

TEATRO VILLA PATRIZI

8

41 Via Manzoni
• Visits on request only: www.teatrovillapatrizi.com

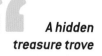

***A hidden
treasure trove***

You only have to ask to visit Villa Patrizi, an old building where, behind a few private rooms, lies the only fully preserved example in southern Italy of an 18th-century theatre "*di palazzo*".

The music room, dating back to the second half of the 18th century, is decorated in an amazingly sophisticated style. Its frescoes and tempera paintings featuring musical scores, notes and instruments were executed in 1771 by Giuseppe Funaro (nicknamed "The Left-Handed"), Giuseppe Baldi and Fedele Fischetti. In the centre of the room, two sensual, sinuous Muses

face one another. On the right, with your back to the terrace, is the stage. On the other side is a splendid gilded wooden gallery with its valuable canvases and frescoes.

The hexagonal terrace has a spectacular view of the Bay of Naples and Vesuvius, that famous panorama with the pine tree immortalised on millions of postcards. The entrance, theatre and terrace are attributed to Ferdinando Sanfelice.

Some of the most sumptuous feasts of the 19th century were held in this villa, named after the family who owned it. Here the Neapolitan nobility met foreign bigwigs, notably the sovereigns of the House of Bourbon, King Ludwig II of Bavaria and the German poet (and count) August von Platen.

In 1998, the little theatre was badly damaged by a fire that destroyed the stage, curtain, floors and ceiling vault with its canvases. Many years of neglect followed this catastrophe.

In 2011, a lawyer named Giose Morgera bought the property and undertook the restoration of the frescoed room in particular, saving it from oblivion.

GUIDO DONATONE PRIVATE MUSEUM ❾

Villa Costanza, 12 Vico Acitillo
• Metro: Line 1 Quattro Giornate
• Tel: 081 5792010 • guido.donatone@alice.it
• Visits only in summer (except August) for cultural associations, on reservation by e-mail or phone (only groups 25 visitors, or more)
• Collection under anti-theft surveillance 24/7

A rare collection of antique ceramics

You can book a visit to the Guido Donatone private museum, an authentic collection of Neapolitan and Campanian ceramics whose most representative pieces have been declared national heritage by the Italian Ministry of Culture. The museum's halls still retain the precious 19th-century Colonnese floor tiles from the renowned manufacturers. Among the many wonderful pieces are two huge and eye-catching plates made in Naples in the 18th century, decorated with vignettes taken from French engravings. These plates are known as "imperial" due to their exceptional size – 60 cm in diameter – whereas the largest pieces manufactured in other Italian workshops measure only 45 cm.

Also not to be missed are the stoups of Borrominian inspiration from

Cerreto (near Reggio Emilia), the rare 15th-century tiles and, displayed in the centre of one room, a beautiful litter for aristocrat transport – a minor masterpiece of Neapolitan Rococo decorated with paintings of Hercules and Diana the Huntress.

Professor Guido Donatone, who has written a couple of dozen specialised works and is one of the greatest ceramics historians, founded the Centro Studi per la Storia della Ceramica Meridionale (Centre for the Study of Ceramics from Southern Italy), based in Naples. The lengthy research of this dedicated historian led to the rediscovery of Neapolitan and Campanian production from the 15th and 16th centuries. These ceramics, found in museums in Italy and abroad, had always been attributed to artisans from Tuscany or Faenza.

It is thanks to Prof. Donatone that we now know that the production of highly sophisticated earthenware was launched in Naples under the Aragonese kings. Around 1447–1448, Alfonso the Magnanimous, the dynasty's first king, brought a great Arab ceramicist from Manises (near Valencia) who specialised in decorative tiled floors. This craftsman worked in the Aragonese Royal Palace of Castel Nuovo where there are records of a ceramics kiln, which so far hasn't been recovered, under a staircase in the courtyard. The late neoclassical Villa Costanza, now Prof. Donatone's residence and museum, was built in the early 19th century by Filippo Angelillo, attorney general and advisor to the Bourbon King Ferdinand II. The villa miraculously escaped the rampant urbanisation of the 1950s.

BAS-RELIEF OF THE *TRIUMPH OF DEATH*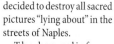

Certosa e Museo Nazionale di San Martino
Largo San Martino
• Funicular: Centrale (Piazza Fuga), Chiaia (Cimarosa), Montesanto (Morghen), then bus V1
• Daily except Wednesday 8.30am–7.30pm

> **Death, which does not yield to the temptation of money**

In the epigraphic section of the remarkable (though little visited) San Martino Museum, the exceptional bas-relief *Triumph of Death* was saved from destruction at the last minute by archaeologist Giuseppe Fiorelli in 1862. In that year, the authorities of recently unified Italy, driven by iconoclastic fury, decided to destroy all sacred pictures "lying about" in the streets of Naples.

The bas-relief was outside the church of San Pietro Martire and dates from 1361. This work, the only bas-relief ever made in Naples, unlike all other similar works in Italy and Europe, is a rare example of folk art: the two characters are addressing one another (instead of the observer) as in a cartoon and the text is written in the vernacular despite its Gothic lettering. The depiction of a mortal who tries to subvert Death is also a first, because all other similar examples date from the 15th century and lack any inscriptions.

Here, Death wears two crowns as a sign of power. The hawk perched on the left arm and the lure in the right hand mean that Death continues its relentless pursuit despite the many victims symbolised by the thirteen corpses lying at its feet. Among these, the crowned head and the prelate indicate that the hunt is indiscriminate and cares little for social status.

To the right is shown the sponsor of the work, Franceschino da Brignale, a Genoese citizen (probably a merchant) who twice survived a shipwreck. He is emptying a bag full of gold coins and saying: "I want to give you all this if you let me go." Death replies: "Even if you gave as much of it as we could ask for, you could not escape death when your hour tolls."

The central inscription, on the other hand, addresses the reader by clearly describing the scene carved on the bas-relief. It ends with a warning and an incentive to behave as a good Christian.

In the border around the carving is the dedication from its sponsor: "I thank God the Father a thousand times [...] for twice saving my life while everyone else drowned. I, Franceschino da Brignale, commissioned this work in memory of this received grace, 3 August 1361."

Above, there are two coats of arms of the Dominican Order, to which the church of San Pietro Martire belonged.

In its original setting, the bas-relief was well known. To refuse a request for a loan of money, Neapolitans used to say: "Why don't you ask Death at San Pietro Martire, who has plenty of it?"

The San Martino Museum, established in 1866 when the Certosa di San Martino (now closed down) was declared a national monument, is rarely visited despite being truly remarkable. Saint Martin's charterhouse itself, dating from 1325, is literally bursting with works of art. The building encompasses various architectural styles, each of the highest order (changes were made until the 17th century), forming a harmonious whole. The church, which is wealthy beyond imagination, is considered the essence of Neapolitan Baroque, with collections that encapsulate the glorious history of the city. To top it all, the building stands on the hill of the same name overlooking the Bay of Naples. From the the monastery's terraces, you can enjoy a 180° panorama. A visit is highly recommended.

SERGIO RAGNI'S PRIVATE COLLECTION

56 Via Aniello Falcone
• Funicular: Centrale (Piazza Fuga) or Chiaia (Cimarosa)
• Visits on reservation by phone or e-mail
• Tel: 081 5584442
• elleboro25@libero.it

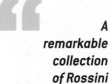

A remarkable collection of Rossini artefacts

The stunning collection that Sergio Ragni has put together in his immense apartment, which occupies part of the splendid Villa Belvedere, is a yardstick for many musicologists. It consists of artefacts relating to music, particularly the work of Gioachino Rossini, who lived in Naples from 1815 to 1822.

Among the rarest pieces are autographed scores, such as the alternative ending to *William Tell* written for the Bologna opera house in 1840, and the *Cantata in Honour of Pius IX*, a very rare composition by the maestro after his decision to give up music and the theatre.

The letters written by Rossini (over 150, many addressed to his father) represent one of the largest collections of Rossini correspondence in existence.

There are also hundreds of documents (contracts, orders, correspondence with impresarios) on Rossini's theatrical activities in Italy from 1809 to 1824; the autographs of musicians he frequented, as well as singers trained in his repertoire; rare portraits of his first wife, the famed Spanish soprano Isabella Colbran; letters and the contract signed by Isabella with impresario Barbaja to perform at the San Carlo and the Fondo (now the Mercadante theatre); a quantity of scores, often first editions printed in Italy, France and Germany, revealing the wide range of the composer's work; an impressive set of biographical and critical works from the first edition of Stendhal's *Life of Rossini* to comprehensive studies by the Rossini Foundation of Pesaro, without equal in any Italian library; an almost complete collection of contemporary press cuttings illustrating the maestro's work; an audio archive including all recordings of his music … In one corner, there is even a pair of stiletto heels that belonged to Maria Callas.

Villa Belvedere, built in 1671 by Flemish banker Ferdinando Vandeneynden, then bought by the Carafa family, opens onto one of the most beautiful views of Naples. The Cenacolo Belvedere reception rooms are on the first floor.

GOTHIC TUNNELS BELOW SAN MARTINO

5 Largo San Martino
• Metro: Line 1 Vanvitelli, then bus V1
• Funicular: Centrale (Piazza Fuga), Chiaia (Cimarosa), Montesanto (Morghen) then bus V1
• Tel: 081 2294541
• accoglienza.sanmartino@beniculturali.it
• Only reservation by mail

The monks' tunnels

After thirty years of work, the underground tunnels of the superb Charterhouse and Museum of San Martino were reopened to the public under the name "Gothic Underground" because they date back to the founding of the monastery (1325), which was designed by the renowned architect Tino da Camaino. There is a profusion of statues, architectural fragments and commemorative plaques from buildings lost during the Risanamento in the late 19th century. Between the powerful arcades of this timeless place, these relics tell of 400 years of the history of Naples, from the 14th to 18th centuries. Among the most saignificant pieces are a Madonna by Tino da Camaino and the *Triumph of Death* bas-relief (see p. 366).

D ON PETRVS DE TOLEDO
MARCHIO VILLE FRANCHE
GES SETCA... AN PRESENTI
REGNO VICE... LOCVM
TENENS GENERALIS CAPI
TANIVS PRE CEPS IVSTINS
MVS EXC... LENTE MILITE
V.D. FER... NANDO EIQ...
ROA PAT... IO HISPANO
REGENTE M... GNIAM CVRIAM
VICARIE S... ANTE A DILLO
RVM MO... M ABOLENDVM
QVNQ.E A... NEMINE SPETTAN
TE BONIS ... DEBANT HVNC
LOCA ... E BIS POSTINC
DRVN... A TIVOLENT
BENEFIC... ... IC ...
SEPIA S... ID COMITAM
SPECTA... NON PROPRIO
MAGA ... ON SAC...

DELLA VICARIA TRIBUNAL COLUMN

Museo Nazionale di San Martino
5 Largo San Martino
• Metro: Line 1 Vanvitelli
• Funicular: Centrale (Piazza Fuga), Chiaia (Cimarosa), Montesanto (Morghen)
• Open every day except Wednesday, 8.30am–7.30pm (ticket office closes 6.30pm)
• Admission: €6, concessions €3

Debtor's "pillory"

In the National Museum of San Martino, on the left side of the passageway where two old coaches are displayed, is a column known as the "colonna della Vicaria", which formerly stood in front of Castel Capuano. Anyone in debt was subject to an infamous punishment – to avoid being condemned to the galleys, he had to lower his trousers and embrace the column while reciting a formula inviting his creditors to confiscate all his property to recover their dues. This "ceremony" was all the more humiliating in that it attracted a crowd of passers-by whose gibes the hapless debtor had to endure. The practice was abolished in 1546 and replaced by a

public "confession" service, followed by the obligation to always wear a hat with distinctive signs sewn on it, recognisable to all.

The column was also a kind of "morgue": all unidentified bodies were placed there in the hope that someone might recognise them. The corpses were left in place until the smell became unbearable. This macabre function wasn't banned until 1856.

A stone for meting out a similar punishment can also be seen in Florence (see *Secret Florence* in this series of guides).

The humiliating exposure suffered by debtors has marked the souls of the Neapolitans: even today, to indicate somebody going away empty-handed, they say *"se ne ji cu na mana annanze e n'ata arreto"* (to leave with one hand in front and the other behind), implying hide one's private parts.

MERIDIAN OF THE CARTHUSIANS

Museo Nazionale di San Martino
5 Largo San Martino
• Metro: Line 1 Vanvitelli, then bus VI • Funicular: Centrale (Piazza Fuga),
Chiaia (Cimarosa), Montesanto (Morghen), then bus V1
• Tel: 848 800288 or 06 39967050
• Open every day except Wednesday 8.30am–7.30pm (ticket office
closes 6.30pm) • Admission: €6, concessions €3
• Group reservations from Monday to Saturday 9am–1.30pm and
2.30pm–5pm

> ***Astronomy
> as an art form***

T he meridian that features in the former prior's apartment at Saint Martin's Charterhouse (room 33) is a superb work of art as well as an astronomical masterpiece.

Despite being lower than the best-known meridians (see next page), it is still one of the most comprehensive and beautiful examples in Italy. It was designed in 1771 by Rocco Bovi, who left his signature in a metal plate set into the magnificent floor with its majolica tiles representing the constellations and signs of the zodiac, made in 1771 by the great ceramicist Leonardo Chiaiese.

On the bronze columnar strips are engraved graduations intrinsic to the diurnal half-day, expressed in hours and minutes in order to determine the daily sunrise and sunset and the height and declination of the Sun.

Note also the indications of the solar cycle, the "Dominical Letter" (assigning the dates on which Sundays fall in a given year following a perpetual calendar), the degrees of the ecliptic that mark the path of the Sun against the background of the celestial sphere, a geometric scale from the Tychonic system (developed in the 16th century by Danish astronomer Tycho Brae to calculate the orbits of the planets as they were known at the time) with respect to the Earth and the Sun, and other related measurements. There are also indications of the winter and summer solstices.

Note also two pretty wind roses in grey marble and copper: on the one with thirty-two winds, four continents (Europe, Africa, Asia and America) are indicated with the north rotated by 90°.

The superb representation of the constellations, defined by little stars along the meridian line, corresponds with the time of year when they transit the local meridian at midnight.

Notable among the various symbols and engraved images are a human face (self-portrait of the artist?), a seascape with boat and seagulls, the Sun with the sign of Cancer and some small houses, as well as a bay (Naples?) and a mountainous landscape: small details that add a poetic note to this superb composition.

For more on meridians and their origin, see following double-page spreads.

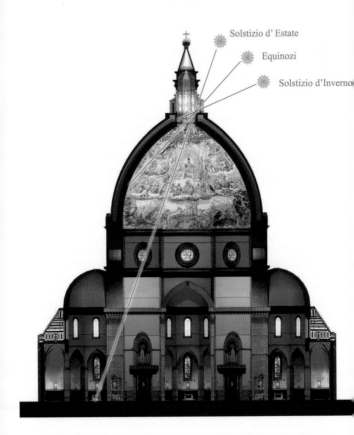

Solstizio d' Estate

Equinozi

Solstizio d'Inverno

HOW DOES A MERIDIAN WORK?

Instead of using the shadow of a gnomon, these use a small hole placed at a certain height, through which the Sun's rays fall onto a meridian line (i.e. one aligned exactly north–south.

The fact that the Sun's rays perform the function of the shadow in a traditional sundial means that the opening is sometimes referred to as a "gnomonic opening".

The higher the opening, the more efficient the meridian, hence the interest in using cathedrals; the circumference of the hole had to be no more than one thousandth of the height above the ground. Obviously, the opening had to be installed on the south side of the building in order to let in the rays of the Sun, which lies to the south in the northern hemisphere. The meridian line should run from the point that stands perpendicularly below the axis of the opening, not always easy to determine using the instruments available to scientists in the past.

The length of the line depends on the height of the opening; in some cases, where the building was not long enough to trace the entire meridian line across the floor (as was the case at Saint-Sulpice in Paris), an obelisk was added at the far end, so that the movement of the Sun's rays could then be measured up the vertical. In summer, when the Sun is highest in the sky, the rays fall onto the meridian line closer to the south wall (where that line begins) than in winter, when the Sun is lower over the horizon and the rays tend to strike towards the far end of the meridian line.

The main principle behind the working of the meridian is that at noon, solar time, the Sun is at its apex and, by definition, its rays fall straight along a line running exactly north–south. So the exact moment when those rays strike the meridian line, which does run north–south, indicates solar noon. Furthermore, the exact place on the meridian line where that ray falls makes it possible to determine the day of the year: the point right at the beginning of the line is reached solely on the day of the summer solstice, whereas the exact end of the line is reached on the day of the winter solstice.

Experience and observation meant that the meridian line could be calibrated to identify different days of the year.

Once this was done, the line could be used to establish the date of various movable feasts, such as Easter – one of the great scientific and religious uses of meridians. Similarly, the different periods corresponding to the signs of the zodiac could be established, which explains why such signs are indicated along the length of a number of meridian lines.

WHY WAS 4 OCTOBER FOLLOWED IMMEDIATELY BY 15 OCTOBER IN THE YEAR 1582?
MEASUREMENT OF TIME AND ORIGIN OF THE MERIDIANS

The entire problem of the measurement of time and the establishment of calendars arises from the fact that the Earth does not take an exact number of days to orbit the Sun: one orbit in fact takes neither 365 nor 366 days but rather 365 days, 5 hours, 48 minutes and 45 seconds.

At the time of Julius Caesar, Sosigenes of Alexandria calculated this orbit as 365 days and 6 hours. In order to make up for this difference of an extra 6 hours, he proposed an extra day every fourth year: thus the Julian calendar — and the leap year — came into being.

In AD 325, the Council of Nicaea (called by Constantine, the first Roman emperor to embrace Christianity) established the temporal power of the Church. The Church's liturgical year contained fixed feasts such as Christmas, but also movable feasts such as Easter, which was of crucial importance as it commemorated the death and resurrection of Christ, and so the Church decided that it should fall on the first Sunday following the full moon after the spring equinox. That year, the equinox fell on 21 March, which was thus established as its permanent date.

However, over the years, observation of the heavens showed that the equinox (which corresponds with a certain known position of the stars) no longer fell on 21 March ... The 11 minutes and 15 seconds difference between the real and assumed time of the Earth's orbit around the Sun led to an increasing gap between the actual equinox and 21 March. By the 16th century, that gap had increased to ten full days and so Pope Gregory XIII decided to intervene. Quite simply, ten days would be removed from the calendar in 1582, and it would pass directly from 4 to 15 October. It was also decided, on the basis of complex calculations (carried out notably by the Calabrian astronomer Luigi Giglio), that the first year of each century (ending in 00) would not actually be a leap year, even though divisible by four. The exceptions would fall every 400 years, which would mean that in 400 years there would be a total of just 97 (rather than 100) leap years. This came closest to making up the shortfall resulting from the difference between the real and assumed time of orbit. Thus 1700, 1800 and 1900 would not be leap years, but 2000 would.

In order to establish the full credibility of this new calendar — and convince the various Protestant nations that continued to use the Julian calendar — Rome initiated the installation of great meridians within its churches. A wonderful scientific epic had begun ...

The technical name for a leap year is a bissextile year. The term comes from the fact that the additional day was once placed between 24 and 25 February. In Latin, 24 February was the sixth (*sextus*) day before the calends of March, hence the name *bis sextus*, to indicate a supplementary sixth day. The calends were the first day of each month in the Roman calendar.

THE HIGHEST MERIDIANS IN THE WORLD

From the 15th to the 18th centuries, some seventy meridians were installed in churches in France and Italy.

Only ten, however, have a gnomonic opening that is more than 10 m above floor level – that height being crucial to the accuracy of the instrument:

Santa Maria del Fiore (Florence)	90.11 m
San Petronio (Bologna)	22.07 m
Saint-Sulpice (Paris)	26.00 m
Monastery of San Nicolo l'Arena (Catania, Sicily)	23.92 m
Cathedral (Milan)	23.82 m
Santa Maria degli Angeli (Rome)	20.34 m
Collège de l'Oratoire (Marseille)	17.00 m
San Giorgio (Modica, Sicily)	14.18 m
Museo Nazionale (Naples)	14.00 m
Cathedral (Palermo)	11.78 m

WHY WERE MERIDIANS INSTALLED IN CATHEDRALS?

To make their measurements more precise, astronomers required enclosed spaces where the point admitting light was as high as possible above the ground: the longer the beam of light, the more accurately they could establish that it was meeting the floor along an exactly perpendicular plane. Cathedrals were soon recognised as the ideal location for such scientific instruments as meridians. The Church had a vested interest as well, because meridians could be used to establish the exact date of Easter.

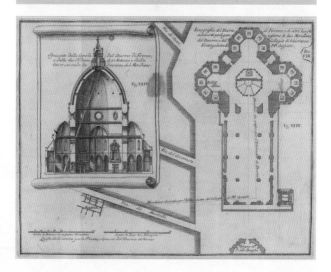

PARCO VIVIANI

Via Girolamo Santacroce (main entrance)
Salita di San Antonio ai Monti (side entrance), Via Cupa Vecchia
• Metro: Line 1 Salvator Rosa
• Open 7am–6pm from 1 to 31 March, 7am–7.30pm from 1 April to
30 June, 7am–8.30pm from 1 July to 31 August, 7am–7pm from 1 to
30 September, 7am–6pm from 1 to 31 October, 7am–4.30pm from
1 November to 28 February

*A green
oasis in a sea
of concrete*

Viviani is a small park of just 2 hectares
on the hillside where some species
of Mediterranean shrub, such as
agave, olive, pine and rosemary, have been
preserved. The site offers panoramic views
with very fine glimpses of sea and city.

A flight of steps also leads to a tunnel dug into the tuff by which you descend to the secondary exit below. Other passages, now blocked up, led to the historic centre of the city, thus linking the "upper" residential neighbourhoods with the popular ones "down below".

The family that owned this domain spread ghost stories by calling themselves "Spiritillo" (Little Ghost) to scare away children who came to steal the fruit from their trees.

Raffaele Viviani (1888–1950), to whom the park is dedicated, is one of the greatest playwrights and poets in the Neapolitan dialect. He particularly liked this place, which he called "a little garden of happiness". Viviani was very close to the people and denounced their situation of extreme poverty in language of great dramatic energy. This author of immense stature is unknown abroad. The markedly Neapolitan spirit of his work is probably why he's been sidelined at the international level.

CENTRALE ABC (ACQUA BENE COMUNE NAPOLI) DELLO SCUDILLO ⓰

Via Serbatoio dello Scudillo
• By car: Tangenziale, Zona Ospedaliera exit
• Public transport: several buses go to the Ospedale Cardarelli terminus
• Information: www.abc.napoli.it

Underground pools three times the size of a football stadium

You can book a visit to the "dello Scudillo" hydro plant, managed by the municipal company ABC, which supplies water to Naples and the surrounding municipalities, 1.6 million

consumers in all. The tours are rather limited as the site is subject to very strict rules because of the sensitive nature of public health facilities, so much so that up to the early 20th century the guards had orders to shoot intruders.

The part open to the sky is littered with relics of the former aqueduct, including a huge section of cast iron dating from 1885. In the covered parts you'll see bronze meters from the same period (the first in Italy) and old tools, as well as invoices from the 1950s with curious advertisements on the back.

After donning protective headgear, the tour continues down to the huge underground pools (the biggest are 330 m long, three times larger than a football stadium). At the end of a long corridor, you'll see a 310 m basin dug out of the rock face and filled with water. The mechanics of routing water to the higher-level districts are very impressive.

OUTSIDE THE CENTRE NORTH & EAST

CASA MUSEO DI PULCINELLA ❶

Piazza Castello
80011 Acerra (suburbs)
• Bus: 171, A37, A31 from Piazza Garibaldi (Napoli Centrale station)
• Tel: 081 8857249
• Open Monday to Friday 9am–1pm; also Monday, Wednesday, Thursday from 3pm–6pm; weekends by appointment
• Admission free

> *Where*
> *Punch first saw*
> *the light of day*

It was at Acerra, one of the Naples suburbs, where *Pulcinella* (Punch) is thought to have first seen the light of day. So it was at Acerra, in a castle dating back to the 9th century that belonged to the feudal lords of the city, that it was decided to pay tribute to this iconic character in a special section of the Pulcinella, Folklore and Peasant Culture Museum. Legends about his origins, old prints, photos of the most famous *Pulcinella* theatres and puppets from around the world take visitors on a trip through the imagination of a people.

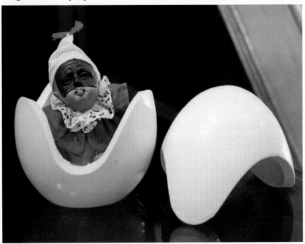

THE SYMBOLISM OF *PULCINELLA*, EXORCIST OF NEAPOLITANS' EXISTENTIAL ANGST

The origins of *Pulcinella* are uncertain. Although the character probably developed from a type of ancient theatre called *atellane* (from Atella, a city near Naples) in the 4th century BC, it was not until the 17th century that he was taken up by the commedia dell'arte. From the 18th century he became the most famous, the most studied and the most represented character (and puppet) in the world.

Far from Naples, he changes his name and sometimes loses some of his typical features. In Paris he's known as *Polichinelle*, in London *Punch*, in Istanbul *Karagoz*, in Spain *Don Cristobal*, in Germany *Kaspar* and in Moscow *Petruska*.

Roberto De Simone, an authority on the subject, claims that *Pulcinella* represents all aspects of Neapolitan popular culture, which, for thousands of years, has exorcised all its existential anxieties by inventing symbols, dances and, in this case, a character.

Pulcinella has in fact a rather funereal aspect: his black face with hooked nose, his spectral complexion, his deformities and his smock as white as a shroud are certainly scary enough; his nasal, croaking voice is not of this world.

His name probably derives from *pulcino* (chick) because, like a chick, he was hatched from a hen's egg – the hen is the creature sacred to Persephone, queen of the underworld. *Pulcinella* thus embodies death and the misfortunes of humanity, but at the same time he wards them off with his cornucopia-shaped cap and his burlesque behaviour. The roles he plays are as numerous as the defects and qualities of a people, for *Pulcinella* is both comic and tragic, simple and smart, affable and arrogant, rich and poor, cowardly and brave, hopelessly stupid and amazingly resourceful, but always able to rise from the ashes, like any genuine Neapolitan.

His inherent and total ambivalence fits perfectly into the Neapolitan culture, where contradictions reign. He has a lover and is frequently lewd, but his Italian name sounds feminine and he is sometimes graphically depicted giving birth to small "clones" from his hump – this is the myth of the hermaphrodite that runs through Neapolitan culture. The androgynous *Pulcinella* also rhymes with *Verginella*, the name the people gave to their great benefactor Virgil, also both man and woman. Moreover, for the alchemists the hermaphrodite is the perfect being insofar as it synthesises man and woman, and therefore the universe.

Pulcinella has a big belly, another allegory of motherhood, but also of hunger because *Pulcinella* is forever hungry. He dreams only of macaroni, an affirmation of his strictly Neapolitan origins. Then, suddenly, his stomach becomes a sign of opulence and he's seen gorging himself on the long steaming ribbons of pasta that he grabs in handfuls to stuff in his mouth.

This is what the poor did in the old days when boiled macaroni sprinkled with grated cheese was sold in the streets. Despite this memorable trademark identity, for the great Roman director Maurizio Scaparro *Pulcinella* is "the world's mask". As for Roberto Rossellini, he has his *Pulcinella* say: "I'm a comedian, not a clown" – for the renowned filmmaker, the character always knows how to keep his dignity.

A Naples theatre, the San Carlino, demolished in 1884, was devoted almost exclusively to so-called *Pulcinellate* plays. Many little street theatres for children, known as *guarattelle*, used hand puppets to tell *Pulcinella* stories. The tradition isn't lost as you can still catch these street performances during festivals and sometimes in the summer.

MARADONA "MUSEUM"   ②

Via Lombardia Isolato 1
• Visits by reservation with Signor Massimo Vignati
• Tel: mobile 3381918907
• Admission free

> *A "temple" dedicated to Maradona*

On display in a cellar is the largest collection relating to the history of Neapolitan football, and especially to Diego Armando Maradona, who played for Napoli from 1984 to 1991. This initiative is due to Signor Saverio Vignati, who was caretaker of the city stadium from 1979 to 2006. On his death, his son Massimo brought all the objects collected by his father together in this room.

So on the entrance walls you can see dozens of pennants offered to the Vignati family by the *Pibe de Oro* in person. The most original exhibit is the bench where the famous footballer sat in the stadium locker room – a bench that's become a veritable altar since Signor Vignati placed the portrait of his idol on it when he finally left Naples. Since that day, nobody has ever dared to sit there.

Also kept in the cellar-museum are the boots worn by Maradona at the 1986 World Cup; his team captain's armband; the gloves he wore to keep out the cold during a game in Moscow; his first professional jersey; the mascot of the 1990 World Cup, a present from Pelé; Ciro Ferrara's parting ball; and Napoli jerseys signed by Maradona and well-known players from other teams who, before leaving Naples, donated some souvenirs to the Vignati family "museum".

NEAPOLITAN COMMUNITY OF THE FRATI MINORI RINNOVATI

• www.fratiminoririnnovati.it

Cloistered in railway carriages

I n a rural district of the Miano suburb of Naples, some carriages from the 1940s and 50s have ended their days on a railway siding inside an engine shed. A ladder leads up to the various compartments that constitute the extraordinary and quite unexpected "house" of the Neapolitan Community of the Franciscan Friars of the Renewal (Frati Minori Rinnovati or FMR). This Roman Catholic institute was founded by Brother Tommaso Maria di Gesù and five other friars of the Capuchin Order, with the aim of sharing and observing the spirit of the teachings of Saint Francis. With about fifty members in all, the FMR has communities in Italy (Palermo, Corleone, Naples), Colombia (Bogotá, San Clemente, El Retiro, San Roque) and Tanzania (Pomerini).

Here in Naples, the choice to live in these old carriages is down to the Order's vow of poverty: the friars bought them from the railway company in October 1976 as scrap metal. At the moment eight of them live here, but their numbers vary. The small compartments of the four "cloister" carriages have been converted into cells where the friars sleep (off-limits to outsiders). A fifth carriage has been turned into a sitting room where guests are welcome. The friars' apostolic work in the outside world, although very intense, doesn't preclude rigorous observation of the rules of Franciscan life: six hours of communal prayer a day, monastery hours, reveille in the middle of the night.

The community survives thanks to the generosity of people who come to visit, sometimes from a considerable distance, and offer food or assistance. The friars don't accept money.

A few metres from the carriages is a prefabricated building with a kitchen and a chapel, which is only open to visitors during the celebration of Mass. Nearby, a dense stand of trees shelters this enclave where peace and silence reign, interrupted only by the chirping of birds.

After your initial bewilderment at the sight of such unusual accommodation, it doesn't take long to appreciate the exceptional spiritual dimension of this place, conducive to reflection and introspection. You don't come here to visit the friars, but to share with them a welcoming experience of brotherhood that can't fail to leave a deep impression.

CIMITERO DELLE 366 FOSSE   ❹

50 Via Fontanelle al Trivio
• Tel: 081 7806933 / 333 1606015
• www.cimiterodelle366fosse.com
• Open Saturday and Sunday 8.30am–1pm

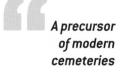

A precursor of modern cemeteries

Constructed in 1762, half a century before Napoleonic edicts banned burials in urban areas, the cemetery of the "366 graves" consists of an area of 80 m² in which 360 communal graves were dug, all numbered and about 7 m deep. The graves, arranged in nineteen rows (the six remaining are below the cemetery church), were used in turn for a single day and then closed up, to be

reopened the following year. Taking into account the population density of Naples (which, at that time, was the third-largest city in Europe after London and Paris), this rotation lessened the risk of spreading germs.

The capacity of these graves was considerable: 900,000 bodies could be buried there. They were however thrown into the pit any old how, which is why an English lady (name unknown), whom, they say, had lost her daughter or niece in a cholera epidemic in 1875, donated a machine that would lower the bodies into place in a more decorous manner. You can still see the remains of this machine in a corner of the cemetery.

This site, designed by Ferdinando Fuga at the request of Charles III of Bourbon, was the first cemetery exclusively for those with no resources. It was part of the social policy of the king, who had commissioned the same architect to build the huge Albergo dei Poveri in the city centre. The cemetery was closed down in 1890.

KELLER ARCHITETTURA STUDIO

106 Via Foria
- Metro: Line 1 Museo, Line 2 Cavour
- Visits on reservation by e-mail or phone
- info@kellerarchitettura.it
- Tel: 081 450707

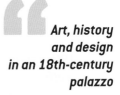

Art, history and design in an 18th-century palazzo

On the second floor of Palazzo Ruffo di Castelcicala, in an apartment of over 400 m², stunning 19th-century majolica floors and French woodwork rub shoulders with prototypes of modern architecture and vintage furniture.

The apartment/office/gallery of architect Antonio Giuseppe Martiniello (Keller Architettura) is typically Neapolitan:

huge rooms, long and very wide corridors and painted ceilings, all decorated with paintings, pop artefacts and a really spectacular suspended bookcase that the owner has had built using the original structure of untreated wood.

At the other end of the apartment, the "Nativity" meeting room takes its name from the ceiling decoration. Next come the "Butterfly" and "Four-leafed Clover" rooms. You can book a visit and even have a drink in this exclusive location, unexpected and charming as it is.

The film *Thus Spake Bellavista* by Luciano De Crescenzo, which was a great success in 1980, was shot in the courtyard of the palazzo.

ORIGIN OF THE NAME "FORIA"

The street name "Foria" probably derives from *fuori via* (beyond the streets) – this district used to be outside the city walls. It was only in the 18th century that the Bourbons built this avenue to connect the capital city with the factories that had sprung up to the north.

CALABRESE ENCLOSED GARDEN

234 Via Foria
• Metro: Line 1 Museo, Line 2 Cavour

19th-century coffeehouse refinement

Founded in 1864 by Francesco Saverio Calabrese, a keen botanist, the Calabrese vivarium was the first in the city and is the only one still operational. The location is a 16th-century garden just opposite the Orto Botanico (entrance 223 Via Foria, bookings 081 2533937, admission free). Despite being in a

densely populated area, the vivarium covers about 4,000 m² and has seven glasshouses which used to be heated by a coal boiler, now preserved in a small building.

The place is redolent with the memory of Calabrese's daughter-in-law Rita Stern, a highly refined aristocrat of German origins whose receptions were attended by the cream of the Neapolitan aristocracy and the intelligentsia. In her offices within the large garden, recently restored and opened to the public, a number of charming objects, paintings, photos and documents are on display.

They trace the history of the family and its relations, who included, among others, Eduardo De Filippo and the great Neapolitan actress Pupella Maggio, who seems to have spent a lot of time in the Kaffeehaus. The beautiful 18th-century architecture is the work of architect Pompeo Schiantarelli.

STATUE OF SAN GENNARO

Via Ponte della Maddalena
• Bus: 194 or 196 from Napoli Centrale station (Parcheggio Brin stop)

> **The statue that halted the lava flow in 1631**

According to a legend recorded by Conrad of Querfurt (Chancellor to Holy Roman Emperor Henry VI, 1194), Virgil had placed a marble knight at the city gates with his bow arched to shoot a arrow in the direction of Vesuvius, in order to protect Naples from the volcano's anger. But one day a reckless peasant, annoyed by this menacing statue, pulled the string of the bow: the arrow flew off and struck Vesuvius, which immediately began to belch fiery lava.

During the eruption of 1631, when burning lava was at the gates of Naples, San Gennaro (Saint Januarius) wrought a miracle: his statue, which had replaced that of Virgil's archer, raised a hand to stop the flood of destruction.

Today, in memory of this miracle, at the southern entrance of the city in Via Ponte dei Francesi the statue of the saint can still be seen, his hand raised in the direction of the volcano. In gratitude, the Neapolitans clubbed together to offer Saint Januarius one of the most sumptuous chapels ever built in honour of a saint, in the cathedral dedicated to him.

In the small square behind the cathedral, Piazza Sisto Riario Sforza, an obelisk was erected for another statue of Saint Januarius. This is the very site where a bronze horse once stood (see p. 236), a miraculous horse that not only cured all animals, but in the guise of Ennosigaïos (the ground-shaker) had the power to repel earthquakes. Another fine example of the assimilation of pre-existing pagan symbols by nascent Christianity, which in order to establish itself preferred to shrewdly absorb local cults rather than struggle against them.

For more on the symbolism of Saint Januarius (San Gennaro), see following double-page spread.

HIDDEN SYMBOLISM OF THE CULT OF SAN GENNARO

On 19 September (anniversary of the saint's death) and the first Saturday of May, in the sumptuous setting of the Treasury chapel, before a crowd of the faithful at prayer, the blood of the patron saint of Naples liquefies. The oldest reference to this event dates back to 1389. The adoption of this saint by the Neapolitans – frustrated by the abolition of their ancestral cults and always looking for extraordinary events – was instantaneous.

Until the 1950s, the miracle was immediately greeted with histrionics that were a mixture of penance and jubilation: crying women tearing out their hair, men shuffling along on their knees, screams of joy and loud applause. On the other hand, if there was a long delay, some old women known as the *zie di San Gennaro* (kinswomen of Saint Januarius) began to hurl insults at the saint using the epithet "Yellow Face" (the colour of the silver statue yellowed by time). This reflected the people's deep-rooted fear that the city might be in danger if the blood did not liquefy. The fear was so great that people could lash out violently at whoever was supposedly responsible for the non-appearance of the miracle. Sometimes it was believed that the saint was protesting against policies hostile to the pope, so people turned against the authorities, who were often forced to reconsider their decisions.

The liquefaction of blood incorporates a mystical aspect dear to Neapolitans: the oracle (concerning the fate of the city) with her priestesses (the kinswomen) and the blood, a key element in some initiation rites (such as those of Mithra and Cybele). During these ceremonies, novices were baptised by having the blood of a specially sacrificed bull poured over them. Note the strong female presence, a fixture in this city's religious practices. Moreover, when waiting for the miracle, the "kinswomen" invoke the Madonna in these terms: "Beloved Mother, take your cloak and the cape of Saint Januarius, and help us, defend us, shelter us, and rid us of all evils, and save us from a bad death. Beloved mother, let us have a good life and a holy death on behalf of the love Saint Januarius vowed to you." According to archival documents, following the beheading of Januarius in 305, the blood was collected and stored in a vial by Eusebia, an old and pious virgin, as ancient and virginal as the Sibyls and the "kinswomen". The vial in question dates from the 4th century.

The blood-centred ceremony also forms part of a collective propitiatory rite celebrated by the Duke and Bishop of Naples (from the 5th to 11th centuries). This involved swinging an ovoid receptacle containing an egg in the presence of four human skulls representing the "four corners of the world", which were supposed to reunite into a single "universal central body" in the form of the egg.

Nowadays, the vial containing the blood is also ovoid, the cardinal too swings the vial, and liquefaction occurs in the presence of the saint's skull. The Vatican has not spoken out clearly on the subject of this "miracle" and prudently defines it as a "marvel". In 1965, Saint Januarius was even demoted and his cult declared "local and voluntary". This loss of status greatly annoyed the Neapolitans and produced one of the best-known examples of graffiti lining the walls of the city: *"San Gennà futtatenne"* (Saint Januarius, don't worry about it).

In 1991, a group of researchers in Pavia, northern Italy, claimed to have reproduced the phenomenon in the laboratory. The liquid in the vial, they declared, was an ordinary type of gel that flows when shaken and coagulates when the vibrations stop. This process of "thixotropy" was already known to the ancient alchemists. In the 18th century the Prince of Sansevero, renowned Neapolitan alchemist and inventor, reproduced this phenomenon before the astonished gaze of his guests.

But the blood of Saint Januarius doesn't necessarily liquefy every time the cardinal shakes the vial – and sometimes it is already found in the liquid state even before the ceremony. Moreover, spectroscopy carried out in 1988 revealed that the substance was indeed haemoglobin, even though the provenance (animal or human) could not be determined. The explanations are many and varied, from alchemical interpretations to quantum theory, not to mention biochemistry and psychophysics. So the case is far from closed.

The ceremony used to take place four times a year. Besides the two dates mentioned above, the miracle was witnessed on 16 December, anniversary of the day the saint's statue raised a hand to halt the lava flow (see p. 399), and 14 January, anniversary of the transfer of his relics from the sanctuary at Montevergine to Naples.

CHURCH OF SAN CARLO BORROMEO ALLE BRECCE ❽

102 Via Galileo Ferraris
• Bus: 192 from Napoli Centrale station (Via Ferraris stop)
• Tel: mobile 349 5939227 (Father Serge Baudelaire)
• Open Sunday at 11am (summer), 10am and 12pm (winter)

> *Painting of the Madonna of the Flies*

In the church of San Carlo Borromeo, high up behind the main altar, is a painting of the Madonna of the Flies. This copy (the original canvas was burned in 1850) depicts, alongside the Virgin, Saint Francis of Assisi and Saint Anthony of Padua, as well as the walls of Constantinople and the glow of the blazing city during the Persian invasion that the Virgin is thought to have halted.

In 1650 flies were painted around the image of Mary, who was originally venerated under the name of Our Lady of Constantinople. The legend goes that that was the year of an infestation of flies in the marshes around Naples. The market gardeners, first to be affected by this scourge and fearful of the disease carried by these insects, promised to build a chapel for the

Virgin in return for her help. The miracle came to pass and the chapel was erected in a swampy area where buffaloes were raised. It was demolished during the construction of the Central Station and moved to the site of the present church. In fact, this legend had its roots in a very old myth concerning one of Virgil's miracles (see opposite).

The cult of Saint Mary of Constantinople spread throughout the kingdom from 1452, when a Byzantine icon with her image was found on a Calabrian beach. In Naples, it was believed that this Madonna kept epidemics at bay and a church in the city centre was dedicated to her.

SYMBOLISM OF THE FLY: FROM VIRGIL'S GOLDEN FLY TO THE MADONNA OF THE FLIES

Belzebuth Signore delle mosche

There is a legend that in the Porta Capuana district, near a swamp, Virgil had a fly made of precious metal: he hung it in a window at the castle (Castel Capuano) to drive away these pests that infested the city.

Flies embody uncleanliness, epidemics, putrefaction and therefore death by disease. Symbolic of evil powers (see Apuleius in his book *The Golden Ass*), these insects are linked to Beelzebub, the Lord of the Flies. This was borne out in the Campanian practice of swatting flies from the body of the deceased during a funeral vigil, in order to ward off evil. This gesture was ritualised to the extent that among the mischief allowed during the feast of Our Lady of Piedigrotta (see p. 32), a fly swatter made from strips of coloured paper could be waved in the faces of passers-by.

During the Angevin period the metal fly – a talisman that had actually existed – was removed. A Christian legend tells of a terrible plague of flies on the outskirts of Naples in 1650, so the market gardeners prayed to the Madonna of Constantinople to save their crops and their families. Once she had got rid of the pests, they commissioned a painting depicting the Virgin surrounded by flies. This painting (a copy of the original which was destroyed during the Second World War) was moved to the church of Saint Charles Borromeo (see opposite).

Questioned by Roberto De Simone, the local priest stated that until the 19th century worshippers prayed to this Madonna for protection against infectious diseases. At the end of each summer epidemic, he added, she was offered golden flies by way of thanks. The last such offerings were made after the terrible cholera epidemic of 1884.

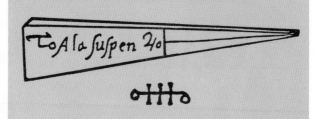

SERPONE & COMPANY ⑨

79 Via Reggia di Portici
• Metro: Line 2 Gianturco
• Admission free, reservations by phone
• Tel: 081 7899211

> **Workshop where the papal vestments are made**

A visit to the Serpone workshop will take you through centuries of Naples' history and throw light on a great local tradition: the production of sacred garments. From the 18th century until today, Neapolitan craftsmanship has carried the city's reputation around the world. Serpone, the historical company founded in 1820, occupies an unusual building: the vast halls of the former Pattison shipyards, one of the first industrial plants in Naples at the beginning of the 19th century (the Guppy & Co workshop could build up to three locomotives a year). "One of my ancestors, Maria Fontana Colonna, was married to a Bourbon army lieutenant who was one of the conspirators in the Parthenopean Republic proclaimed in 1799," says Paolo Serpone, one of the owners. "He was murdered and his belongings immediately confiscated from

his family. And so my homeless and penniless grandmother sought refuge with the monks. They welcomed her, but on one condition: she had to embroider their habits." Shortly afterwards, thanks to her talent, the first embroidery shop opened in Via San Domenico Maggiore. Today, in the

Via Reggia di Portici workshop – now mechanised but respecting traditional techniques – artisans continue to produce banners and standards, as well as robes for magistrates and lawyers and for the ceremonies of several institutions. Few people know that this workshop also has the exclusive warrant to produce all the liturgical vestments for the papal sacristy, the popes (since John Paul II) and all pontifical ceremonies (election of cardinals, bishops, deacons, etc.). The two hundred chasubles required for the election of Cardinal Jorge Mario Bergoglio as Pope Francis are some of the recent important pieces from this workshop. During the visit, you'll see hundreds of holy water stoups, Baby Jesus images, crucifixes, kneelers and altars. You can also admire some valuable private collections, old (and rare) embroidery, dozens of photographs of famous people, and possibly witness the restoration of vestments sent to this workshop in the hope that they'll be "resurrected" by expert hands.

ARCHIVIO NAZIONALE E STORICO ENEL

24 Via Ponte dei Granili
• Metro: Line 2 Gianturco; Bus: 2 or 4
• Tel: 081 3674213
• archiviostoricoenel@enel.com
• paolo.deluce@enel.com
• Visits on reservation

> *The entire history of the Italian electricity industry*

The historical archives of Enel (Ente Nazionale per l'Energia Elettrica – the result of the nationalisation and merger of Italy's 1,270 electricity suppliers in 1962) – contain the complete documentation relating to the history of the Italian electricity industry from the 19th century to the present day. In 2006, the archives of various Enel headquarters throughout Italy were combined with those of Naples to become the national archives. They extend for 13,000 m and contain, among other documents, the first original contract of 1894 for the city lighting, signed by the mayor at the time, about 100,000 photos, thousands of sketches, hundreds of instruments, incandescent lamps for street lighting …

Among the curiosities is a rare example of a 1940s meter with a capacity of 1,382 kilowatts, equipped with a system that let you pay for your electricity consumption with one-lira coins. This device was removed after eighteen months – some very astute Neapolitan consumers had made fake coins the same weight and size that worked perfectly. In the 1980s, a more efficient blue-coloured meter was introduced: technicians called it the "Maradona meter" in honour of the famous footballer of the local team.

ART WORKSHOPS OF THE TEATRO SAN CARLO⓫

23 Stradone Vigliena – San Giovanni a Teduccio
• Trolleybus: 4 from Piazza Garibaldi
• Tel: 081 7972205
• Visits on request
• Admission: €4

A former factory in the service of art

This building, which consists of two rectangles of different heights dating from 1928, belonged to Cirio, a canned food manufacturer which in the 1960s and 1970s was the largest in Europe.

Since the 1990s, Naples' inner industrial suburbs had been largely depopulated and so became run-down. Thanks

to a scheme designed by the prestigious San Carlo theatre, art came to the rescue of this declining district that until the beginning of the 20th century had been renowned for its beautiful beaches. The absurd policy of "industrialisation at any price" had literally made a clean sweep of the most beautiful coastal sites of Naples, both east and west along the bay.

The former Cirio establishment, now rehabilitated, has seen its machines replaced by scenery and its workers by artisans.

In this way, Naples has followed the example of other major European cities which have transformed their abandoned factories into creative spaces. Plans are also afoot for these huge premises to host educational exhibitions that are open to the public.

This spectacular site can be visited on request.

MUSEO FERROVIARIO NAZIONALE DI PIETRARSA

⑫

6 Via Pietrarsa
• From Napoli Centrale station, Salerno–Torre Annunziata line (Pietrarsa stop) • museopietrarsa@fondazionefs.it • Visits: Thursday: 2pm-8pm; Friday 9am-4.30pm; Saturday and Sunday: 9am-7.30pm
• www.ferroviedellostato.it; www.museopietrarsa.it
• Guided tours Thursday, on reservation: 081 472003 • Admission: € 7, concessions € 5 (children 6–10 years, senior citizens 65 and over)

> ### *Trains from the glory days of Naples*

Housed in a disused factory at Pietrarsa, the National Railway Museum is the first in Italy and among the largest in Europe. Among the exhibits are railcars, the first electric trains with a driver's cab, wagons for transporting coal, royal carriages and those of the first "fast" trains, steam locomotives including the "Bayard", twin of the "Vesuvio", which inaugurated the first Italian railway linking Naples to Portici (7.5 km), and a giant model 18 m long that a railway worker spent his entire life building.

Founded in 1840 on the decision of Ferdinand II of Bourbon, the factory, known as the "Real Opificio Borbonico di Pietrarsa", was the most modern steel plant in Italy as well as the largest. It not only produced locomotives, but also steam engines as well as artworks such as the huge cast iron-statue (4.5 m high) of Ferdinand II. The factory was in the vanguard even in the social sphere: the employees – almost 1,000 of them (982 workers, including 224 soldiers and 40 prisoners being reintegrated into society, plus administrative staff) – worked only eight hours a day and were entitled to a pension.

After the unification of Italy in 1861, the Real Opificio Borbonico was gradually downgraded to the rank of locomotive repair shop: production was relocated to the north of Italy and the staff were reduced to 100. In 1863, the ensuing workers' revolt was bloodily suppressed by the army – seven protesters were killed and twenty seriously wounded (see memorial plaques on the outside wall of the museum). Pietrarsa closed on 15 November 1975.

The site where the factory was built was originally called "Pietra Bianca" (white stone), a name that was changed to "Pietrarsa" (burnt stone) after the terrible 1631 eruption of Vesuvius when the entire area was covered with lava.

NAPLES AND THE SOUTH BEFORE 1860: A WEALTHY AND PROGRESSIVE KINGDOM

Until it was annexed to the Kingdom of Italy on 21 October 1861, the Kingdom of the Two Sicilies had aroused the admiration of many foreign travellers. A prosperous and highly industrialised country with its 9 million inhabitants (among a total of 22 million in what would become Italy), its 5,000 industries employing 51% of the peninsula's population and its 9,174 merchant ships, the kingdom had gold reserves that were twice the size of all the other Italian states combined. The most modern taxation system in Italy, controlled prices of essential goods, the lowest infant mortality in Europe thanks to vaccination (from 1818) and the high number of doctors guaranteed people a very agreeable life. Prestigious universities, a plethora of publishing houses and newspapers (1,289 publishers/printers against Milan's 1,255),[1] and fifteen theatres open nightly, all made Naples a city of culture with an international reputation.

Under these conditions, it isn't surprising that the south put up fierce resistance to the Piedmontese occupier. The price of Italian unification was extremely heavy for the south: indiscriminate acts of barbarism against tens of thousands of resistance fighters and civilians (the former accused of banditry, the latter of complicity), hundreds of villages razed to the ground ... In protest, Austria, France, Prussia and Russia even broke off diplomatic relations with the new government.

But the spoliation of the south didn't stop: its thriving economy was literally destroyed and relocated to the north. All the laws governing the former kingdom were abolished and nothing put in their place, the upkeep of order was entrusted to pardoned criminals and the country, plunged into chaos, has never recovered. Emigration became the only means of survival for millions of southerners, who left their homeland for the first time in thousands of years.

The veils that hid the historical truth have only recently been lifted. These excerpts from testimonies (selected from the hundreds rediscovered to date) are very enlightening:

A. Bianco di Saint-Jorioz (Commander of the Piedmontese army): "The year 1860 found these people dressed, shod, industrious, with economic reserves ... Now it's just the opposite ... Nobles and commoners, rich and poor, all here aspire, with a few rare exceptions, to an imminent return of the Bourbons."[2] Senator Brignole Sale (during the vote in the Piedmontese Senate for the annexation of the Kingdom of the Two Sicilies): "That kingdom belongs to an independent prince who is still in place, who with a group of loyal soldiers resists the revolutionary hordes. Were we not at peace with him? ... What reason will we invoke to justify such a crime?"[3]

Colonel Massimo d'Azeglio (former Minister of the House of Savoy): "I can understand that Italians have the right to fight against those who would keep the Austrians in Italy, but we do not have the right to shoot Italians who, while remaining Italian, do not wish to join with us."[4]

Napoleon III to General Fleury: "I informed Turin of my reproaches. [...] Not only are misery and anarchy at their height, but the most culpable and unworthy acts are a matter of course ..."[5]

Lord Henry Lennox (speech in the British House of Commons, 8 May 1863): "The so-called Italian unity primarily owes its existence to the moral support and protection of England ... and it is in the name of England that I denounce such barbaric atrocities ... The description of the attitude and condition of the tortured in Dante's Inferno would give the best idea of the scene that presented itself in that prison yard ..."[6]

The socialist Gaetano Salvemini (letter of 1923): "If the Mezzogiorno [the south of Italy] was ruined by unity, Naples was frankly assassinated ..."[7]

G. La Farina (Sicilian unitarist deputy): "... Four or five jobs all done by the same person ... important posts given to minors ... pensions for the wives, sisters and sisters-in-law of so-called patriots although they are not entitled to them [...] Thieves, escaped prisoners, looters and murderers, pardoned by Garibaldi and paid off by Crispi and Mordini, have been implanted in the carabinieri, in the security services, in the revenue guard corps and even in the ministries ..."[8]

Letter (28 October 1861) from Minister Ricasoli to the Prefect of Naples: "... The transfer of these documents to the General Archives could be extremely dangerous ... His Majesty's Government [Victor Emmanuel], which wishes to put an end to the era of Italian discord, cannot allow retrospective recriminations to be constantly fuelled by a publicity of which he alone can determine the shape and opportunity."[9]

Over a thousand books have been published on the subject in Italian, some of which are included in the bibliography on p. 430.

1. Information from CLIO, *Catalogo dei libri italiani dell'ottocento* [Catalogue of Italian books from the nineteenth century] (1801–1900).
2. A report from 1864. See G. Turco, "Brigantaggio, legittima difesa del Sud" [Brigandry, the South's Legitimate Defence], *Il Giglio* magazine, Naples, 2000, p. xxxi (& others).
3. Declaration at the Senate's sitting of 16 October 1860 during the vote to annex the Kingdom of Naples (before the plebiscite of 21 October).
4. Letter of 2 August 1861 to the Hon. Matteucci, published in the *La Patrie* and *Monarchia Nazionale* newspapers.
5. Letter of 21 July 1863 sent from Vichy. See O'Clery, *La Rivoluzione italiana* [The Italian Revolution], Ares, Milan, 2000.
6. O'Clery, *La Rivoluzione italiana*.
7. Letter no. 58, dated 14 June 1923.
8. Account given to Carlo Pisano, 12 January 1861. See A. Pellicciari, *L'Altro Risorgimento* [The Other Risorgimento], Ares, Milan, 2011.
9. *Istituto Storico Italiano per l'Età moderna e contemporanea*, [Italian Historical Institute for the Modern and Contemporary Era], Vol. XVIII, 28 October 1861, no. 401; cited by U. Pontone, "Due Sicilie" [Two Sicilies], *L'Alfiere*, no. 46, Naples, 2003.

MUSEO PRIVATO DELLE CARROZZE DI VILLA BIANCHI ⑬

c/o Clinica Bianchi
342 Via Libertà – Portici (Naples)
• Rail: Circumvesuviana station, direction Torre Annunziata–Sorrento
• Visits (free) on reservation • napolisegreta@gmail.com

Incredible treasures on wheels

Professor Leonardo Bianchi's private collection of carriages, completely overlooked by Neapolitans, definitely merits a visit both for its location (the former stables of the castle where the kings of Naples often stayed on hunting trips) and for its superb vehicles, all in perfect working order. In the 1940s Professor Bianchi, a renowned neurologist and

accomplished horseman, collected unique examples of carriages produced in Italy and abroad between 1820 and 1920. These vehicles have all belonged to eminent personalities of the time, such as the hunting car of the Duke of Aosta, Emmanuel Philibert, who often took part in hunting expeditions organised by the Bianchi family.

Note in particular the splendid black and yellow model that belonged to the Thurn und Taxis (a rich, aristocratic German family who were key players in the postal services of Europe in the 16th century) which the ladies would hire to join their husbands for a picnic lunch after the hunt; and the lovely "Clarence" coupé designed by the English Duke of Clarence, later William IV … not to mention the German "Landau" sedan with its refined upholstery and, among the oldest vehicles in the collection, the small and fast "American" made in New York in the early 19th century.

ALPHABETICAL INDEX

ALPHABETICAL INDEX

ALPHABETICAL INDEX

NOTES

NOTES

NOTES

ACKNOWLEDGEMENTS

Valerio Ceva Grimaldi Pisanelli di Pietracatella

To my grandfather, Ugo Stellato, a remarkable man of culture and a great lover of Naples
To Amato Lamberti, a treasured teacher

Special thanks to:
Fernando Pisacane, Antonio Speranza, Laura Giusti, Augusto Cocozza, Serenella Greco, Roberta Stellato

For their contributions to the texts:
Augusto Cocozza, Serenella Greco, Antonio Speranza, Elena Regina Brandstetter, Serena Riviezzo, Roberto Fedele (Fondazione De Felice), Giuseppe Balsamo (Palazzo Nunziante), Tommaso Luongo (delegate of the Italian Association of Sommeliers of Naples, Vigne Metropolitane), Claudia Grieco (NapoliStreetArt), Sergio Riolo and the staff of the Historical Archive Museum of the Banco di Napoli (Museo dell'Archivio Storico del Banco di Napoli), Andrea Milanese, Alessandro Gioia, Daniela Savy, Serena Venditto, Angela Luppino (Mann), Luisa Maradei (Museo di Capodimonte)

This guide has been produced in collaboration with the Geositi project of Napoli Servizi – Comune di Napoli, directed by Salvatore Iodice

Also:
Massimo Marrelli, Luigi de Magistris, Fabrizio Vona, Annachiara Alabiso, Rossana Muzii, Fabio Speranza, Simona Golia, Soprintendenza Speciale per il Patrimonio Storico, Artistico ed Etnoantropologico e per il Polo Museale della Città di Napoli e la Reggia di Caserta, Fondo Edifici di Culto del Ministero dell'Interno, Ufficio per i Beni Culturali Ecclesiastici della Diocesi di Napoli for kindly granting reproduction rights, Comando Provinciale dei Carabinieri di Napoli, Francesco Pinto, Antonello Perillo, Carlo Sbordone, Sergio Sciarelli, Lida Viganoni and Università Orientale, Luciano Gaudio, Gennaro Rispoli, Paolo Jorio, Riccardo Carafa d'Andria, Flavio Zanchini, Michele Iodice, Italo Ferraro, Agostino Caracciolo and the entire board of Circolo dell'Unione, Imma Ascione, Paola de' Liguoro di Presicce, Massimo d'Orta, Ignazio Frezza di Sanfelice and secretariat of Arciconfraternita dei Bianchi, Francesco Rossi and Seconda Università degli Studi di Napoli, Nino Daniele, Niccolò Rinaldi, Guido Donatone, Marco de Gemmis, Sergio Ragni, Serena Lucianelli, Rita Pagliari, Mario Pagliari, Manuela Sorice, Natalie de Saint Phalle, Jole Lianza, Andrea Rea, Fondazione Monte Manso di Scala, Carla Travierso, Franco Abbondanza, Arciconfraternita della Santa Croce, Antonio Martiniello, Giuseppe Zevola, Rosaria Russo, Silvano Focardi, Enzo De Nicola, Mimmo Galluzzo, Maria Francesca Stamuli, Università Parthenope, Circolo Artistico Politecnico, Giuseppe Messina, Bernardo Leonardi, Salvatore Miranda, Leonardo Bianchi, Giuseppe Morra, Giampiero Martuscelli, Fabio Chiosi, Mariano Cinque, Gabriele Flaminio, Marina Andria, Susy Cacace, Imma Cuomo, staff of NapoliServizi, Antonio Loffredo, Adelina Pezzillo and staff of San Gennaro and San Gaudioso catacombs, Luca Cuttitta, Gianluca Minin and staff of Galleria Borbonica, Gianpaolo Leonetti, Insolitaguida Napoli, Associazione Nartea, Lello Scuotto, Antonio Caliendo, Maurizio Di Cresce, Francesco Licastro, Giovanni Lucianelli, Gennaro Giorgio, Associazione La Paranza, Pierluigi Sanfelice di Bagnoli, Livio Barone, Carlo Ferrari, Maria D'Ambrosio, Alessio Postiglione, Grazia Formisano, Imma Sansone Perrella, Adriana Pascale, Fulvio Mamone Capria, Palmiro Camerlengo, Enzo Colimoro, Antonella Rizzo, Pietro Fusella, Francesco Russo, Michele Iacobellis, Arturo Castellano, Carlo Leggieri, Daniela Del Monaco, Giuliana Sandulli, Piero Bizzarro, Alessandra Basile, Fabrizio Masucci, Davide Tartaglia, Stefano Cortese, Donatella Monti, Clemente Esposito, Vincenzo Esposito, Giobby Greco, Antonio Gargano, Maria Girardo, Roberto Vernetti, Salvatore Maffei, Carmen Credendino, Luca Marconi, Marco Giglio, Vincenzo Pisano, Rosario Serafino, Trianon – il Teatro della Musica a Napoli, Vincenzo Dina, Angelo Mazzagatti, Francesco (Monastero delle 33), Massimo Vignati, Carmelo Raiti, Giuseppe Serroni, Luciano Iovinella, Gaia Mautone, Nicoletta Diamanti, Lanificio25, Antonio Iaccarino (Locus Iste), Paolo de Luce, Francesco Esposito, Press Office of Teatro San Carlo, Rosaria Torre, Vincenzo and Davide Canzanella, Gianfranco Wurzburger, Pasquale Catalano, Giuseppe Talotti, Pasquale Ferraioli, Silvana Casale, Giuseppe Brancaccio, Antonio Daldanise, Massimo Rippa, Antonio De Gregorio and Paolo Giordano for their collaboration on the text

and illustrations for Cimitero delle 366 Fosse, Sisters of Ospizio Marino, Giuliana Ricciardi, Francesco Quaratino, Giulia Milanese, Antonio Moccia, Tiziana Grassi, Pasquale de Luca, Reale Arciconfraternita di Santa Maria del Popolo, Stefania Salvetti, Alice Bartoli, Cristina Di Stasio, Giovanni Brun, Antonio Denunzio, Carla Celestino, Andrea of San Giorgio Maggiore church, Isabella Tarsi, Serena Amabile, Fabiana Mendia, Antonio Pariante and Comitato di Portosalvo, Gruppo Archeologico Napolitano, Associazione Roots Discovery, Carmine G., Saverio Dionizio, Roberto Conte, Università degli Studi Suor Orsola Benincasa, P. Edoardo Parlato, Renato Previtera, Rossana Spadaccini, Agnese Iardino, Davide Lazzaro, Clelia Santoro, Chicca Pagliari, Maria Esposito, Mauro Giancaspro, Gennaro Oliviero, Stefano e Mario de Felice, Lavinia De Rosa, gruppo Grimaldi, Paul Kyprianou, Chiara Palmiero, Archivio Fotografico Carbone, Maurizio Morra Greco, Alessia Volpe, Antonio Busiello, Massimo Faella and association "Respiriamo Arte", Associazione News and Secrets, Casa Morra, Paolo Giulierini, Sylvain Bellenger, Alessio Cuccaro, Museo di Capodimonte, Frati Minori Rinnovati, Paolo Serpone and whole Serpone's family, Renato Ruotolo, Enzo De Luzio, Donatella Bernabò Silorata.

Maria Franchini

Special thanks to Maestro Roberto De Simone for his immense contribution to my knowledge of Neapolitan culture.
With great appreciation for their invaluable help: Raffaele Bracale, tireless researcher; Prof. Giuseppina Buonaiuto of Liceo Genovesi; Dr Lucio Fiorile, head of Biblioteca Majoli; Dr Paola Milone of Istituto di Storia Patria; Prof. Mirella Scala of Istituto Pimentel Fonseca; Dr Anna Sicolo of former Ospedale Bianchi; Fondazione Giambattista Vico.

All texts are by Valerio Ceva Grimaldi Pisanelli di Pietracatella except: 19-21, 228, 277, 311, 325, 295 (nearby and thematic boxes) and pages 26, 27, 29, 30, 31, 32, 33, 60, 61, 70, 78, 79, 82, 83, 84, 85, 90, 91, 92, 93, 110, 111, 113, 114, 126, 127, 128, 129, 130, 131, 134, 147, 152, 153, 154, 155, 160, 164, 190-191, 204-211, 240, 241, 252, 253, 262, 263, 264, 265, 317, 322, 340, 341, 345, 346, 347, 286, 287, 288, 289, 366, 367, 386, 387, 399, 400, 401, 402, 403, 412, 413 (Maria Franchini) and 234, 235 e 237 (VMA).

Select bibliography (in Italian - untranslated works)
Arturo Fratta : "Il patrimonio architettonico dell'Ateneo Fridericiano", ed. arte tipografica
Michele Fatica : "Sedi e Palazzi dell'Università degli Studi di Napoli l'Orientale", ed. U. N. O
Vittorio Gleijeses : "Chiese e palazzi della città di Napoli" ed. del Giglio
B. Capasso : "Napoli greco-romana"
Italo Ferraro : "Atlante della città storica", Oikos
P. Aprile : "Terroni", Piemme 2011
G Viesti : "Abolire il Mezzogiorno", Laterza 2003
L. Del Boca : "Indietro Savoia, controcorrente del Risorgimento italiano", Piemme 2004
G. Ressa : "Il Sud e l'unità d'Italia", 2003. www.olevano.it/biblioteca/Sud-Unita.italia-Ressa.pdf
E. Bianchini Braglia : "La verità sugli uomini e sulle cose del Regno d'Italia"
Ass. Solfanelli 2010
F. Molfese : "Storia del brigantaggio dopo l'unità" West Indian, 2012
O. Ferrara : "Addio Sud, o briganti o emigranti" Capone 2012
D. Liguori : "Memento Domine. Le verità negate sulla tragedia del Sud fra Borbone, Savoia e briganti", Sibylla, 2007
V. Gulì : "Il Saccheggio del Sud" Editoriale Campania Bella, 1998
N. Zitara : "L'unità d'Italia. Nascita di una colonia", Jaca Book, 2011
Collettivo : "Napoli Nobilissima", A. Berisio, 1969
B. Croce : "Storie e leggende napoletane", Adelphi 1990
R. De Simone : "Il segno di Virgilio", Sezione editoriale Puteoli, 1982
A. Gambardella, G. Amirante, "Napoli fuori le mura. La Costigliola e Fonseca da platee a borgo", Edizioni Scientifiche italiane, 1994
V. De Dominici, "Vite de' pittori, scultori ed architetti napoletani"
Adsi, Associazione dimore storiche italiane, "12-Restauri", Umberto Allemandi & c.
Guida alla Collezione Egizia del MANN" (Electa, 2017)